SURVEY OF LONDON
VOLUME IX

The Parish of St. Helen, Bishopsgate

(Part I)

AMS PRESS
NEW YORK

STAINED GLASS, WITH THE MERCHANT'S MARK OF SIR JOHN CROSBY IN THE BORDER, AND A SHIELD OF THE ARMS OF LADY CROSBY.

LONDON COUNTY COUNCIL

SURVEY OF LONDON

ISSUED BY THE JOINT PUBLISHING COMMITTEE
REPRESENTING THE LONDON COUNTY COUNCIL
AND THE LONDON SURVEY COMMITTEE

UNDER THE GENERAL EDITORSHIP OF

SIR JAMES BIRD (*for the Council*)
PHILIP NORMAN (*for the Survey Committee*)

VOLUME IX

THE PARISH OF ST. HELEN, BISHOPSGATE
(PART I)

PUBLISHED FOR THE LONDON COUNTY COUNCIL BY B. T. BATSFORD, LTD.
94, HIGH HOLBORN, LONDON, W.C.
1924

Library of Congress Cataloging in Publication Data

Reddan, Minnie.
The Church of St. Helen, Bishopsgate.

Reprint of the 1924 ed. published for the London County Council by B. T. Batsford, London, which was issued as v. 9 of the Survey of London.
Bibliography: p.
Includes index.
1. London. St. Helen, Bishopsgate (Church) I. Clapham, Alfred William, Sir, 1883–1950, joint author.
II. Title. III. Series: Joint Publishing Committee Representing the London County Council and the London Survey Committee. Survey of London; v. 9.
NA5470.S4R42 1979 726′.5′094212 74-6179
ISBN 0-404-51659-9

First AMS edition published in 1979.

International Standard Book Number:
Complete set: 0-404-51650-5
Volume IX: 0-404-51659-9

MANUFACTURED IN THE UNITED STATES OF AMERICA

THE CHURCH OF ST. HELEN, BISHOPSGATE, BEING THE NINTH VOLUME OF THE SURVEY OF LONDON. BY MINNIE REDDAN AND ALFRED W. CLAPHAM, F.S.A., MEMBERS OF THE LONDON SURVEY COMMITTEE

JOINT PUBLISHING COMMITTEE REPRESENTING THE LONDON COUNTY COUNCIL AND THE LONDON SURVEY COMMITTEE.

Chairman.

E. L. MEINERTZHAGEN.

Members appointed by the Council.

GRANVILLE-SMITH, R. W.
JOHNSON, W. C.
MEINERTZHAGEN, E. L.
TAYLOR, ANDREW T.

Members appointed by the London Survey Committee.

GODFREY, WALTER H.
LOVELL, PERCY.
NORMAN, PHILIP.

MEMBERS OF THE LONDON SURVEY COMMITTEE DURING THE PERIOD OF THE WORK.

The former Presidents of the Committee were—
The late LORD LEIGHTON, P.R.A.
The late Rt. Hon. and Rt. Rev. Dr. CREIGHTON, LORD BISHOP OF LONDON.

President.

The Most Hon. the MARQUESS CURZON OF KEDLESTON, K.G., G.C.S.I., G.C.I.E., F.R.S.

Honorary Members.

The Rt. Hon. Lord Aberdare of Duffryn, D.L.
A. A. Allen.
The Rt. Hon. Lord Aldenham.
The Society of Antiquaries, of London.
William Sumner Appleton.
The Royal Institute of British Architects.
The Society of Architects.
The Architectural Association.
The Athenæum.
John Avery, F.C.A., F.S.S.
E. Burrell Baggallay.
J. S. Baines.
P. A. Bayman.
Boylston A. Beal.
Walter G. Bell.
The Bermondsey Public Libraries.
The Ven. Archdeacon Bevan.
Henry Forbes Bigelow.
Harry W. Birks.
The Birmingham Central Library.
The Bishopsgate Institute.
Arthur Bonner, F.S.A.
The British Museum.
E. W. Brooks.
A. Herve Browning.
The Carnegie Library, Pittsburgh.
The Worshipful Company of Carpenters.
Miss A. G. E. Carthew.
W. J. Checkley.
The Chelsea Public Library.
G. H. Chettle.
The Chiswick Public Library.
Sir Cyril S. Cobb, K.B.E., M.V.O., M.P.
E. C. Colquhoun.
The Columbia University Library.
The Constitutional Club.
William W. Cordingley.
Lady Courtney.
The Rt. Hon. the Earl of Crawford, K.T., V-P.S.A.
The Most Hon. the Marquess of Crewe, K.G.
W. E. Vernon Crompton, F.R.I.B.A.
The Croydon Public Library.
George H. Duckworth, C.B., F.S.A.
Herbert L. Eason.
Eustace Erlebach.
The Rt. Hon. the Earl Ferrers, F.S.A.
The Fulham Public Library.
Miss Agnes Garrett.
Richard L. Giveen.
Sir Rickman J. Godlee, Bt., K.C.V.O.
The Goldsmiths Library, University of London.
Sir Albert Gray, K.C.B., K.C.
Miss I. I. Greaves.
Hubert J. Greenwood, J.P.
The Guildhall Library.
The Hackney Public Library.
Richard Walden Hale.
E. Stanley Hall, M.A., F.R.I.B.A.
The Hammersmith Central Library.
Arthur F. Hill.
The Rt. Hon. Sir Samuel Hoare, Bt., C.M.G., M.P.
Victor Tylston Hodgson.
J. J. Holdsworth.
E. J. Horniman, J.P.
Constant Huntington.
Maj. Douglas Illingworth.
Mrs. Illingworth Illingworth.
Miss Edith F. Inderwick.
The Rt. Hon. Viscount Iveagh, K.P., G.C.V.O., F.R.S.
C. H. F. Kinderman.
James E. King, M.A., F.S.A., F.R.Hist.S.
C. L. Kingsford, F.S.A.
G. C. Lawson.
Lady Leconfield.
The Rt. Hon. Viscount Leverhulme, F.R.G.S.
H. W. Lewer, F.S.A.
Owen C. Little.
The London Library.
J. Lort-Williams, K.C., M.P.

Gilbert H. Lovegrove, F.R.I.B.A.
Mary Countess of Lovelace.
Alexander Macdougall.
The Manchester Public Libraries.
The Manchester Society of Architects.
Rev. William MacGregor.
Mrs. John Markoe.
Miss B. A. Meinertzhagen.
The Metropolitan Public Gardens Association.
G. Vaughan Morgan.
Mrs. John H. Morison.
John Murray, F.R.I.B.A.
The New York Public Library.
Mrs. Richard Nicholson.
R. C. Norman.
Mrs. Robert Norman.
Vere L. Oliver.
The Oxford and Cambridge Club.
Reginald H. Pearson.
F. W. Peters.
The Free Library of Philadelphia.
Mrs. W. Wilton Phipps.
H. A. Piehler.
F. W. Platt.
Arnold Danvers Power.
Sir D'Arcy Power, K.B.E.
F. W. Procter.
The Public Record Office.
Colin E. Reader.
The Reform Club.
Mrs. F. W. L. Richardson.
The John Rylands Library.
The Shoreditch Public Library.
Sion College.
Commander Skinner.
Mrs. Vernon Smith.
W. J. Songhurst.
H. C. Sotheran.
The Southwark Public Library.
The Stoke Newington Public Library.
R. T. D. Stoneham.
R. Clipston Sturgis.
Hamilton H. Turner.
The Victoria and Albert Museum.
Lewis Huth Walters.
The Library of Congress, Washington.
The West Ham Public Library.
The City of Westminster Public Libraries.
Mrs. Wharrie.
J. Barrington White.
Miss M. J. Wilde.
The Woolwich Public Libraries.
H.M. Office of Works.
John E. Yerbury
Keith D. Young, F.R.I.B.A.

Active Members.

C. R. Ashbee, M.A.
Oswald Barron, F.S.A.
A. H. Blake, M.A.
*J. W. Bloe, O.B.E., F.SA.
*W. W. Braines, B.A. (Lond.)
*A. E. Bullock, A.R.I.B.A.
*A. W. Clapham, F.S.A.
A. O. Collard, F.R.I.B.A.
*H. W. Fincham, F.S.A.
Mrs. Ernest Godman, A.R.E.
*T. Frank Green, F.R.I.B.A.
Edwin Gunn, A.R.I.B.A.
*Richard Harriss.
Osborn C. Hills, F.R.I.B.A.
*Philip S. Hudson, A.R.I.B.A.
T. Gordon Jackson, F.R.I.B.A.
*Max Judge.
*P. K. Kipps, A.R.I.B.A.
*Ernest A. Mann, Licentiate R.I.B.A.
W. McB. Marcham.
*Ellis Marsland, F.S.Arc.
W. Monk, R.E.
*Sydney Newcombe.
*E. C. Nisbet, Licentiate R.I.B.A.
*Robert Pearsall.
Francis W. Reader.
*Miss M. Reddan.
T. Maxwell Scott.
*Joseph Seddon.
*Mill Stephenson, F.S.A.
*Francis R. Taylor, Licentiate R.I.B.A.
*T. O. Thirtle, A.R.I.B.A.
*George Trotman.
Miss E.M.B. Warren, A.R.B.A.
A. Grayston Warren.
W. Wonnacott, A.R.I.B.A.
*E. L. Wratten, A.R.I.B.A.
*Edward Yates.
*W. Plomer Young.
*Philip Norman, F.S.A., LL.D., *Hon. Editor of the Committee.*
*Walter H. Godfrey, F.S.A., *Hon. Assistant Editor of the Committee.*
E. L. Meinertzhagen, J.P., L.C.C., *Hon. Treasurer of the Committee.*
*Percy W. Lovell, B.A., A.R.I.B.A., *Secretary of the Committee*, 27 Abingdon Street, S.W. 1.

* Denotes those who have co-operated in the production of the present volume.

CONTENTS

DESCRIPTION OF THE PLATES.

ILLUSTRATIONS IN THE TEXT

HERALDIC ILLUSTRATIONS

15. PICKERING – – – – *Gules*, a cheveron between three fleurs-de-lis *Or*.
16. KIRWIN – – – – *Argent*, fretty *Gules*, a chief *Azure* with three fleurs-de-lis (*Or?*) therein.
17. STAPER – – – – *Argent*, a voided cross between four stars *Sable*.
18. SPENCER – – – – *Argent*, two gimel-bars between three eagles *Sable*.
19. LANGHAM – – – – *Argent*, three bears' heads razed *Sable*, muzzled *Or*.
20. CHAMBERLAIN – – – *Gules*, a scutcheon *Argent* within an orle of cinqfoils *Or*.

PREFACE

THE first volume of the Parish of St. Helen is also the first volume of the Survey dealing with any portion of the City of London, although a monograph by the Survey Committee on Crosby Hall was published as far back as 1908. That the volume on St. Helen's Church should be placed in such a position in the series needs no excuse when it is recalled that St. Helen's, on account of its monuments if not from its architecture, is easily the first of the ancient Churches of the City, while to the interest of its being one of the oldest Parish Foundations of London it adds the history and part of the buildings of a rich Benedictine nunnery, where for three hundred years the daughters of the merchant princes took the veil. St. Helen's has so far been the subject of but one monograph, written by a late vicar, the Rev. J. E. Cox, and published in 1876. Since that time much additional information, both historical and architectural, has come to light; students of archæology have also learned to discard much that passed current in the 19th century, and being better equipped are able to acquire more from a closer critical study both of the building itself and of its records.

The historical portion, dealing with the pre-Reformation period, is entirely the work of Miss M. Reddan, who, as the author of the compressed account of the Priory in the Victoria History of London, most kindly consented to undertake this, the most onerous part of the literary work of the volume.

The thanks of the Committee are due to the Rev. S. T. H. Saunders, Rector of St. Helen's, for the kindness and help which he has ever extended to its members during their survey of the building. Acknowledgment should also be made to the Clerk of the Leathersellers' Company, Mr. G. F. Sutton, F.S.A., for giving access to the records and drawings in possession of the Company; to the Society of Antiquaries and the Merchant Taylors' Company for permission to reproduce certain engravings and drawings from their Libraries; to Major V. Farquharson, F.S.A., for his notes on the funeral helm in the Church; to Mr. F. S. Eden for his description of the ancient glass, and to Mr. G. Gordon Godfrey for his drawings of the heraldic shields. My own personal thanks are due to Mr. Challoner Smith, F.S.A., to Mr. Charles Lethbridge Kingsford, F.S.A., to Mr. H. L. Hopkinson, F.S.A., and to Mr. Philip M. Johnston, F.S.A., for freely placing at my disposal facts and information from unpublished documents with which I should otherwise have been unacquainted.

A. W. CLAPHAM.

ST. HELEN, BISHOPSGATE

I.—HISTORY : PRE-REFORMATION PERIOD

THE PARISH CHURCH OF ST. HELEN, BISHOPSGATE

The Church of St. Helen, Bishopsgate, was probably founded before the Conquest,* though of this there is no proof. Nothing is really known about it until the middle of the 12th century,† when it is mentioned as one of the churches in the jurisdiction of St. Paul's Cathedral.‡ At this time it was customary for the chapter to make over its churches to men who became responsible for the cure of souls and for the payments due to the canons. By an agreement of a date after 1140,§ a certain Ranulf and Robert his son, who themselves appear to have been canons of St. Paul's,|| were to hold the church of St. Helen for their lives paying 12d. yearly to the chapter, and after the death of both, a third member of their family or community chosen by them was to have the church, paying, however, 2s. a year to the chapter. On the death of this third person the canons were to enter into complete possession of the church.¶ The three successive holders must have all died before 1181, for in the time of Dean Hugh ** the canons granted St. Helen's to Peter, son of Edmund the Alderman, who was to pay them 10s. yearly.††

A few years later Dean Ralph de Diceto and the chapter of St. Paul's gave to William, son of William Goldsmith, and his heirs the patronage of St. Helen's, providing that the priest chosen by them should be presented to the canons and should swear fealty to them for the church and promise to make an annual payment of a mark, which they for their part undertook not to increase, and providing that William and his heirs should not alienate the advowson to any religious house.‡‡

During the 12th century two visitations of the church are recorded. At the first visitation, *c.* 1160–81,§§ when Alberic was priest,|||| the church

* As to the early foundation of many of the City churches, including St. Helen's, see W. Page, *London, Its Origin and Early Development*, pp. 159–61.

† A grant to the canons of St. Mary, Southwark, of 12d. rent from land in front of the Church of St. Helen (Cart. Cotton. xxvii, 100) is dated *c.* 1160 in the calendar of B. M. charters.

‡ These and all the deeds entered in Liber C. (*Doc. of D. and C. of St. Paul's*) are considered to be not later than the 12th century. (*Hist. MSS. Com. Rep.* IX, App. I, 64b.)

§ The canons promised Ranulf to celebrate yearly the anniversary of Thurstan, Archbishop of York, who died 1140.

|| The canons are called Ranulf's " Confratres."

¶ *Hist. MSS. Com. Rep.* IX., App. I, 64b.

** Hugh de Marny was dean *c.* 1160 to 1181. (*Victoria County History, London*, I, 431.)

†† *Hist. MSS. Com. Rep.* IX, App. I, 64b.

‡‡ *Doc. of D. and C. of St. Paul's*, Press A, Box 12, No. 1111. If William wants to give the patronage to two or more clergy serving God in that church, he may do so on condition that the chief of the number shall swear for himself and the others before the canons not to transfer the patronage to any religious place or convent, and shall promise fealty and payment of one mark annually.

§§ *Victoria County History, London*, I, 181.

|||| Among the donors and witnesses of the grant to Peter, son of Edmund Alderman, was Master Alberic.

possessed a missal, the third part of a breviary, an antiphonary, a manual, a hymnary, a complete vestment with chasuble of cloth, two altar towels, an altar-cloth and a silver cross.* The return made after the second visitation, *circ.* 1181–86,† recites that the church of St. Helen belongs to the canons and pays 20s. to them by the hand of Master Cyprian, 12d. for synodals, and 12d. to the archdeacon. It has a cemetery. The ornaments of the church are as follows: a silver chalice gilded inside weighing 16*s.*; a good and new antiphonary of the use of St. Paul; a copy ‡ of the four gospels; a cross with relics; a painted picture; part of a breviary; a complete vestment with silk chasuble; a silk altar frontal; two maniples; a banner; two altar frontals, one of silver, the other linen; two old altar-cloths; § one mass vestment ||; a good iron-bound chest for storing books and vestments. At this time the church was served by Ailnod.¶

THE PRIORY OF ST. HELEN, BISHOPSGATE

Early in the 13th century** [*circ.* 1210] Dean Alard and the chapter of St. Paul's gave William, son of William Goldsmith, permission to establish a nunnery in the church of St. Helen and to confer on the convent the advowson of the church. They ordained that the prioress on election was to be presented to the dean and chapter and to swear fealty to them for the church and promise to make the annual payment to them of half a mark. She was to undertake not to alienate the right of patronage nor to subject herself to any other community. The dean and chapter for their part gave the convent leave to convert to their own uses all the obventions of St. Helen's except the pension.†† The nunnery thus founded was of the Benedictine Order.

At some time a form was drawn up as to the procedure to be observed on the death of a prioress of St. Helen's and the election of her successor.‡‡ This ordered that on the death of the prioress the convent through their steward and chaplains were immediately to inform the dean and chapter as their patrons. Two canons were then to be sent from St. Paul's to take possession of the priory, in token of which they were to be given the keys of the church by the sub-prioress. After the body of the prioress had been committed to the grave by the two canons, the convent had to send their confessor, steward and household chaplains with their letters patent under their common seal to ask leave of the dean and chapter to elect, and leave was to be granted without delay. When the election had taken place notice

* *Hist. MSS. Com. Rep.* IX, App. I, 64b. † *Victoria County History, London*, I, 181.

‡ "Textus." The word generally means the four gospels in a richly ornamented cover.

§ "Due [palle] super altare veteres." || "Parura."

¶ Transcription of the document at St. Paul's by W. Sparrow Simpson. (*Archæologia*, LV, 295.)

** Dean Alard de Burnham died August, 1216.

†† W. Sparrow Simpson, *Documents Illustrating the History of St. Paul's Cathedral* (Camden Soc.), 107.

‡‡ Transcribed from the *Statuta Majora* of St. Paul's. (*Ibid.* pp. 107–11.)

Dean and Chapter of St. Paul's.

was to be sent to the dean and chapter who appointed a day for the convent to present the prioress elect at St. Paul's. The election being examined and confirmed, the prioress elect was to be led to the high altar during the singing of the "Te Deum Laudamus," and while she knelt on the steps a psalm was to be sung and certain prayers* were to be said.

The prioress was then to be led back to the chapter, the charge of the monastery was to be committed to her and she was to swear fealty and obedience to the dean and chapter, promising to subject her house to no other, and to pay the half-mark due yearly.

Permission was then to be given to the prioress and nuns accompanying her to visit their friends for the three days following, since except on the election of a prioress the nuns never went outside the nunnery's walls.† On the fourth day, two canons from St. Paul's were to meet the prioress and nuns at the gates of the quire of St. Helen's, and leading the prioress between them up the quire were to place her in front of the altar. After two or three prayers had been said, they were to conduct her to the stall, chanting meanwhile the psalm "Levavi oculos," and install her by authority of the dean and chapter. Subsequently she was to be led into the nuns' chapter house and assigned the highest seat; then the chief canon was to deliver to her the rule of St. Benedict with the spiritual government and afterwards the common seal with the temporal government of that house, enjoining the nuns to obey her as their spiritual mother. The nuns were then to kiss her and do obedience as was customary.

The early history of the house is scanty. With the exception of a dispute, soon after the foundation,‡ about property included in the endowment, the first mention of the nunnery seems to be in the will of William Longespee, Earl of Salisbury, in 1225.§ In the same year|| the prioress of St. Helen's put in a claim to half the advowson of Eyworth church under a grant of Maud de Bussy.¶ Shortly afterwards the prioress figures in a suit about half a mill called Old Ford Mill on the Lea,** which apparently had been recently bought by the convent. Then come two or three grants or events of more intimate concern to the house. Such is an agreement in 1242–43†† over the will of Mary Duket, which provides for a chantry to be established in the priory of St. Thomas of Acon, or

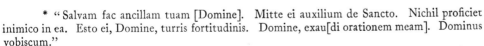

* "Salvam fac ancillam tuam [Domine]. Mitte ei auxilium de Sancto. Nichil proficiet inimico in ea. Esto ei, Domine, turris fortitudinis. Domine, exau[di orationem meam]. Dominus vobiscum."

† The nuns in a petition to Edward III describe themselves as "les povres recluses . . . de la Mesoun de Seinte Eleine en Londres."

‡ In the time of A. [i.e. Alard], the Dean, and therefore before August, 1216.

§ *Close Rolls*, ii, 71.

|| The house of St. Helen, London, to the master of which Henry III made a gift of logs in 1224 (*Close Rolls*, i, 601b) was apparently not the nunnery in the City, but a hospital for lepers outside London (*Parliament Rolls*, I, 323b), almost certainly that of St. Giles in the Fields under an alternative or additional dedication.

¶ Maitland, *Bracton's Note-book*, iii, 107; *Victoria County History*, *Bedford*, II, 233.

** Maitland, *op. cit.*, I, 340.

†† *Cart. Harl.*, 49, F, 51.

that of St. Helen in London. Of domestic importance too was the leave given by the king to the convent in March, 1249, to enclose a lane which crossed their property.* This must have been the lane described at the inquisition of 1274–75 as leading to the church of St. Mary Axe and as having been blocked some years before with an earthen wall.†

Edward I on 4th May, 1285, went on foot with a company of nobles and bishops to present to the nuns of St. Helen's the Holy Cross called "Neit," apparently a piece of the True Cross,‡ which he had found in Wales.§ This gift may have caused an addition to the dedication of the house, for *c.* 1299 the nunnery is mentioned as the priory of Holy Cross and St. Helen, London.||

During the interdict on the City in 1290 by John Peckham, Archbishop of Canterbury, the prioress and convent as a special favour were granted permission to have service in the nunnery on the Day of the Invention of Holy Cross.¶ Then comes a link between the nunnery and the social life of the trading community. The Fraternity of Puy, established at the end of the 13th century by Gascon merchants in London, chose this priory for the annual celebration of a solemn mass for dead companions of the brotherhood. **

About this time the convent seems to have been in need of financial help, probably for building. In 1290 Pope Nicholas IV granted relaxation of a year and 40 days of enjoined penance to penitents visiting the nuns' church on the feasts of St. Helen and Holy Cross; †† and sixteen years later Ralph Baldock, Bishop of London, offered an indulgence of 40 days to those of his diocese who should go to the conventual church of St. Helen for devotion or pilgrimage, hear the divine office there, or give aid to the fabric or to the maintenance of the ornaments.‡‡ The will of Thomas of Basing,§§ enrolled in 1300, implies that he and his brother Salomon had erected the church or nunnery buildings: the remainder of a rent of 45s. 8d. after deduction of 5 pittances of 6s. 8d. each to the convent of St. Helen's was to be devoted to the maintenance of their church which,

* *Calendar of Patent Rolls*, 1247–58, p. 38.

† *Hundred Rolls*, 409, 410.

‡ The Cross "Gneyth" as a sacred relic is mentioned in connexion with other religious houses. (*Liber Quotid. Contrarot. Garderobae*, 28 *Edw. I*, pp. 32, 35, 36)

§ *Chron. of Reigns of Edw. I and Edw. II* (Rolls Ser.), I, 93–4.

|| Mortuary Roll of Amphelissa, Abbess of Lillechurch (Highham), Kent. (*Camb. Ant. Soc.*, X, 386). The priory is called Holy Cross and St. Helen by Hasted. (*Hist. of Kent*, ii, 151). The obituary roll of Thomas Hatfield, Bishop of Durham, 1381, and that of Priors Ebchester and Burnby (Surtees Soc.) in the second half of the fifteenth century, give the simple dedication of St. Helen. Possibly the double dedication was little used in order to avoid confusion with the Priory of Holy Cross established in Hart Street shortly before 1300 by the Crossed Friars. (*Victoria County History, London*, I, 514.)

¶ *Epist. Joh. Peckham* (Rolls Ser.), iii, 970.

** *Munim. Gildhall* (Rolls Ser.), II (1), 4; 216–18.

†† *Cal. of Papal Letters*, I, 521.

‡‡ Fowler, *Regit. Rad. Baldock* (Cant. and York Soc.), 39.

§§ Thomas of Basing was sheriff in 1269–70

Basing.

he says, Salomon my brother and I "construximus."* Whatever the exact meaning of these words may be, they signify undoubtedly that the benefactions to St. Helen's of Salomon and Thomas Basing were considerable.†

The connexion of this family with the priory extended over a long period: Felicia of Basing was elected prioress in 1269; ‡ Dionisia of Gloucester, granddaughter of Thomas Basing, was a nun there; § and Henry of Gloucester, goldsmith of London, a relative of Thomas Basing, was a benefactor to the house by his will in 1332, leaving 11 marks a year to the prioress and convent for 12 years to provide two chantries in the church of St. Helen during that time,|| and providing for the perpetual payment of a silver mark to the convent every year for a pittance.¶

The nuns made an agreement in 1344 with Walter Dieuboneye of Bletchingley, cheesemonger of London, in return for his benefits to them, to establish a chantry for him in their church and give the chaplain a salary of two marks a year besides food and drink and a suitable house within the priory such as the parish priest had.** Property was left to the convent to endow chantries in their church for varying periods under the will of John of Etton, rector of Great Massingham, in 1346††; by Robert Atte Hyde, rector of St. Mary Wolnoth, in 1348‡‡; and by Walter of Bilyngham by will enrolled in 1349.§§ Although the income of the house must have been increased by these legacies and in other ways, there was evidently little margin beyond ordinary expenditure. In 1350, as a result of a petition to the Pope, a papal indulgence of a year and 40 days was granted to those who visited the nuns' church on Good Friday or on the feasts of the Invention and Exaltation of the Cross, or who made a substantial contribution to the fabric of the church, "which was in danger of going to ruin."|||| The truth of this statement receives corroboration from the will of William of Thorney¶¶ in 1349, in which bequests were made to

* *Husting Rolls*, 29, m. 54.

† A garbled account of these was probably the basis of Stow's mistakes about the foundation of the priory: "William Basing Deane of paules was the first founder, and was there buried, and William Basing, one of the Shiriffes of London, in the second yeare of Edward the second, was holden also to be a founder, or rather a helper there." (*Survey of London*, Kingsford's edn., I, p. 171.) The priory was not founded by a dean of St. Paul's and there is no record of a dean called William Basing. Moreover there is apparently no evidence extant of gifts made to the priory by William Basing, sheriff in 1308–9.

‡ See under Prioresses.

§ *Husting Rolls*, 29, m. 54.

|| After the 12 years his heir was to maintain one chaplain for 5 years more.

¶ *Husting Rolls*, 60, dors. 152.

** *Cart. Harl.* 44, F, 45; *Hist. MSS. Com. Rep.* IX, App., p. 57b. They made themselves responsible for certain payments, among them one for a pittance of half a mark to the convent.

†† Sharpe, *Cal. of Wills proved in the Court of Husting*, I, 687.

‡‡ *Ibid.* I, 512–13

§§ *Ibid.* I, 581.

|||| *Cal. of Papal Petitions*, I, 198.

¶¶ Sheriff, 1339–40.

the prioress and nuns of St. Helen's not only for the establishment of chantries, but for repairing their church, dormitory and cloister.*

Francis.

An important addition to the church was made a few years later when Adam Francis,† mercer, of London, built a chapel in honour of the Holy Ghost. In August, 1363, he obtained from Pope Urban V an indulgence for those who visited the chapel at Christmas and other great festivals, and on the feasts of Holy Cross and All Saints.‡ Francis by his will in August, 1374,§ left directions for the establishment of a perpetual chantry of St. Mary and of another in the chapel of his foundation. The chaplain of the first chantry was to celebrate a mass by note daily at the high altar of the conventual church, and at the conclusion he was to commemorate the faithful departed and Adam Francis by name; this mass was to be said before the nuns' hour of prime,|| and six nuns chosen by the prioress every Saturday¶ were to be present and remain until the commemoration of the dead was over; each nun for her attendance and services was to receive 4d. at the end of the week. The chaplain of the St. Mary chantry was to be paid £8, the other chaplain £7 a year. Francis's anniversary was to be observed by special services in the nuns' quire and the parish church, and by the feeding of 13 poor persons in the priory.

It is interesting to note that Richard II, alleging a crown right after coronation, nominated a nun to St. Helen's.** If the king had such a right, this seems to have been the sole instance of its exercise, and the conclusion may be drawn that entrance to the convent was at that time considered a privilege.

An affair which occurred shortly afterwards†† certainly indicates that the priory was supposed to possess ample means. Joan Heyroun, one of the nuns, represented to Pope Urban VI that she was suffering so badly from gout that she was unable to perform her canonical duties, and asked that she might be excused from them, and that on account of her great poverty he would grant her food and clothing from the monastery's goods. In response the pope in February, 1384, ordained that she should have for life two corrodies from the prioress,‡‡ such as two other nuns received, that she should be cared for as they were, and should have

* He left to the convent moreover a cup with silver-gilt cover to hang by his silver seal-chain behind the High Altar for keeping the Host, his portifory, psalter and silver-gilt chalice with vestments, towels or other necessaries for service in the church. (Sharpe, *op cit.*, I, 649–50.)

† Mayor in 1352–3 and 1353–4.

‡ *Cal. Papal Petitions*, I, 445. Shortly afterwards the indulgence was extended to those visiting the chapel during the Octave of Whitsuntide.

§ A copy of the will, which is extremely detailed, is given by Cox in his *Annals of St. Helen's, Bishopsgate*, 362–76.

|| This early mass had for some time been celebrated, and it had been customary for some of the nuns to be present, but up to now it had not been endowed.

¶ If the numbers in the house permitted, no nun was to do two weeks' service consecutively.

** *Cal. of Pat.*, 1377–81, p. 20.

†† *Doc. of D. and C. of St. Paul's*, Press A, Box 25, No. 1112.

‡‡ Worth £10 a year.

a suitable dwelling, viz. a hall with two chambers annexed within the precinct of the cemetery of the parish church. Joan, however, met with opposition from the prioress, and seems then to have obtained other bulls ordering the prioress to answer in the papal court. The prioress and two of her supporters retaliated, it was said, by keeping her a close prisoner on insufficient food,* whereupon the dean and chapter of St. Paul's intervened, ordering the prioress to release Joan, and to permit her to have the comforts sent her by friends and to communicate with her relations. The prioress and the other two nuns, who had meanwhile appealed to the court of Canterbury, refused, pending their appeal, to recognise the jurisdiction of the dean in the matter, and were on 18th July, 1385, declared by him to have incurred the threatened sentence of excommunication. Here information ceases, so how the case ended is unknown. The facts as disclosed are not favourable to Joan. If she was poor, her friends were obviously rich or influential, and she was apparently trying to benefit herself at the expense of the convent and in defiance of the authority of the prioress. On the other hand her action may have been a protest against injustice or favouritism: an attempt to get what had been given to others and denied to her.

Three years afterwards the domestic affairs of the convent again called for the dean's intervention. One of the nuns, a certain Joyce, who had taken the veil of her own free will, became so discontented a year or two later as to cause a rumour that she wanted to leave the priory. Examined on this point by the dean in July, 1388, Joyce declared that she had never repented her profession, but in September she escaped by stealth from the priory, put off the nun's habit, and in October was reported to have married. The dean and chapter therefore ordered her to be denounced as excommunicated until she returned to her cloister.†

A set of inquiries and injunctions for a visitation of St. Helen's, though undated, may in all probability be referred to the time of this same dean, John of Appelby,‡ possibly between 1385 and 1389. Notification of a visitation to be held at St. Helen's on Thursday before the feast of St. Nicholas was given to the convent by John the dean, and the inquiries were to be made at a visitation on a Thursday; moreover, in the Joan Heyroun case Thomas Feckenham is mentioned as one of three clerks prosecuting the appeal of the prioress and her supporters, while questions about grants to "Feckenham" were among the inquiries. These are as follows: 1. On Thursday former injunctions given to the prioress are to be shown. 2. Restitution of the quit-claim made to Feckenham at the

* At some stage of the proceedings the civil authorities ordered Joan's arrest under the Statute of Præmunire, so that the prioress' action may not have been as arbitrary as it appears.

† *Doc. of D. and C. of St. Paul's*, A, Box 25, No. 1110.

‡ In *Victoria County History, London*, I, 431, John of Appelby is said to have been succeeded in 1376 by Robert Brewer. The author of the article, however, gives Robert Brewer as a dean whose tenure was doubtful; and John of Appelby was certainly dean at the time of the cases of Joan Heyroun and Joyce in 1385 and 1388.

time of the visitation is to be required as was formerly enjoined on the prioress. 3. The state of the house is to be shown: the rental and accounts with a copy of those accounts for delivery to the dean and chapter. 4. The said Feckenham is to show the corrody formerly granted to him before the time of the present prioress, in which Feckenham is bound, as is said, to do certain services to the prioress and convent for life, in order that it be known whether he has duly performed them, and can thus perform them in future. 5. Full inquiry is to be made of the prioress and each nun whether the house is burdened of old or lately with any other corrody and if so with a corrody to what person, notwithstanding inquiries and full replies made before in this matter. 6. It is to be enjoined on them publicly in chapter that they shall sing and say divine service day and night, and especially *Placebo* and *Dirige*,* fully and distinctly, and not too fast as up to now they have been accustomed to do; nay rather with due and proper pauses. 7. It is to be enjoined on them that henceforth they abstain from kissing secular persons, a custom to which they have hitherto been too prone. 8. The prioress is to give up little dogs † and to be content with one or two. 9. The nuns are to wear veils according to the rules of their order and not such as are unduly ostentatious unless necessity so demands. 10. Margaret Senior, one of the prioress's maids, is to be removed from the service and company of the prioress owing to certain causes moving the dean and chapter, and this for the better reputation of the prioress. 11. The prioress is to be enjoined that in future she is not to have or keep with her any guests either at table or otherwise. 12. The prioress is to show missals and books, chalices and all other ecclesiastical ornaments, and to say who has the custody of them and how they are kept, and if by indenture, that indenture is to be shown. 13. Inquiry is to be made how many seals they have, whether two, viz. one, common, and the other "ad causas," and whether by the seal "ad causas" the house can be bound.

These injunctions show perhaps that life in the priory, especially in the case of the head, was not very austere, but that on the whole there was not much fault to be found. About fifty years later there was a great deal that needed amendment, to judge from the ordinances issued by Dean Reginald Kentwood on 21st June, 1439, after a visitation of the priory.‡

1. He ordered that divine service was to be performed by the convent night and day, and that silence was to be kept in due time and place as prescribed by their rule. 2. He enjoined the prioress and every nun to make due and complete confession to the confessor assigned by him. 3. The prioress and convent were ordered to appoint a place for an infirmary, where the sisters in sickness might be properly kept and tended at the expense of the house, as is customary. 4. The prioress was enjoined to

* These occur in commemorations of the dead.

† Cf. Chaucer's Prioress, *Canterbury Tales*, *Prologue*, l. 146 *et seq.*

‡ Dugdale, *Mon. Ang.*, IV, 553–4, transcribed from *Brit. Mus. Rot. Cotton.* V, 6. It is stated in *Hist. MSS. Com. Rep.* IX, App. I, that the date is wrongly given in Dugdale and should be 1432, but the *Cotton. Roll* says 1439, 17th year of Henry VI.

keep her dormitory and lie therein by night according to the rule, except when the rule permits otherwise. 5. The prioress and convent were not to allow secular persons to be locked within the bounds of the cloister, nor to enter after the compline bell except women servants and little girls at school ("mayde childeryne lerners") there. No women were to be allowed to reside there without the dean's permission. 6. The prioress and sisters were not to frequent any place within the priory through which evil suspicion or slander might arise, such places to be notified later by the dean to the prioress; and there was to be no looking out, through which they might "fall in worldly dilectation." 7. A serious and discreet woman of the Order, of good conduct and repute, was to be appointed to shut the cloister doors and keep the keys, so that nobody could enter or leave the place after compline bell nor at any other time by which the place might be slandered in future. 8. The prioress and convent were enjoined that no secular women were to sleep by night in the dormitory without special permission given in chapter among them all. 9. They were not to speak nor commune with secular persons; they were also not to send letters or gifts to secular persons nor receive such from them without permission of the prioress, and except in the presence of another nun assigned by the prioress to hear and report the rectitude of both parties, and except the letters and gifts have a good not bad motive and cause no scandal to the nuns' reputation and Order. 10. The prioress and convent were to admit to office only such sisters as were of good name and fame. 11. They were to choose one of the sisters, upright, competent and tactful, who could undertake the task of training the nuns who were ignorant, so that they might be taught their service and the rule of their religion. 12. Forasmuch as various perpetual fees, corrodies and liveries had been granted in the past to officers of the house and others to the injury of the house, and because of the dilapidation of the goods of the house, they were forbidden to make any such grants without the consent of the dean and chapter. 13. All dancing and revelling in the priory were forbidden except at Christmas and other proper times of recreation, and then only in the absence of seculars. 14. The prioress was commanded to have a door at the nuns' quire so that strangers could not look at them, nor they at strangers while they were at divine service; she was also to have made "a hache of conabyll heythe, crestyd withe pykys of herne" before the entrance to their kitchen, so that no strangers might enter, "with certeyne cleketts avysed be yow and be yowre steward to suche personys as yow and hem thynk onest and conabell." 15. The prioress alone was to have the keys of the postern door leading from the cloister to the churchyard, "for there is much coming in and going out unlawful times." 16. No nun was to receive children or keep them in the house unless "the profite of the comonys turne to the vayle of the same house." 17. These injunctions were to be observed in their entirety and were to be read four times a year in the nuns' chapel before them, so that they were remembered and kept, under pain of excommunication and other lawful penalties.

It is clear that some of the nuns were inclined to frivolity, or at any rate had not taken their profession with sufficient seriousness. There is also no doubt that the financial affairs of the house had at some period been mismanaged, and the priory was then suffering from the consequences. If the house righted itself, it was not for long. It was again in monetary difficulties in 1459, for the prioress and convent then assigned to their steward £76 16s. 8d. in part payment of a larger sum, to be taken by him from rents which were due to them, and in the collection of which he was promised the help of their rent collector.*

Crosby.

The will of Sir John Crosby† proves that the house in 1471 was still in economic straits and that money was then especially needed for contemplated alterations of the church. After arranging for his burial and tomb in the chapel of the Holy Ghost, Crosby bequeathed to the high altar of the church £66 1s. 4d. for offerings delayed or forgotten,‡ 400 marks to endow a chantry for 40 years; 100 marks for keeping his anniversary; and in consideration of "the great damages that the prioress and convent stand in by means of the great duties they owe" . . . £40 to diminish their debts; "also upon the renewing and reforming the said church 500 marks sterling."

Practically nothing more is heard of the priory's affairs § until 1528, when a vacancy gave rise to much intriguing for the position of prioress. A nun named Margaret Vernon, not a member of the convent, was promised it by Wolsey, and she and her friends made assiduous application to Cromwell.|| Meanwhile "Parson Larke," no doubt the rector of St. Ethelburga,¶ pressed at court the claims of the sub-prioress,** and in the end was successful. The incident offers more than one point for comment. The dignity was sufficiently important to attract several candidates ready to pay a considerable sum.†† Presumably the nuns had ceded the nomination willingly or otherwise to Wolsey or the king,‡‡ for there is no mention of the convent's right to elect. Altogether the transaction is not very creditable to any of the parties concerned, and was not calculated to improve discipline

* *Doc. of D. and C. of St. Paul's*, A, Box 77, No. 2043. The whole amount owing was apparently £110, as this is the sum for the repayment of which the convent gave its bond.

† Proved 1475. Cox, *op. cit.*, pp. 231–3.

‡ He was a parishioner of St. Helen's.

§ A nun of St. Helen's was chosen by Bishop FitzJames to be prioress of Holy Cross, Castle Hedingham. (*Victoria County History, London*, I, 459.)

|| *L. and P. Hen. VIII*, IV (3), 5970; V, 19, 20.

¶ John Larke was presented to the rectory of St. Ethelburga 30 Jan., 1504, and resigned 1542. (Newcourt, *Repert. Eccles.*, I, 346.)

** *L. and P. Hen. VIII*, IV (3) 5970; V, 15.

†† *Ibid.* V, 19, 20. According to Margaret Vernon they were offering 200 marks, and although she was shocked at them, she herself had earlier made an offer of £100 for it to Wolsey.

‡‡ The appointment seems at first to have been in Wolsey's hands, but afterwards the king gave the nomination to a certain Mr. Harper.

in the house. Still the spread of the new doctrines or fear of recent legislation rather than laxity of conduct may account for the flight of some of the nuns about 1534.*

The prioress and convent did their best to propitiate the authorities: in September, 1534, they gave Cromwell an annuity of four marks for life†; and they also subscribed to the declaration of the king's supremacy.‡

In 1537 and 1538, either to provide for their friends while they could, or as a kind of insurance for themselves, they completely set aside the Kentwood injunction and granted annuity after annuity: December, 1537, to their auditor a life annuity of 40s.§; 21st January, 1538, one of 4 marks to John Sewstre, gent.; 30th March, one of 40s. to Edward Rollesley, gent.||; 26th June, one of 4 marks to John Rollesley, gent.¶; 30th June, an annual rent of 10s. and an annuity of 2 marks to Henry Bowsell, gent.; 9th July, an annuity of 4 marks to Jerome Shelton, gent.; one of 20s. to Roger Hall, and another of 4 marks to John Staverton, gent.; and 1st October, an annuity of 20s. to John Melsham, gent.** These were about the last recorded acts of the convent.

Property of the Priory.

There is no surviving account of the original endowment of the house, nor does the priory figure in the *Taxatio Papae Nicholai*, *c.* 1297, so that a comparison of its possessions and income at different periods is impossible. The *Valor Ecclesiasticus* of 1535 gives the most satisfactory summary of its property at the end of its existence, and details that are lacking here can sometimes be supplied from the Ministers' Accounts, 32 Hen. VIII.††

* John Stanton had complained to Parliament on behalf of his master who was then in the Bishop of London's prison, and the Chancellor replied that it ill became him to be attorney for his master, adding that he was at the conveying of certain nuns from St. Helen's. (*L. and P. Hen. VIII*, V, 982.)

† Hugo, *The Last Ten Years of the Priory of St. Helen, Bishopsgate*, 7. In Cromwell's Accounts, Dec., 1537, there is the entry, "my lady of St. Ellyn's," 4, m. (*L. and P. Hen. VIII*, XIV (2), 782.)

‡ *Ibid.* VII, 1025 (2).

§ They gave him also the nomination to Eyworth vicarage for one turn. Hugo, *op. cit.*, 14.

|| *Ibid.* 13–15, 16.

¶ *Ibid.* 16. Edward and John Rollesley were probably related to the prioress, Mary Rollesley, who leased much conventual property to them. After the dissolution a person writing to Cromwell for a farm, formerly the property of St. Helen's, said that it was in the hands of one Rollesley by lease of the prioress not long before her suppressing "with most part of her tenements." (*L. and P. Hen. VIII*, XIII (2), 1177.)

** Hugo, *op. cit.*, 17–19. The annuity to Hall was for good and faithful service, the others were for good counsel, past and future. They were all allowed by the Court of Augmentations. The two Rollesleys and John Melsham were receiving them in 1556. (*Add. MS.* 8102, fol. 3.)

†† Both of these are printed in Dugdale, *Mon. Ang.* (ed. 1846), IV, pp. 554–5.

ST. HELEN, BISHOPSGATE

Income.

	£	s.	d.
CITY OF LONDON AND MIDDLESEX.			
Rents of assize with other rents within the city of London and suburbs *	312	6	4
Manor of Bordeston†	9	0	0
Edmonton	0	7	6
Wood in the demesne of Edmonton,‡ usually	1	8	0
Rectory of St. Helen in the hands of the Lady Prioress with tithes there	11	0	0§
BEDFORDSHIRE.			
Eyworth,‖ rent of assize, etc.	12	10	6
KENT.			
Barming,¶ rents of assize, etc.	4	0	0
Wood in the demesne, 5 acres, price per acre 1s.	0	5	0
*ESSEX.***			
In Balaamsmede	1	10	0
Manor of Marck	10	6	8
HERTFORDSHIRE.			
Rents of assize, etc., in Ware ††	2	0	0
BUCKINGHAMSHIRE.			
Firm of the manor of Datchett ‡‡	8	12	0
The sum of the whole value §§ is	376	6	0

* The Mins. Accts. give the 24 parishes in or near London in which the property lay. They include: parish of St. Helen within the close (£32 0s. 8d.); St. Helen outside the close (£35 9s. 4d.); St. Ethelburga (£32 11s. 4d.); St. Mary Axe (£8 18s. 8d.); St. Michael Cornhill where the nuns had tenements in 1224–25 (*Anct. D.* (*P.R.O.*) A, 1630) and acquired more under the will of Margery of Abingdon *c.* 1307–8 (Sharpe, *Cal. of Wills*, I, 196); St. Matthew, Westcheap (£10), where rents had been left to them by William of Paris in 1271 (*ibid.* I, 10); Philiplane in the parish of St. Stephen, Coleman St., where a tenement had been bequeathed to them *temp.* Edw. I (*Cal. of Pat.*, 1321–24, p. 127); St. Faith, where the convent already owned property in 1334–35 (*Hist. MSS. Com. Rep.* IX, App. I, 9b); the parish of St. Gabriel (£19 11s. 4d.) where they had a holding *c.* 1348 (Sharpe, *op. cit.*, I, 512), and held 19 messuages at the dissolution (*L. and P. Hen. VIII*, XIX (2), 166 (68)); parishes of St. Swithin and St. Mary Wolnoth, where Robert Atte Hyde in 1348 had left them property (Sharpe, *op. cit.*, I, 512–13); St. Mary, Whitechapel, and Stepney where they had land as early as 1248 (*Doc. of D. and C. of St. Paul's*, Liber A, fol. 44).

† In 1307 Edward I, at the instance of Queen Margaret, granted the nuns a weekly market on Tuesday and annual fair in their manor of Burston or Bordeston in Brentford (*Cal. of Chart. R.*, 1300–26, p. 81), but apparently they soon lost these privileges, possibly owing to the opposition of the Abbot of Westminster, who was lord of Brentford. (*Parl. R.* (Rec. Com.), II, 403.)

‡ Omitted from the Mins. Accts.

§ In the Mins. Accts. the value of the rectory is given as £15 9s. 8½d.

‖ The Mins. Accts. say Eyworth Firm of Manor—£11. For St. Helen's holding in Eyworth see *Victoria County History, Bedford*, II, 231; it included the rectory, for the church was appropriated to the Convent in 1331. (*Cal. of Pat.*, 1327–30, p. 446; *Cal. of Papal Letters*, II, 368.)

¶ The wood is omitted from the Mins. Accts. The prioress of St. Helen's held in 1346 a small part of a knight's fee in East Barming. (*Inq. relating to Feudal Aids*, III, 45.)

** The Mins. Accts. run: Marke £8, Leyton Firm of land £1 10s. Balaamsmede was probably the meadow in Fritheye given to the priory in 1265 for the nuns' clothing. (*Anct. D.* (P.R.O.), 791.) The St. Helen's manor of Marks was in Leyton. (Wright's *Hist. of Essex*, II, 497.)

†† The priory acquired property in Ware and Amwell in 1392. (*Cal. of Pat.*, 1391–96, p. 156.)

‡‡ The Mins. Accts. give: Firm of a messuage £8 12s.; Quitrents £7 18s. 10d.

§§ The sum total in the Mins. Accts. is £295 19s. 8½d.

ST. HELEN, BISHOPSGATE

OUTGOINGS.

	£	s.	d.
RENTS PAID.			
Rents paid from the above,* mainly to religious houses	6	14	5½
FEES.			
To James Butteyn, Knt., chief steward of the priory	2	0	0
To Richard Berde, receiver of all the demesnes, etc.	8	0	0
To John Dodington, auditor	2	8	8
PENSIONS.			
To David Netley, chaplain of the chantry of B. V. Mary founded in the church of St. Helen	8	0	0
To Thomas Criche, chaplain of the perpetual chantry of the Holy Ghost in that church	7	0	0
To the wardens of B. Mary Bothaw for the salary of one chaplain	6	0	0
To the wardens of the fraternity† in the church of St. Mary le Bow	4	0	0
To Thomas More, chaplain of the chantry of St. Michael Cornhill	4	13	4
In money paid to poor people in the City of London praying for the soul of Adam Francis on his anniversary in St. Helen's	0	6	8
And for the soul of Robert Knollys ‡ on his anniversary	0	3	4
To the vicar of Eyworth	4	0	0
To the Bishop of Lincoln per annum	1	0	0
For sinodals and procurations paid to the same bishop	0	10	8
Sum total of reprises	55	10	3½
There remains clear	§320	15	8½

To the priory belonged, then and in 1303,|| the advowsons of four city churches: St. Mary Axe, St. Mary Wolnoth, St. John on Walbrook and St. Ethelburga.

PRIORESSES

D. (? Dionisia), (*circ.* 1210).

A letter from the convent about some property was taken by D., the prioress, to A. the dean; ¶ and there is another letter on the subject from D. the prioress to A. the dean.** As the priory was founded in the time of Dean Alard (d. 1216) this appears to be the first prioress. A document at St. Paul's,†† of a date not later than the beginning of the 13th century, records that Aliz the prioress and the convent of St. Giles of Woodchurch, i.e. St. Giles's in the Wood, Flamstead, granted to the church of St. Helen and the nuns dwelling there Dionisia, a nun of their house, free from all subjection to their church. It seems possible that the first prioress D. was Dionisia from Flamstead.

* Among them 6s. 8d. to the rent collector of the Guildhall, London; probably the half mark payable under the agreement with Walter Dieuboneye.

† The Fraternity of Holy Trinity (*Doc. of D. and C. of St. Paul's*, A, Box 77, No. 2042). Probably the fraternity was responsible for Walter Dieuboneye's chantry. (*Cart. Harl.* 44, F, 45.)

‡ Robert Knollys, Esq., usher of the King's Privy Chamber, bequeathed to the Prioress and Convent in 1520 a suit of copes and £20. (Harris Nicolas, *Testamenta Vetusta*, 562.)

§ This does not agree with the total (£295 13s. 8½d.) of the Mins. Accts. Some household accounts, apparently of an earlier date than the *Valor*, give the income of the house as £356 14s. 6d. (*Doc. D. and C. of St. Paul's*, A, Box 77, No. 2042.)

|| *Munim Gildhall, London* (Rolls Ser.), II (1), 236.

¶ *Hist. MSS. Com. Rep.* IX, App. I, p. 5.

** *Brit. Mus. Cart. Cotton.*, V, 6 (2).

†† A, Box 25, No. 1109.

ST. HELEN, BISHOPSGATE

Maud.

The sale of a quitrent by this prioress was witnessed by William FitzAlice and John Travers.* William FitzAlice was sheriff in 1200–1201; John Travers was sheriff 1215–16; 1223–24 and 1224–25.

Helen (1230–31–1255).

The Prioress Helen in 1230–31 was party to a transaction about property in "Popleset," co. Midd.; in 1236–37 and 1249–50 about property in "Herghes," and 1244–45 about tenements in Greenford.† A grant of land in the parish of St. Mildred, Canterbury, was made to the master and brethren of the hospital of Ospreng in 1247 by a prioress called Helen.‡ In 1248 E. (? Elena) the prioress figures in an agreement about suit of court for land in Stepney.§ The nuns on 9th May, 1255, asked leave to elect a prioress in place of H., their late prioress, deceased.||

Scolastica (1261–62–1269).

The Prioress Scolastica in 1261–62 bought a rent of 100s. in Southminster and Althorne, co. Essex, from Holywell Priory.¶ A grant was made to the Prioress Scolastica and the convent in 1265–66.** She died July, 1269.††

Felicia of Basing (1269).

She was elected on the Tuesday before the feast of St. James (25th July), 1269.‡‡

Joan of Winchester (d. 1324).

The convent on 30th July, 1324, asked leave to elect to the vacancy caused by her death.§§

Beatrix le Boteler (d. 1332).

The convent informed the dean and chapter of her death on 3rd November, 1332.||||

Eleanor of Winchester (1332–44).

Notification of the election of Eleanor of Winchester, the sub-prioress, was made to the dean and chapter on 10th November, 1332.¶¶ She is mentioned by name as prioress in documents concerning property, 1334–35***; and in the agreement with Walter Dieuboneye, June, 1344.†††

Margery of Honeylane (1354–55).

In December, 1354, Margery of Honeylane, prioress of St. Helen's, London, was granted a papal indult to choose a confessor who might give her plenary remission at the hour of death.‡‡‡ She gave an acquittance for a rent on 16th December, 1355, to the wardens of London Bridge.§§§

Constance (1385).

The prioress during the case of Joan Heyroun in 1385 was named Constance.||||||

* *Guildhall MS.* 122, fol. 263.
† Hardy and Page, *Cal. of Fines for London and Middlesex*, I, 18, 22, 28, 32.
‡ *Cal. Chart. R.*, I, 318.
§ *Doc. of D. and C. of St. Paul's*, Liber A, fol. 44.
|| *Hist. MSS. Com. Rep.* IX, App. I, 27b.
¶ Kirk, *Feet of Fines for Essex*, I, 249.
** *Anct. D.* (P.R.O.), A, 791.
†† *Hist. MSS. Com. Rep.* IX, App. I, 57a.
‡‡ *Ibid.* §§ *Ibid.* 27b. |||| *Ibid.* 28a.
¶¶ *Ibid.* *** *Ibid.* 9b.
††† *Cart. Harl.* 44, F. 45; Sharpe, *Cal. of Letter-bk.*, F, 115.
‡‡‡ *Cal. of Papal Letters*, III, 528.
§§§ Sharpe, *Cal. of Letter-bk.*, G, 44.
|||||| *Doc. of D. and C. of St. Paul's*, A, Box 25, No. 1112.

ST. HELEN, BISHOPSGATE

Constance Somerset (d. 1398).

The date of her death, 15th April, 1398, is given in the convent's petition for leave to elect.* This lady was probably not the Prioress Constance of 1385. One of the injunctions, which appear to have been made by Dean John of Appelby,† and therefore not later than 1389, concerns a corrody granted *before the time of the present prioress* to a man called Feckenham. But as Feckenham had acted for and supported Prioress Constance in 1385 she is the most likely person to have given him the corrody.

Joan (1399).

This prioress presented in May, 1399, to the chantry of the Holy Ghost.‡

Margaret Stokes (1446–49).

Margaret Stokes as prioress on 21st July, 1446, gave a formal acquittance for a rent.§ A grant in mortmain of property in East Barming was made to the Prioress Margaret on 26th February, 1449.||

Alice Wodhouse (1459).

Her bond for payment of a debt is dated 20th April, 37 Hen. VI¶ [1459]. She appears to have resigned, for she witnessed as a nun the lease granted to Crosby in 1466, her name coming next to that of the prioress.**

Alice Ashfield (1466).

She figures as prioress in the lease to Crosby.††

Alice Tracthall (1498).

As prioress she granted a lease of premises in Birchin Lane on 20th March, 1498.§§ She was a member of the convent in June, 1466.‡‡

Isabel or Elizabeth Stamp (1512–28).

Isabel Stamp as prioress granted leases of conventual property on 3rd December, 1512, and 1st November, 1526.¶¶ In 1518 Elizabeth Stamp, prioress of St. Helen's, was enrolled a member of the Fraternity of Parish Clerks.|||| An entry in the Lord Treasurer's Memoranda Roll 32 Hen. VIII states that Isabel Stamp resigned on 12th November, 20 Hen. VIII [1528].***

Mary Rollesley (1528 or 1529–38).

Mary Rollesley was a nun at St. Helen's in 1513, when her mother, Elizabeth Rollesley, bequeathed £5 to her and £5 to the prioress and convent.††† She became sub-prioress, and according to the Lord Treasurer's Memoranda Roll ‡‡‡ was elected prioress on 22nd August, 21 Hen. VIII. She was certainly, however, acting as prioress before, for on 21st December, 20 Hen. VIII [1528], a lease was granted by Dame Mary "Rowlisley," prioress of St. Helen's. §§§

* *Hist. MSS. Com. Rep.* IX, App. I, 27b.

† See above, p. 8.

‡ *Hist. MSS. Com. Rep.* IX, App. I, 28a.

§ Christie, *Some Account of Parish Clerks*, 87–8.

|| *Cal. of Pat.*, 1446–52, p. 215.

¶ *Doc. of D. and C. of St. Paul's*, A, Box 77, No. 2043.

** *Brit. Mus. Addit. MS.* 15664, fol. 230.

†† *Ibid.*; *L. and P. Hen. VIII*, XVII, 881 (17). See also London Survey Committee's monograph, *Crosby Place*.

§§ Hugo, *op. cit.*, p. 4.

‡‡ *Addit. MS.* 15664, fol. 230.

¶¶ Hugo, *op. cit.*, p. 5.

|||| Christie, *op. cit.*, 38.

*** *L. and P. Hen. VIII*, V, 20, note.

††† Madox, *Formulare Anglicanum*, 440.

‡‡‡ See above.

§§§ *Exch. Aug. Convent. Leases, London*, No. 24.

Other offices held by nuns were those of sacristan and cellarer, the first being mentioned in 1344 and both in 1375.*

PRIESTS

In the "form of electing a prioress" mention is made of the nuns' confessor and the household chaplains.† Probably the foundation of the two chantries for Adam Francis made more than one conventual chaplain unnecessary. It is certain that in the last days of the priory only one priest, Thomas Wynstanley, was actually called the nuns' chaplain. He had a salary of £6 13s. 4d.,‡ and as a quarter of this sum, 33s. 4d., was entered in the convent's accounts of an earlier date as owing "to the chaplain celebrating high mass," § it looks as if for some time there had been only one household chaplain. Wynstanley evidently continued to officiate in the church until the suppression of chantries,|| and was then given an annual pension of 100s. which he was still receiving in 1556.¶

OFFICERS

The officials comprised a chief steward, a man of some social standing, an under-steward or rent collector, and an auditor.

In 1459 William FitzWater, gent., was steward, and Thomas Deryngton was rent collector.** Another steward, John Gower, is mentioned in Stow as buried in the church in 1512.††

Sir James Bolleyne, kt., was appointed steward in December, 1534, at a salary of 40s. a year ‡‡; and in January, 1535, Richard Berde, citizen and girdler of London, who rented from the convent *The Black Bull* in the parish of St. Ethelburga, was made steward, receiver and collector for life at a stipend of £12 a year and 20s. for his livery, an allowance of food and drink, 2 cartloads of fuel and 10 qrs. of charcoal, and use of an apartment within the priory precinct.§§ John Dodyngton is mentioned as auditor in the *Valor* and in 1537.||||

There were probably also minor officials.¶¶

* *Cart. Harl.* 44, F, 45; Cox, *op. cit.*, 366.

† W. Sparrow Simpson, *Docts. Illust. the Hist. of St. Paul's Cathedral.* (Camden Soc.)

‡ Hugo, *op. cit.*, 22. The information is taken from Mins. Accts. 31–32 Hen. VIII.

§ *Doc. of D. and C. of St. Paul's*, A, Box 77, No. 2042.

|| In the Mins. Accts. 31–32 Hen. VIII the salaries of the two Francis Chantry Chaplains and Wynstanley are entered. (Hugo, *op. cit.*, 22.) In 1547 the B. V. Mary Chantry must have been vacant, as only Wynstanley and the Chaplain of the H. Ghost Chantry were paid. (*Chantry Certif.* 34, No. 101.)

¶ *Addit. MS.* 8102, fol. 4.

** *Doc. of D. and C. of St. Paul's*, A, Box 77, No. 2043.

†† *Survey of London* (Kingsford's edn., I. p. 172).

‡‡ Hugo, *op. cit.*, 9. He is called James Butteyn in the *Valor*.

§§ Hugo, *op. cit.*, 9.

|||| *Ibid.* 14.

¶¶ Such as the janitor of the west gate of the close. (*Ibid.* 21.)

ST. HELEN, BISHOPSGATE

The house was surrendered on 25th November, 1538, but there are no signatures to the document.* The sixteen members of the convent were allotted pensions on 29th January, 1538–39, as follows:—†

Mary Rollesley (Rowlesley),	prioress	£30
Mary Shelton‡	nun	£4
Agnes Stavarton§	,,	66s. 8d.
Anne Webbe	,,	,,
*Joan Pawntlyver‖	,,	,,
Godclyff Laurence	,,	,,
*Eleanor Hannam	,,	4 marks
Elizabeth Marten	,,	,,
*Margaret Samson	,,	,,
Alice Gravenar	,,	,,
*Katharine Glossop	,,	,,
*Elizabeth Graye	,,	,,
Ursula Thwaytes	,,	,,
Joan Holdernes	,,	,,
Cecilia Cope	,,	66s. 8d.
*Anne Aleyne¶	,,	4 marks

The six whose names are prefixed by an asterisk were still receiving their pensions in 1556.**

The priory may be described as essentially a London religious house. It was founded by a London goldsmith, nearly all its benefactors were London citizens and merchants, and the convent was most probably recruited mainly from London homes and families. One of the prioresses belonged to the important City family of Basing; the name of another, Margery of Honeylane, proves her a native of the City; Joan of Winchester may have been a relative of Nicholas of Winchester, sheriff in 1280–81, and Beatrix le Botiller, a relative of James le Botiller, sheriff 1308–9; Constance Somerset probably came from the parish of St. Mary Somerset, and the last prioress was almost certainly a Londoner.†† Nearly all existing

* Hugo, *op. cit.*, 20; *L. and P. Hen. VIII*, XIII (2), 908.

† *Augment. Off. Misc. Bks.* 233 ff., 101–103b.

‡ A messuage within the close was held by Jerome Shelton, 1543. (*L. and P. Hen. VIII*, XVIII, 346 (54).)

§ Possibly a relation of John Staverton to whom the convent had granted an annuity. See above.

‖ Called Pamplyn in *Addit. MS.* 8102, fol. 3.

¶ Hugo suggests that she may have been the daughter of John and Agnes Alen to whom the convent in 1520 had granted a lease of "the Sun" or "the Salutation" in the parish of St. Olave's, Hart St. (*Op. cit.*, 201). They held the property at the Dissolution. (*L. and P. Hen. VIII*, XVIII, 346 (54).)

** *Add. MSS.* 8102, fol. 3.

†† Her mother, Elizabeth Rollesley, left by will to St. Botolph's without Aldgate 40s. "for tithes of her beerhouse named 'the Swan,' negligently forgotten," and she died within the jurisdiction of St. Mary Graces' Abbey. (Madox, *op. cit.*, 440.)

references to individual nuns point in the same direction. Most of these occur in wills proved in the Court of Husting. Besides the granddaughter of Thomas Basing already noticed, Lucy the daughter of John de Bancquell* was thus mentioned in 1328,† the sister of John of Etton in 1355, the sister of John atte Pole in 1361 and the sister of Thomas of Frowyk in 1374.‡ Property in Sopers-lane left to St. Helen's in 1373, was charged with an annual payment of 40s. to one of the nuns, Katharine Wolf,§ so probably she was a Londoner. It may be remarked that Chausier or Chaucer, the name of the lady nominated to the convent by Richard II, was by no means uncommon in London at that period, and moreover that Chaucer the poet, himself a Londoner, was related in some fashion to the Heyrouns,|| hence a possible connexion of Joan Heyroun's family with the City. The one exception is that of the nun Joan of Bures mentioned in 1418 in an agreement to pay during her lifetime to the prioress and convent 100s. from lands in Great and Little Whelnethan.¶ It seems clear that she was a native of Suffolk, but even in this case there was a close connexion with London if, as seems likely, Joan was related to Andrew of Bures who in 1331 established a chantry in the Crossed Friars.**

SEAL

The Seal of the Convent, a pointed oval, bears a representation of the Cross with St. Helen on the left, turning towards the right. She has her left arm round the shaft of the Cross and holds the three nails in her left hand. On the right, turning towards the left, are several women, two on their knees, some with arms extended to the Cross. Under an arch below is a half figure in prayer.

SIGILL · MONIALIVM · SANCTE · HELENE · LONDONIARVM ·

Note—This seal, attached to a deed of 1333–34 in the Augmentations Office, described in Dugdale (*Mon. Eng.*, IV, 552), evidently exactly resembles that appended to *Harl. Chart.* 44, 45, dated 1344, and the seal attached to a document of 1534, depicted in Malcolm's *Londinium Redivivum*, III, 548.

* Sometime alderman of Dowgate. (Sharpe, *Cal. of Wills*, I, 342.)

† Will of Cecilia de Bancquell. (*Husting R.*, 56, dors. 22, m. 168.) A half mark a year was left to Lucy.

‡ Sharpe, *op. cit.*, I, 687; II, 47, 170.

§ Will of Adam Francis. (Cox, *op. cit.*, 372.)

|| Riley, *Memorials of London*, xxxiii–xxxv.

¶ *Brit. Mus. Cart. Topham* 39. Joan was to have 40s. of the amount for her own use.

** *Victoria County History, London*, I, 514.

ST. HELEN, BISHOPSGATE

II.—HISTORY : POST-REFORMATION PERIOD

The parish records of St. Helen's do not, as in the case of several City parishes, include any of pre-reformation date. The Vestry Minutes begin in 1558, but there is a serious gap between 1578 and 1676. The churchwardens' accounts begin in 1563. These records contain a certain amount of information relative to the fabric, and the material portions have been printed in Cox's work.*

The nuns' church, together with the rest of the priory buildings, was granted in 1542 to Sir Richard Williams (*alias* Cromwell).† The Leathersellers' Company acquired their property in St. Helen's in 1543, and with it the nuns' quire.‡ In 1561 the Vestry Minutes refer to a conference with the Leathersellers' Company as to "the repairing and amendement of certaine decayeed places on the outside of the north Ile of the church." Some time therefore between these two dates the parish had come into possession of the fabric of the nuns' church, but whether by gift or purchase does not appear. It is likely, however, that the transfer happened very shortly after 1543, as otherwise the nuns' church would probably have been stripped of its lead and unroofed as of no use for domestic purposes.

Cromwell.

Leathersellers' Company.

In 1548 the church was considerably affected by the dissolution of the chantries. The chantry certificates give the following particulars of St. Helen's§ at this date :—

The paroche of Seint Ellens.

The kinge's majeste findeth within the saied churche two chauntry prestes and payethe them out of thaugmentacions xiij li xiijs. iiijd.

* J. E. Cox, *The Annals of St. Helen, Bishopsgate*, 1876, pp. 100–226.

† *Patent Roll*, 33 Hen. VIII, pt. 6. The property is described as follows :—

"All that site, close, circuit, ambit and precinct of the late priory of St. Helen, within the City of London, and also the church commonly named the Nonnes Churche of Seynt Helyns, and all and singular messuages, houses, edifices, structures, yards, dovecotes, gardens, orchards and the land and soil of the same, profits, commodities, emoluments and other hereditaments whatsoever within the same site, close, circuit, ambit or precinct of the same late priory being, or which as part or parcel of the same late site were commonly reputed or esteemed lying or being, in the parish of Saint Helen, within our said City of London, and also all and singular messuages, houses, edifices, lands, tenements and other our hereditaments whatsoever lying or being in the parish of Saint Helen, in our City of London, and now or lately in the several tenures or occupations of William Baker, Jane Julyan, Edmund Brewer, Guy Sturdye and Lancelot Harryson, or their assigns, or the assigns of any of them, and to the said late priory of Saint Helen formerly belonging and pertaining, and being parcel of the possessions of the same late priory."

‡ *Add. Ch.* 39406 A. The purchase price was £380, and the description of the property given in the indenture of 28th April, 35 [Henry VIII], i.e., 1543, between "Sir Richard Wyllyams otherwise Crumwell" and Thomas Kendall, who acted for the company, is practically identical with that in the grant of the previous year. For further particulars of this transaction see W. H. Black's *History of the Worshipful Company of Leathersellers* (1871), p. 88.

§ *P. R. O. Chantry Cert.* 34, No. 101. The two chantry priests are presumably those serving the Francis chantries.

ST. HELEN, BISHOPSGATE

Ther is of howsling people within the same paroche the nombre of ccxx.

The kinges majestie is parsone of the same churche and no vicar there but a parysshe prest.

John Goldesburgh by lycence of king Edward the thirde founded one chauntery within the seid churche and gave certen quitrentes to the sustentacion of a priest ther oute of dyverse tenements in the tenure of the parischeners of Saint Bennet ffynckes of the yerely value by yere.	iiij li vjs viijd. whereof	To Sir John Bedell Incumbent for his Salary iiij li vjs. viij and then remayneth clere nil.
Thomas Wilforde by lycence of Kyng Henry the ffourthe founded one chauntery in the seide churche and gave for the mayntenaunce of a priest to syng ther for ever landes and tenementes by yere.	lxvijs. iiijd.	wherof To Sir John Meryalle Incumbent for his salary lxvijs. iiijd. and ther remeyneth clere nil.

The religious changes of the early years of Queen Elizabeth are reflected in the following entry in the Minutes under the date 14th January, 1564–65: "It is ordered and agreade be the whole assent of the parishioners here present that the residue of oure roode lofte yet standinge at this daie shallbe taken downe according to the forme of a certain writing made and subscribed by Mr. Mollyns, Archdeacon of London. . . . And further that the place where the same doeth stande shallbe comelie and devoutlie made and garnished againe like to St Magnus Church or St Dunstone in the East." Other indications of the arrangements of this period are provided by various entries: a mention of the price of burials indicates that the chancel was flanked by Sir Thomas Gresham's pew (probably on the north) and the vestry (probably in the south chapel, its later position); a further mention of burial in the porch seems to indicate that the western part of the nave was used for that purpose. In 1568–69 the roof at the west end was repaired, and the "cloke house" moved (possibly from the apex of the west gable) for greater safety to "the corner of the wall so as ytt shall be borne uppon the wall and not to beare any pt of ytt on the roof of the churche"; this position is still occupied by its successor. Small alterations included the taking down of the organ and the removal of the two upper steps of the altar-pace in 1576.

Gresham.

Sir Thomas Gresham (d. 1579) promised to build a steeple "in recompense of ground in their church filled up with this monument," but this was never done. Stow, writing in 1598,* mentions that the partition between the nuns' church and the parish church had then been taken down.

In 1632–33 a general repair of the church became necessary, and free

* *Survey of London* (Kingsford's edn.), I, p. 171.

subscriptions were obtained towards the cost, from the City of London Corporation (for Gresham's College), the Merchant Taylors', East India, Skinners', Mercers' and Leathersellers' Companies, Sir Julius Caesar, Sir Henry Machin, Mr. Thomas Audley and others. The indications of the work undertaken, from the churchwardens' accounts are very meagre, but the disbursement of £122 to the carpenters, £35 to the bricklayers, the same sum to the smiths, £139 to the plumber, £78 to the painters, £299 (part payment) to the masons and £463 to the joiners, indicates considerable structural alterations, including large repairs to the roof. Mention is made separately of the new font and cover (£20), 10½ ells of canvas for the "commandements," the clock tower, the church porch (£23 10s. 9d.), and the glass painter (£15 16s. 6d.). Of the last two items it seems probable that the first refers to the cost of the existing south doorway and the second to the cost of the stained-glass shields of contributors, some of which still remain in the nuns' church. The total cost of the restoration, entered under the date 1632, was £1322 3s. 2d. It has been asserted that these alterations were made under the direction of Inigo Jones (*vide* Cox, *op. cit.*, page 40), but the statement, apparently, rests on no contemporary evidence.

The religious troubles of the middle of the 17th century are reflected in two entries in the churchwardens' accounts of 1643–44, relating to the taking down of the cross on the belfry, and the defacing of "superstitious" inscriptions. A sundial was set up on the church in the latter year.

Few alterations seem to have been made to the fabric or its fittings during the second half of the 17th century. There is, however, mention of a new organ in 1683, and to the pulling down of the old engine house (for the fire engine), in 1694. At a vestry meeting held on 8th October, 1696, it was agreed that Sir Christopher Wren should be consulted about the repairs of the church. Something was done and finished in 1697, but no particulars of the work are available.

In 1696 an agreement was entered into between the parish and Thomas Armstrong that, in consideration of the sum of £100 and taking down the bells, wheels and ropes in the belfry (over St. Helen's Gate in Bishopsgate Street), and delivering them safe and sound in the church, Armstrong should have the lease of the belfry for 61 years, evidently with a view to rebuilding the structure. From this it appears that the bells hung, and probably had hung since the 16th century, over the gate-house at the entry to Great St. Helen's, and that only a clock bell hung in the clock tower, or steeple, over the church. On 18th June following it was decided to sell three of the four bells for the repair of the church, the best of the four to be kept for the use of the parish. In 1699 the belfry and church were repaired and a bell hung up to give notice of burials.*

The church was repaired in 1710 at a cost of £155 10s., and in

* According to Hatton's *New View of London* (1708), i, p. 274, the small tower (probably the existing one) was built in this year.

1722 a further sum of £127 was expended. In 1736 an estimate of £550 3s. 1d. for repairs, was referred back for reduction. There is no evidence as to the work done on any of these occasions.

In 1742 a new organ and organ loft were built from the specifications of Mr. Thomas Griffin at an estimated cost of £500, including a "compleat butifull outside case or frame of mahogany, the work to be masterly finished with beads, mouldings, carvings, frees, cornishes, and other ornaments."

In 1763 a partition was set up across the western part of the church, under the organ loft, forming an ante-chapel (it is represented in the engraving reproduced in Plate 7). At the same time (1764) £1000 had to be raised for the repair of the church.

At the end of 1764 various inhabitants of Little St. Helen's had leave to open a door out of the garden of Leathersellers' Hall into the church at the east end. This doorway was covered externally by a small porch of renaissance design which figures in several late-18th-century views of the east end of the church. This feature is not shown in Ogilby and Morgan's map (1677), and was almost certainly added when the door was pierced. It was destroyed soon after 1799.

The various restorations of the 19th century have very materially altered the internal aspect of the church, but though much of interest has been removed and much 17th and 18th-century work has been wantonly destroyed, the Gothic revival has not swept the church so bare of non-Gothic features as in many another instance.

The following are the details of the restorations and of the principal alterations effected thereby.

In 1809–10 £2994 17s. 3d. was spent, an external roof covered with slates being erected over the existing roof. At this time the staircase in the north wall of the nuns' church was discovered, and the outside repaired with brick. An ancient window was uncovered on the south side and another on the west side; these were probably both in the south transept or chapels. The seating was rearranged and the pavement relaid.

In 1841 the outer roof of 1809 was repaired and recovered with slates, and subsequently the external walls were protected by dry areas.

In 1865 the screen at the west end was removed, the organ repaired and removed to the Holy Ghost chapel; part of the floor of the nave was lowered and the nuns' stalls moved from the nuns' quire to their present position in the parish chancel.

In 1874–76, at a cost of £1560, the chapels were restored, the floors lowered and the roofs renewed.

In 1888 the most important restoration took place. The external walls were stripped of plaster and repointed; the floors of the parts of the church, not previously dealt with, were lowered to their present level; the outer roofs of 1809 were removed and the old roofs repaired and covered with lead, the parapets rebuilt and the belfry restored or rebuilt. The vestry in the south chapel was removed and the new vestries on the south side of the nave built; new windows were inserted in the north wall and various alterations and additions made to the fittings.

By Order in Council dated 5th May, 1873, the benefices of St. Helen and St. Martin Outwich were united, and on the demolition of the latter church 18 monuments from it were transferred to St. Helen's.

III.—THE MONASTIC BUILDINGS

Apart from the nuns' church nothing now survives of the buildings of the Benedictine Priory, which covered a considerable area of ground immediately to the north of the existing buildings. The eastern range, with gardens to the east of it, was acquired by the Leathersellers' Company in 1543 and the buildings adapted for use as their Livery Hall. This range, altered in the time of Elizabeth and no doubt subsequently, survived until 1799, when the whole site was cleared and the new St. Helen's Place laid out.

Information available as to the plan and disposition of the monastic buildings is to be derived, mainly, from three sources: (*a*) a fairly detailed survey of the buildings of the priory taken at the Dissolution*; (*b*) plans and drawings of the remains taken before the demolition of Leathersellers' Hall in 1799, and (*c*) the excavations undertaken when the site was cleared in 1922.

The survey of 1541 runs as follows:—

The late Priory of St. Elenes within the City of London.

The View and Survey ther taken xxist daye of June in the xxxiij yeare of the raigne of our Soveraigne Lord Kinge Henrye the VIIIth by Thos. Mildmay, one of the King's Auditors thereunto assigned.

First the cheaf entre or comminge in to the same late Priory is in and by the street gate lying in the parishe of St. Elenes in Bysshopsgate Streat which leadeth to a little cowrte next adjoyning to the same gate having chambers, houses and buyldinges environning the same, out of which cowrte there is an entre leading to an inner cowrte which on the north side is also likewise environed with edificyons & buildings called the Stewardes lodging with a countinge house appurteining to the same.

Item next to the same cowrte there is a faire kechinge with a "Pastery house," larder houses & other houses of office appurteininge to the same & at the East ende of the same kitchen & entre leadinge to the same hall with a little parlor adjoining having under the same hall & parlour sondrie howses of office next adjoining to the cloyster ther & one howse called the Covent parler.

Item iij fair Chambers adjoininge to the hall whereof the one over the entree leadinge to the cloyster thother over the Buttree & the third over the larder.

Item from the said entre by the hall to the cloyster which cloyster yet remaneth holly leaded & at the north side of the same cloyster a fare long howse called the fratree.

* *MS., Soc. of Antiquaries*, 521—printed in *Archæologia*, XVI, p. 29, *London and Middlesex Archæological Society*, II, p. 192, and in Cox, *op. cit.*, pp. 29–30.

Item at the est ende of the same cloyster a lodginge called the Supprior's lodging with a litle gardin lieing to the same And by the same lodginge a pare of staires leading to the Dortor at the southend whearof ther is a litle hows wherein the evidence of the sd. hows nowe dou remayne with all howses & lodginges under the same Dortor.

Item at the westende of the same cloyster a dore leadinge into the miñes late Quire extending from the dore out of the churcheyarde unto the lampe or particyon deviding the priorye from the parisshe which is holly leaded.

Item at the estende of the said cloyster an entre leading to a little garden & out of the same littell garden to a faire garden called the Covent garden contening by estimacon half an acre. And at the northend of the said garden adore leading to an other garden called the ketchin garden & at the west ende of the same ther is a dovehowsshe & in the same garden a dore to a fair woodyerd with houses, particons & gardens within the same woodyerd & tenement with a garden a stable & other the appurtenances to the same belonginge called Elizabeth Hawtes lodginge All which premisses ben rated extendyd & valued. The Kinges Highnesse to be discharged of the reparations of the yerely value of £6 13s. 4d.

Item one ten$^{t.}$ there in the hold of Willm. Baker by the yeare 20s.

Item one other ten$^{t.}$ in the hold of Jane Julian by the yeare 13s. 4d.

Item one other ten$^{t.}$ there in the hold of Edmunde Brewer by the yeare 13s. 4d.

Item one other ten$^{t.}$ there in the hold of Eye Sturdye by the yeare 13s. 4d.

Item one other ten$^{t.}$ there in the hold of Lance Harryson by the yeare 13s. 4d.

iii £ 13s. 4d.

Sum, £10 6s. 8d.

Ex$^{nd.}$ per/by me THOMAM MILDMAIE, *Auditor.*

There is also a short inventory* of moveables of slightly later date which gives some further particulars :—

Inprimis in the kechyn a dowble cestern of leade, thre dressynge boords, a choppyng blokke, a shelffe, a covering of an oven of iron, a shelffe boorde, a skrene.

Item yn the larder house a cupborde and twoo dressyng boordes.

Item yn the pultry house a greate cowpe.

Item yn the pastrye house fower pastyng boordes and fower bowtyng bynnes.

Item yn the drye larder house twoo cupbordes with a dowble hangyng shelffe and a chyeste.

Item yn the pantry a brede bynne, fyve shelffs, a joyste for byere, a perche to hang on table clothes.

* *Add. Char* 39406 B.

Item yn the hall twoo portalls, a cupborde, and the sayd hall selyd rowndeabowt with waynscotte.

Item yn the frater two standyng tables . . . frater celyd rownde about with waynescotte.

Item yn the lowe p'lure, under the hall a portall with a lytell shelffe.

Item yn the beere celler thre joystes for beere and a chese rakke.

Item yn the chappell a closet.

Item yn the chamber over the entre a cupborde celed rownde about with waynescott.

Item a lodgyng nowe yn the occupyeng of Master Wate. Crumwell two portalls of waynescotte with all the doores.

Item yn the gardeyn the same rayled rownde about, a dyall, three rakkytes to hange clothes upon with polles.

Item a welle whele with one bukkytt and a wynche. All the glasse and all the other portalls, doores, lokks, keyes, and boltes to theym belongyng and all the other tymber, stones and ironwoork.

Item one cheste above yn the house for easement callyd the Jake or Jaks.

It is evident from the description in Mildmay's survey that the normal arrangement of a Benedictine house was followed at St. Helen's, the chief buildings being grouped in their traditional positions round the cloister. The survey begins with the west range, containing on the ground floor the buttery, larder, passage to the cloister, the convent parlour* and various houses of office no doubt appertaining to the cellaress. On the first floor was the hall (no doubt the Guest Hall) a little parlour (perhaps the guests' solar) and three fair chambers, over the entry, buttery and larder respectively. On the north of the cloister was the conventual Frater, a large hall on the ground floor, occupying the whole length of the range and extending to the west beyond it. The view of it in ruins given by Wilkinson,† and another in the *Gardner Collection* show it to have been a 13th-century structure, lit by a range of lancets in the north wall, of which four are shown as still intact. That the Frater range extended beyond the western limit of the cloister is indicated in this view by a break in the south wall, where the west wall of the cloister joins it, and is also clearly shown in Ogilby and Morgan's map, where the building of the Frater appears in block; the western part, however, was probably the kitchen or offices and the three lancet-shaped windows in the west wall are evidently, from the Gardner drawing, a more or less modern arrangement.

The cloister itself was a rectangle 71¼ feet north to south and probably about 70 feet east to west. Portions of the foundations of the arcade walls of the north, south and east were uncovered during the excavations of 1922 and are shown on the plan. The alleys were 10 feet wide and the arcade walls 1¾ feet thick. Near the middle of the east side

* In large monastic houses there were commonly two parlours, the inner on the east and the outer on the west of the cloister. The outer parlour was often used as the entry from the outer court, and as a parlour and entry are mentioned at St. Helen's it seems likely that the inner parlour was here dispensed with.

† *Londina Illustrata.*

was an added buttress projecting into the garth. No trace was found of the western arcade wall, and the foundations of the south arcade appear to indicate that the cloister on this side was not conterminous with the west end of the church. As, however, Ogilby and Morgan's map shows a building on the site of the west range and closing the cloister in at this point, it must be supposed that the overlap, if any, cannot have been more than a foot or two in extent. The Frater was entered from the cloister by a doorway at the end of the west walk, shown in the view of the ruins. The position of the kitchen, mentioned in the Survey, is not certain; it may have adjoined the west end of the Frater or the north end of the western range or may even have formed part of the western range itself. The eastern range is that which till 1799 formed part of Leathersellers' Hall. According to the Survey it contained on the ground floor, the "sub-prior's" (sub-prioress') lodging,* a passage to the garden appertaining to it and various houses and lodgings and on the first floor the nuns' Dorter, with the Muniment room at the south end of it. The existing plans and drawings of these buildings together with the recent excavations give considerably more information than the survey. Adjoining the church was a narrow building ($46\frac{1}{2}$ feet long by 13 feet wide in the eastern part and 12 feet in the western part), undoubtedly the sacristy. The western part was roofed with two bays of 13th-century quadripartite vaulting with chamfered ribs springing from moulded corbels. It was entered from the cloister by a doorway of two recessed orders, and opened into the eastern part of the building by an arch springing on the south from a plain respond with two attached shafts on the east face. The eastern part of the sacristy was not vaulted, and the roof was at a higher level. It has a plain pointed recess in the south wall (the church wall) and east of it is a 13th-century piscina with a shouldered head. The various openings in the wall between the sacristy and the church will be described under that building. The whole of the south side of the sacristy with the base of the west doorway was uncovered in 1922, and showed that Wilkinson's plan was not accurate in several particulars, notably in the projection of the west wall into the cloister, which projection was non-existent.

The Chapter House adjoined this building on the north. It was $46\frac{1}{2}$ feet long by 21 feet wide, and portions of the north, south and west walls were recently uncovered. The plans and views of this building before its demolition show that it had four bays with a ribbed quadripartite vault of stone, three lancet-windows in the east wall and a doorway from the cloister in the west wall having a central and two side shafts.†

* That the lodging of the sub-prioress or even of the prioress was in this position is very unlikely; the apartment referred to was more probably a checker.

† Portions of the mediæval pavement of red tiles were found during the recent excavations. They showed that the original level of the chapter-house floor must have been below that of the cloister, a not uncommon arrangement, to provide greater height, without interrupting the level of the dorter above. Traces were also found of a subsequent raising of the floor, probably also mediæval.

Extending north from the Chapter House was a vaulted undercroft ($63\frac{1}{2}$ feet by $26\frac{1}{2}$ feet) of similar date and character to the rest of the range, and divided into five bays in length and two in breadth by a row of octagonal columns with moulded capitals and bases. The ribbed vault, in quadripartite bays, rested on these columns and on moulded corbels in the side walls. The narrow second bay from the south probably formed a passage and was entered from the cloister by a pointed doorway.

The two passages shown on Wilkinson's plan extending to the west and south of this undercroft, were probably neither of them mediæval, the western not according with the known position of the Frater walls and the northern extending much too far (56 feet) to have served any monastic purpose.*

The Dorter, extending over probably the whole of this range (except the south end), was so entirely altered by being transformed into the Leathersellers' Hall and Court Room as to leave no traces of its mediæval features in the drawings of it that have survived. The Muniment Room, or place where the evidences of the house were kept, must have been above the sacristy already described. The Dorter was approached by the night stairs (see church) from the church and by the day stairs, mentioned in the Survey, somewhere near the east end of the Frater. Before leaving this range, it may be mentioned that during the excavations two masses of foundation were discovered projecting, at a slight angle, eastwards from the Chapter House. They no doubt formed the substructure of the Elizabethan or Jacobean building added by the Leathersellers' Company, and indeed the massive southern foundation exactly represents in plan a chimney stack shown on several old views of the building.

Three buildings, essential to the later monastic economy, are absent from the list in the Survey—the Infirmary, the Rere Dorter and the lodging of the prioress. The Infirmary is mentioned in the Kentwood Injunctions (*ante* p. 8) in a way that implies that there was then no separate building for that purpose; possibly it had been put to other uses or leased to a lay tenant. The Rere Dorter is referred to (as the Jake or Jaks) in the Inventory of moveables. The Infirmary should lie east of the Dorter Range, the Rere Dorter in immediate connection with the Dorter and the lodging of the prioress in any position dictated by local conditions.

The buildings of the outer and inner courts are also lightly touched upon by the surveyor. The gate house in Bishopsgate Street is indeed mentioned, but the bake and brew-houses, stables, etc., must be included in the general terms—"Chambers, Howses and Buildings," surrounding the courts. The gate house is undoubtedly represented by the present entrance from Bishopsgate Street and the taking down of the old building in 1696 has already been referred to (p. 21).

* There is a view of this passage in the *Gardner Collection*. It was built entirely of brick and apparently was of no great antiquity.

IV.—PRIESTS AND VICARS OF ST. HELEN, BISHOPSGATE

No vicarage was instituted in St. Helen's church before the Reformation. The church was served by a parish priest, generally referred to as the parochial chaplain. The names of two are recorded in the 12th-century visitations of the church (pp. 1–2 *ante*) :

Alberic in *c.* 1160–81.
Ailnod in *c.* 1181–86.

The parochial chaplain is referred to, but not by name, in 1344* and again in 1374 in the will of Adam Francis. In both cases the context makes it perfectly clear that the chaplain was quite distinct from the chantry priests.

The following list of parish priests, vicars and rectors is taken from Newcourt's *Repertorium*, ed. Hennessy, 1898, p. 210 :—

1541. John Weste.
1571. Thomas.
1575. John Olivar.
1586. . . . Lewis.
1592. Nicholas Felton.
1600. Lewis Hughes.
1603. Richard Ball, S.T.B.
1613. Thomas Downing.
1618. Thomas Evans.
1619. William Laurence.
1621. Joseph Browne, A.M.
1635. Richard Maden, S.T.B.
1639. Matthias Milward.
1642. Thomas Edwards.
1645. Samuel Willis.
1647. Arthur Barham.
1663. John Sybbald, A.M.
1666. Thomas Horton, S.T.P.
1674. Edward Pelling, A.M.
1678. Henry Hesketh, A.M. (nominated Bishop of Killala, 1689).
1695. Thomas Willis, A.M.
1701. Samson Estwicke, S.T.B.
1713. William Butler, LL.B. (Prebendary of St. Pauls).
1773. John Naish.
1795. Robert Watts, M.A.

* *Harlean Charter*, 44, F, 45.

ST. HELEN, BISHOPSGATE

1799. James Blenkarne, M.A.
1835. Charles Mackenzie, M.A.
1847. John Thomas How Le Mesurier, M.A. (Archdeacon of Gibraltar).
1849. John Edmund Cox, D.D.

RECTORS

1873. John Bathurst Dean, M.A.
1887. John Alfred Lumb Airey, M.A.
1909. Silvanus Taylor Hingston Saunders, M.A.

ST. HELEN, BISHOPSGATE

V.—ARCHITECTURE

There is ample documentary evidence of the existence of a church of St. Helen, on or near the present site, in the 12th century, but it has been generally assumed that this building was entirely removed about the time of the foundation of the priory. A close study of the plan of the existing building reveals, however, the significant fact that the existing south doorway, together with the earlier one which it replaced, is set unusually far east, being indeed about the middle of the south wall. This easterly position of the south doorway is in itself presumptive evidence of a lengthening of the nave westwards, and that the earlier nave terminated a short distance to the west of the doorway, which would thus assume its normal position. Now the ordinary proportions of a 12th-century parish nave are roughly two squares, that is to say, the length is double the width; the position of the division between the nave and chancel is, for various sufficient reasons,* very seldom altered, so that by setting out two squares from the existing screen the approximate position of the early west end should be arrived at. This setting out marks a point in the Spencer monument (in the south wall), and the same point is marked externally by the only buttress on the south wall. The logical conclusion is that this buttress was added by the 13th-century builders to mask the junction of the earlier work with their extension, as otherwise the buttress is meaningless.

The reconstruction in the early years of the 13th century appears to have begun with the nuns' quire, as indicated by the small lancet window in the north wall, which is of early 13th-century type, and to have been followed by the parish nave and chancel and the south transept, lancet windows, of about the second quarter of the century, still remaining in the south transept and nave. About 1300 the western of the two arches, between the nuns' quire and the parish chancel, was inserted, and shortly afterwards the west doorway of the parish nave was built; these appear to be now the only structural evidences of the extensive rebuilding mentioned in the will of Thomas of Basing (*ante* p. 4).

Before 1363 Adam Francis appears to have built (*ante* p. 6) the two chapels (of the Holy Ghost and St. Mary) east of the south transept, together with the arcade opening into them. Early in the 15th century the eastern arch between the nuns' quire and the parish chancel was inserted. The nave arcade was built and other alterations carried out about 1470–75. For certain of the works provision was made in the will of Nicholas Marshall, ironmonger, 1472,† and others were due to a bequest of 500 marks made by

* Commonly the divided responsibility of the parish and the rector.

† *P.C.C.* 16 Watlys, proved 1474. He desires to be buried at St. Elene in the chapel of the Holy Ghost there, under the marble stone "there by me ordeyned." The Ironmongers were to keep an obit for him and his wife Elizabeth, to be said as well by the Prioress and Convent in their common "quere" as by the priests and clerks in the parish "quere." His executors were "to fynysh in godely maner both the stone walles and the rofe coveres of the

Sir John Crosby in 1475, and the character of the existing work agrees well with this attribution. To Crosby also must be assigned the two arches on the south of the parish chancel (one of which spans his tomb),* the mouldings and other details being the same as those of the nave arcade. The west doorway of the nuns' quire and the doorway to the night stairs from the dorter are both late 15th-century insertions or reconstructions, and to the early years of the succeeding century belong the north clearstory windows of the nuns' quire, and the three windows on the south side of the parish nave. The two large west windows of the church are possibly due to the restoration of 1632, and the two main east windows appear also to have been reconstructed at the same time; they survived until they were "restored" to their present form in the last century. Perhaps early in the 17th century the south window of the transept was inserted, and in 1633 the south doorway of the nave was built.

The various modern restorations of the church have been already dealt with and it will be unnecessary to recapitulate them here.

Architectural Description

The *Nuns' Quire* is a simple rectangular building 119½ feet long by 26½ feet wide. The large five-light east window dates entirely from 1888, when it took the place of a window of five-pointed lights in a pointed head, shewn on old engravings, and probably of 17th-century date. In the north wall there are nine windows, of which the four to the east are modern and are set very high in the wall. The next four windows further west are at a rather lower level, but set sufficiently high to be above the level of the roof of the former cloister; they are of early 16th-century date and are each of three plain pointed lights in a segmental-pointed head; externally they have been much restored. The westernmost window is an early 13th-century lancet light, with wide internal splays and much restored. Remains of the external sills of three similar windows are visible further east. In the lower part of this wall is a series of squints and doorways, all connected with the now destroyed monastic buildings which adjoined the church on the north. Taking these in succession from east to west, the first is an elaborate squint formerly opening into the eastern part of the sacristy (see Monument 5). Immediately west of this is the east jamb of a blocked doorway formerly opening into the west sacristy. It is not now visible externally, the wall-

quere and rere-quere of the Nunnes church . . . from the parkeclose betwene the chauncell and the Nonnes quere unto the west end of the same church after the neue werke made from the high auter unto the foresaid parkeclose and that they provide in the same werke a convenient steple for the said Nonnes so alway that the Prioresse and Convent there suffre myn Executors to have all the lede tymber irne stone and glass and all other stuffe now being in the church and steple of the old werke there in furtheryns of the said neue werke." If the work was done before his death the money was to be applied to find a priest.

* The direction in Crosby's will as to his burial in the chapel of the Holy Ghost, in conjunction with the position of the tomb, still remaining, is conclusive evidence that this chapel was the northern of the two still existing transeptal chapels.

arch containing it being blocked with brickwork. Farther west is a second squint, probably of late 15th or early 16th-century date, and of two square-headed openings with traces of the mortices for an iron grille. It is set externally in a recess with a segmental-pointed head. The early 13th-century doorway further west is of two continuous chamfered orders with a two-centred head. It is now blocked, but formerly opened into the west part of the sacristy, and must have served as the eastern processional entrance to the church. A third squint of uncertain date is rectangular with chamfered reveals and has traces of the fixing of a former grille. Higher up in the wall and below the third window from the east is a small square opening which must have communicated with the building above the sacristy. Below the fifth window from the east is a staircase in the wall; enclosed

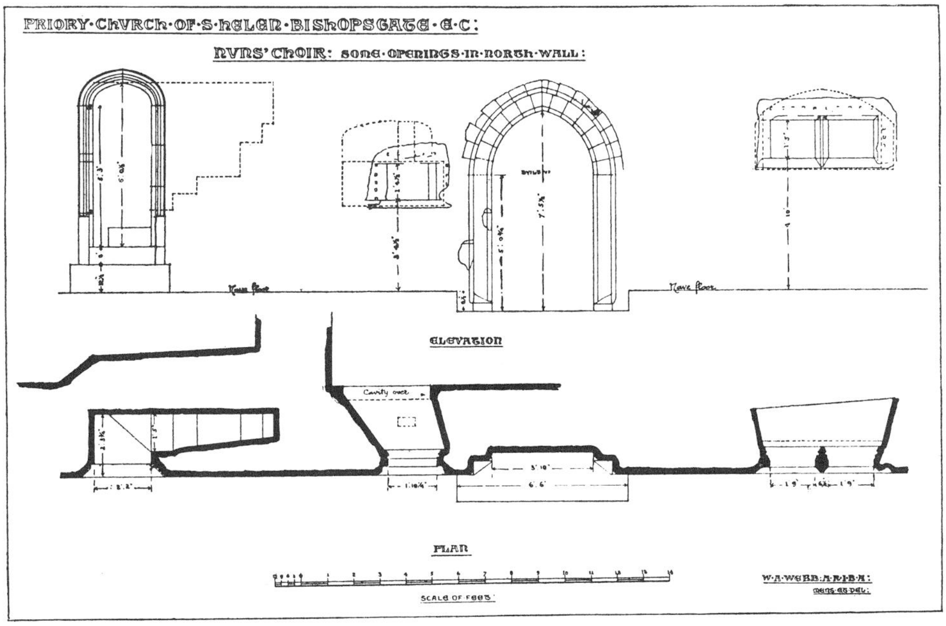

PRIORY·CHURCH·OF·S·HELEN·BISHOPSGATE·E·C:
NUNS' CHOIR: SOME·OPENINGS·IN·NORTH·WALL:
ELEVATION
PLAN
SCALE OF FEET
W·A·WEBB:A·R·I·B·A:
MENS·ET·DEL:

externally in a brick projection, and probably used as the night stairs from the dorter. The doorway into the church is of late 16th-century date, and has moulded jambs and a four-centred head; two iron door-pins remain in the west jamb. Below the westernmost window in the north wall is a four-centred relieving arch, marking the position of the western processional entrance from the cloister.

In the south wall of the nuns' quire are two arched openings into the parish chancel and four into the nave. The easternmost arch is of early 15th-century date, four-centred and moulded; the east respond has an attached shaft with a moulded capital carrying the inner member of the archivolt; the west respond has a similar shaft cut short by a modern corbel and a second shaft on the north side. The second arch is of early 14th-century date; it is two-centred, and of two chamfered orders, with a moulded label on each face; the responds have each an attached shaft with a moulded capital and base. Above the west haunch of the eastern arch are traces of the jambs and segmental head of a clerestory window, probably of early 15th-century date. The late 15th-century nave arcade is of four bays with two-centred and moulded arches; the columns have each four attached shafts, divided by wave mouldings and having moulded capitals and bases, raised on tall plinths. The responds have attached half columns. In the west wall of the nuns' church is a five-light window of 16th or early 17th-century character; the stonework, however, is modern, but the form of the window reproduces the earlier work except for the added transom. The late 15th or early 16th-century west doorway has a four-centred arch in a square head with a moulded label and quatrefoiled spandrels; the arch, spandrels, and perhaps part of the jambs are original, but the rest is modern restoration.

The *Parish Chancel* is 42½ feet long by 22½ feet, and is not structurally divided from the nave. The modern east window is in place of a 16th or 17th-century window of seven lights in a depressed head, removed at the restoration of 1888. On the south side are two late 15th-century arches opening into the chapels and transept. The eastern is two-centred and the western four-centred, and both correspond in detail to the arches of the nave arcade.

The *Parish Nave* is 77 feet by 22½ feet, and has in the south wall at the east end a blocked lancet window of mid 13th-century date, now largely concealed by the pulpit. Further west are three early 16th-century windows, each of three pointed lights in a segmental pointed head, and having moulded internal reveals. The sill of the middle window is kept high to clear the south doorway. This doorway was inserted or rebuilt in 1633, and is an interesting if somewhat coarse example of Renaissance work. The opening has moulded imposts and a round arch with an architrave moulding and three key blocks; surrounding it is an "eared" architrave with rusticated pilasters supporting the ears, and surmounted by a frieze, cornice, and pediment. The tympanum encloses a carved cherub-head, and the middle part of the frieze is brought forward as a panel and inscribed in large Roman capitals LAVS DEO S HELENA. On the key blocks is inscribed REP^{d} 1633. To the east of this doorway are traces of an earlier doorway, visible externally. Below the westernmost window in the south wall is a modern doorway opening into the modern vestries. In the west wall of the nave is a window of five lights and of 16th or early 17th-century type, but completely restored on the old lines. Below it is a much-restored 14th-century doorway with a moulded two-centred arch and label; the jambs have each an attached shaft with a moulded capital and base.

The *South Transept* is 26½ feet by 22 feet, and has a late 14th-century arcade of two bays in the east wall. The two-centred and deeply moulded arches spring from a column having four attached shafts with moulded capitals and bases, and divided by hollow chamfers. The responds have attached half columns. Above the arcade is a modern timber clerestory. In the south wall is a large Jacobean Gothic window of three cinquefoiled lights with tracery in a two-centred head. The upper part of the wall is cut back and has probably been rebuilt; in it is a small restored window, cut across by the modern boarding of the roof. In the south-east angle is a small doorway of doubtful date, with a pointed head and opening into a stair turret communicating with the leads of the roof. In the west wall are two blocked lancet windows of mid 13th-century date; the northern is open internally to the face of the jambs, but the southern is entirely blocked.

The *Chapel Aisle* is 16¾ feet wide and contains the two chapels of the Holy Ghost and St. Mary. In the east wall are two almost entirely modern windows, of 14th-century character, and each of three cinquefoiled lights with tracery in a two-centred head. In the south wall are two equally restored windows, also of 14th-century character, and each of two cinquefoiled lights, with an octofoil in a two-centred head; they are enclosed under a 14th-century wall arcade with two-centred, moulded arches, resting on attached shafts with moulded capitals and bases, standing on a stone base and all much restored.

The *Roofs* throughout the building are of timber. Those over the nuns' church and the main parish church are of flat pitch with the purlins resting immediately on the tie-beams. In form, and no doubt partly in structure, they are of late 15th-century date, but have been frequently repaired during the numerous restorations. The tie-beams are moulded and have curved brackets or braces under the ends. The timber bell-turret, standing over the middle of the west front, is of late 17th or early 18th-century date. It is square, and has a segmental-headed, louvred opening in each face, a cornice and an ogee-shaped roof, covered with lead, and supporting a small lantern with a round-headed opening in each face; this is also finished with a cornice and ogee-shaped roof supporting a ball and vane.

The *Ritual Arrangements* of the nuns' quire, previous to the dissolution of the priory, must be briefly considered. The position of the various squints and doorways in the north wall is sufficient evidence that the nuns' stalls must have been placed to the west of the doorway from the night stairs. The existing stalls (now removed to the parish quire) occupy a length of 21 feet on the north side, and to this must be added an allowance for the returned stalls at the west end, and possibly for others which have been destroyed. This leaves at the west end a space of some 25 to 30 feet in length forming the retro-quire or ante-chapel. These main divisions are referred to in the will of Nicholas Marshall, already quoted,* as the "quere" and "rere-quere." The pre-Reformation altars and images in the church included the chapels of the Holy Ghost and St. Mary founded by Adam Frauncys,† the chapel of St. Katherine and St. Margaret,‡ the image of St. Helen§ on the north of the nuns' quire, the light on the "beam" and the "lights de la Pité,"|| and the Trinity.¶

* See *ante*, p. 31. † See *ante*, p. 6.

‡ Will of Joan Cokayne, 1509, *P.C.C.* 9, Bennett. The double dedication is mentioned in the will of John Hudson, who desires to be buried in the parish church of Saint Helen within the chapel of Saint Katherine and Saint Margaret. *Cons. Ct. of London*, Book i. Palmer.

§ See *post*, p. 55. || Will of Alice Sewale, 1419, *P.C.C.* 44, Marche.

¶ Strype's Stow, see *post* p. 94.

ST. HELEN, BISHOPSGATE

VI.—FITTINGS

1. *Altar.*

In the Chapel of St. Mary is a stone altar-slab in dark marble with modern consecration crosses, repolished, found buried under the St. Mary's Chapel.

2. *Bells.*

The three bells were all cast by Pack and Chapman in 1779–80 and rehung in 1893. They are as follows:

Tenor, weight about			5	cwt.	D.
Second	,,	,,	4	cwt.	E.
Treble	,,	,,	$3\frac{1}{2}$	cwt.	F♯.

3. *Brasses.*

On the floor of the south chapel:

(1) Robert Cotesbrok, 1393.

Inscription in French, 21 × 3 inches, two lines, black letter (the latter half of the first line defaced):

> Robert Cotesbrok gist ycy [*dieu de sa alme eyt mercy et pite*]
> morust le xi jo' de marcz lan de g'ce mil ccclxxxxiii

Relaid in a new stone.

On the floor of the south chapel.

(2) Civilian and wife, unknown, *c.* 1465.

Full-length effigies, $35\frac{1}{2}$ inches, of a man in civil dress, feet lost, with short curly hair, gown with fur cuffs and edging, and fur-lined mantle buttoned on the right shoulder, and wife in mitre head-dress, kirtle, and high-waisted close-fitting gown with fur edging and cuffs. Inscription lost.

Relaid in a new stone with the feet of the man, the outline of the inscription plate, and six shields indicated on the stone. An old drawing in the possession of the Merchant Taylors' Company shows the brass in its original slab, 8 feet 5 inches by 3 feet 8 inches, with indents for the inscription, four children, each separately inlaid, and six shields. The feet of the man then missing.

On the floor of the south chapel.

(3) Nicholas Wotton, LL.B., rector of St. Martin Outwich, 1482.

Full-length effigy of a priest, 25 inches, in academical costume, cassock, tippet and hood.

Inscription in Latin, 18 × 3 inches, three lines, black letter:

> Orate ꝑ aīa dn̄i Nich̄i Wotton quodm Rector istius eccl̄ie Et
> Baccallarii legis qui obiit Septimo die mensis Aprilis Anno
> dn̄i millim̄o ccccº lxxxijº Cuius Anime ꝓpicietur deus Amen

ST. HELEN, BISHOPSGATE

Removed from the church of St. Martin Outwich and relaid in a new stone.

On the floor of the south chapel.

(4) Thomas Wylliams, gentleman, 1495, and his wife Margaret.

Full-length effigies, 29½ inches, both side-face, of a man in civil dress with long hair, gown with large fur cuffs, pouch and rosary at girdle, and broad round-toed shoes, and wife in pedimental head-dress with broad lappets, low-necked close-fitting gown with turned-back fur cuffs, and narrow girdle with large buckle and long pendant end terminating in a metal tag.

Inscription in Latin, 23×3¾ inches, four lines, black letter (the greater part of the last line defaced):

> Hic jacet Thomas Wylliams Generos' et Margareta uxor ejus qui quidē Thomas obiit xvi° die mens' Januarii A° dn̄i m°cccc° lxxxxv° Et p'dicta
> Margareta obiit —— die mens' —— Anno dn̄i m°cccc —— quorum [*animabus propicietur deus Amen*]

Below the inscription are indents for two groups of children and at the corners of the slab for four shields, now filled with cement.

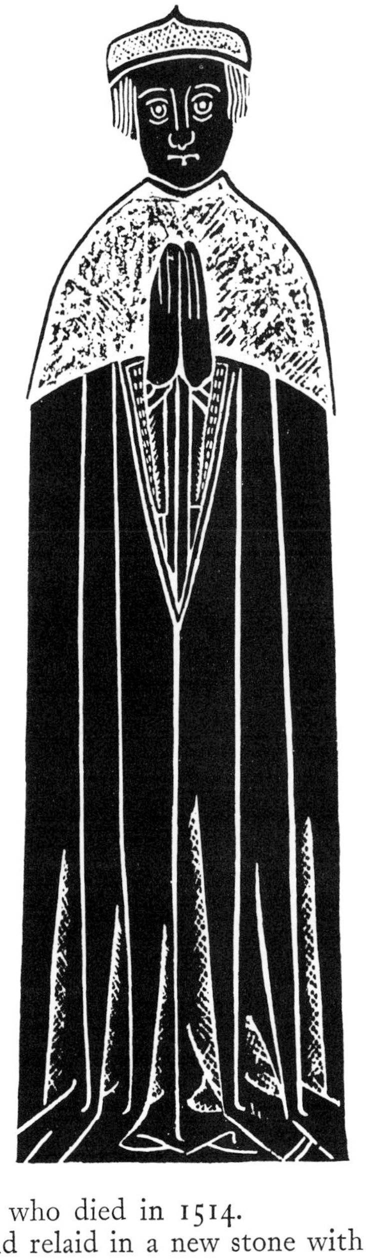

On the floor of the south chapel.

(5) A priest in academicals, *c.* 1500, inscription lost (see adjoining figure).

Full-length effigy of a priest, 18 inches, in the dress of a doctor of divinity, pointed cap, hood and gown.

Usually attributed to John Breux, D.D., rector of St. Martin Outwich, died 1459, whose inscription is given by Weever, but the style of the figure is much later, about 1500, and it may possibly represent Edmund Crome, D.D., rector of St. Martin Outwich, who died in 1495, or William Robson, D.D., who died in 1514.

Removed from St. Martin Outwich, and relaid in a new stone with Nicholas Wotton, 1482.

On the back of a high tomb in the north wall of the north aisle.

(6) Hugh Pemberton, alderman of London, 1500, and his wife Katherine.

All that now remains of this brass is a broken plate, 8×6½ inches, with the figures of seven sons, a portion of a group of ten sons, all kneeling, and all with long hair and fur-trimmed gowns; a scroll from the mouth of the lost figure of the eldest son, 11×1¼ inches, inscribed: "Pater de celis deus miserere nobis" in raised black letter, and two shields, the dexter bearing . . . a cheveron . . . between three buckets . . . for Pemberton, impaling checky . . . and . . . on a fess . . . three martlets . . ., for Thorpe(?), and the sinister the arms of the Merchant Taylors' Company, with the Holy Lamb on the chief as granted in 1486.

The indents show that the brass originally consisted of the kneeling figures of Hugh Pemberton and his wife Katherine with their children kneeling behind them, scrolls from their mouths addressed to a figure of the Trinity, alongside which was another small kneeling figure. The indent for the wife and daughters has been partly destroyed by the insertion of a tablet now removed. The inscription-fillet is modern, inserted when the tomb was removed from St. Martin Outwich.

On the floor of the north chapel at east end.

(7) John Leventhorp, esq., one of the four ushers of the chamber to Henry VII, 1510.

Full-length effigy of a man in armour, 31½ inches, bare-headed with long hair, head resting on helmet with crest of a man's head, feet on dog, wearing a standard of mail, breastplate with projecting ridge and lance-rest, shoulder and elbow-pieces alike in size and shape, short skirt of taces with longer skirt of mail, over which are strapped two tuiles. The usual knee- and shin-pieces with large round-toed sabbatons and rowel spurs. The sword is suspended from a narrow belt crossing the taces diagonally, and a long dagger hangs behind the body, but with no visible means of support.

Inscription in Latin, 17½×3½ inches, three lines, black letter (the precatory clause in the last line defaced):

> Hic iacet Joh̄es lēenthorp armig' nuꝑ unus quatuor
> hostiarior' camere dn̄i reg' h̄erici septimi qui obiit vi die
> augusti a^{o} dn̄i $m^{l}v^{o}$ x [*cuj' anime p̄'picietur deus amen*]

In original slab with indents for two shields at the top.

On the floor of the south chapel.

(8) Robert Rochester, esq., serjeant of the pantry to Henry VIII, 1514.

Full-length effigy, 26 inches, in armour, bare-headed with long hair, wearing a collar of SS. His armour much resembles that of John Leventhorp, but is without a lance-rest, the skirt of mail is longer, and the feet rest on a mound. The figure is now much worn.

Inscription in English, 21×5½ inches, five lines, black letter (the first and last lines defaced):

ST. HELEN, BISHOPSGATE

[*Humbly to crave you of yoʳ charite to p'y for the soule of me*] Robt' Rochester esqier late s'geant of the pantry of oʳ sov'ain lord king henry the viii which deptid this p'sent lyff the first day of may the yere of oure lord god a thousand five hundrith & xiiii on [*whose soule Ihu of his ĩfinyte grace have mercy Amen*]

In original slab. An old drawing in the possession of the Merchant Taylors' Company, made about 1810, shows that originally there were four shields, of which the lower dexter still remained in position. It bore the arms of Rochester of Terling, Essex, . . . a fess between three crescents . . ., the fess charged with another crescent for difference, impaling quarterly 1 and 4 . . . three cocks . . . 2 and 3 . . . 3 bars . . . with an anulet for difference. Possibly for Cockayne quartering Harthull.

On the floor of the south chapel

(9) Lady in heraldic mantle, *c.* 1535, inscription lost.

Full-length effigy, 32 inches, of a lady in pedimental head-dress, partlet, gown with striped sleeves and frilled cuffs, confined round the waist by a girdle with three rosettes as a buckle, and mantle charged with heraldic bearings: a lion rampant with three wounds on the shoulder. Round her neck is a chain, from which hangs a large Tau cross. The arms may be either Bolbec or Robsart, both families bearing the wounded lion.

Relaid in a new slab. An old drawing in the possession of the Merchant Taylors' Company shows this figure in its original slab, 6 feet 3 inches by 3 feet 2 inches, with indent for a large shield above the head, but with no indication of any inscription.

On the floor of the north aisle at west end.

(10) Elizabeth Robinson, 1600.

Shield, $5\frac{1}{2} \times 4\frac{1}{2}$ inches, inscription, $25\frac{1}{2} \times 12$ inches, and text, 21×7 inches, for Elizabeth, daughter of Sir Richard Rogers of Brianston, Dorset, knt., wife of John Robinson, 1600, had issue one son and one daughter.

Arms: Quarterly I and IV (*argent*) a molet (*sable*), on a chief (*gules*), a fleur-de-lys (*or*) for Rogers of Brianston; II and III (*azure*) a fret (*argent*) for Etchingham.

HERE VNDER LYETH THE BODIE OF ELIZABETH
ROBINSON THE WIFE OF JOHN ROBINSON, SONNE
AND HEIRE OF JOHN ROBINSON LATE CITTIZEN
AND MARCHANTAILER OF LONDON & MARCHANT
OF THE STAPLE OF ENGLAND, AND DAVGHTER OF
SR RICHARD ROGERS OF BRIANSTON IN THE
COVNTIE OF DORSCET KNIGHT, WHO HAD ISSVE
BY THE SAID JOHN ROBINSON HER HVSBAND
ONE SONNE AND A DAVGHTER AND DIED ON
THE 23TH DAY OF OCTOBER ANNO DOMINI 1600

CHRIST IS MY LIFE DEATHE IS MY GAINE
MY BODY SLEEPES IN HOPE TO RAIGNE
THRICE HAPPIE CHANGE IS IT FOR MEE
FROM EARTHE TO HEAVEN REMOV'D TO BEE
ELIZABETH ROBINSON

In original stone.

On the floor of the south chapel.

(11) Thomas Wight, 1633.

Shield, $6\frac{1}{2} \times 5\frac{1}{2}$ inches, inscription in Latin on an oval plate $22 \times 15\frac{1}{2}$ inches and eight English verses on a rectangular plate, $19\frac{1}{2} \times 8$ inches.

Arms: A cheveron *ermine* between three bear's heads couped and muzzled, a crescent for difference, for Wight.

CERTA
RESVRGENDI FIDE REQVIESCIT
THOMAS WIGHT
IVVENIS, PARITER AC SENEX
COELEBS & DESPONSATVS;
ÆTATE IVVENIS SAPIENTIA SENEX
MUNDO COELEBS CHRISTO DESPONSATVS
QVI
FAMILIAM VIRTVTE CLARAM
VERA PIETATE EXORNAVIT
QVI
POST EXTERAS REGIONES PERLVSTRATAS
(SPRETA SÆCVLI & LOCORVM VANITATE)
SEIPSVM PERLVSTRAVIT
SVVMQ PROTINVS ANHELANS IESVM
TANDEM PRO VOTO
POSITIS MORTALITATIS SVÆ EXUVIIS
MATVRÂ LICET FESTINA
IMMORTALITATE
CŒLOS PRÆOCCVPAVIT
DIE 16° IAN: ANNO SALVTIS.
MDCXXXIII
ÆTAT: SVÆ.
24°

READER: THOV MAYST FORBEARE TO PVT THINE EYES
TO CHARGE FOR TEARES, TO MOVRNE THESE OBSEQVIES
SVCH CHARITABLE DROPS WOVLD BEST BE GIVEN
TO THOSE W^{CH} LATE OR NEVER COME TO HEAVEN
BUT THERE YOV WOVLD IN WEEPING ON THIS DVST
ALLAY HIS HAPPINESSE WITH THY MISTRVST
WHOSE PIOVS CLOSINGE OF HIS YOVTHFULL YEARES
DESERVES THY IMITATION NOT THY TEARES.

In original slab, removed from St. Martin Outwich.

ST. HELEN, BISHOPSGATE

Lost Brasses.

(1) In the Craven Ord collection (*Brit. Mus. Add. MS.* 32478, fol. 31) and in other collections are reversed impressions from the brass of a lady, *c.* 1420, in veil head-dress, kirtle and mantle, with the words " Ih̃u m̄cy " in black letter on her breast. Height 20 inches. This brass probably represents Joan, daughter of Henry Seamer, first wife of Richard, son and heir of Robert, Lord Poynings, who died in 1420. An old drawing in the possession of the Merchant Taylors' Company shows the figure in its original slab, 3 feet 2 inches by 2 feet 8 inches, with indents for a foot inscription, two shields, one on each side of the figure, and two large roundels in the upper part of the slab. Hatton, in his *New View of London* (1708), I, 282, gives one of the shields as bearing " two bars surmounted by a bend quartered with a bend and impaled with a fess indented." The quartered coat is no doubt Poynings and Fitzpain. The impalement is doubtful. The arms of Seamer or Seymour were two cheverons, which Hatton may have misread and called " a fess indented."

(2) Amongst the collections of the Society of Antiquaries is a sketch of the brass to Thomas Benolt, Clarenceux King of Arms, 1534, and his two wives. The sketch shows Benolt in his official robes with crown on head and sceptre in hand, standing between his two wives, two of the corner shields and the greater part of the marginal inscription. A foot inscription, three groups of children, and two other shields were then lost. The slab, 7 feet 4 inches by 3 feet 5 inches, with indents for this brass was in existence in 1889 on the floor of the north aisle. It has since disappeared.

The inscription reads :

> Here und' lieth ye bodi of Thom̄s Benolt esquyer Somtȳe Sauāt & Offycer of Armes by ye name of Widēsore herault unto the right high & mighty Prince of . . . most drade soũaye lord kȳg her̄y ye viii which Thom̄s benolt otherwyse namyd Clarenceux kȳg of armes decesid the viii daye of May in the yere of our lord God M^{o} V^{c} xxxiiij in the xxvi yere of o^{r} said souerāye lord . . . A.

The two shields bear the arms and quarterings of Benolt.

Amongst the collections of the Merchant Taylors' Company is a careful drawing of the three figures, and another showing the figures in position on the slab.

Also amongst the Merchant Taylors' collections are drawings of the following :

(3) A black letter inscription to John More, 1495 :

> Hic jacet Joh̃es More qui obiit xx^{o} die
> mensis Novembris Anno Dom mll^{o} cccc^{o} lxxxxv^{o}.

(4) A black letter inscription, 17 by $3\frac{1}{4}$ inches, to Nicholas, son of John Skinner of Reigate, 1517:

> [defaced] Nichi Skynner jun ffilii Johis
> Skynner de Reygate in com̄ Surr' qui
> obiit xii die Marcii A^e^ dn̄i m° vc xvii [defaced].

(5) Figure of a lady in pedimental head-dress and gown, *c.* 1540, standing on shield charged parted fesse-wise a crowned eagle displayed, with indents for a foot inscription and for a marginal inscription. Size of slab 47 by 24 inches. Into this slab has been inserted a later inscription with four verses to James Lomeley, 1592, and wife Joan, the date for whose death is left blank:

> And allso here lyeth buryed ye bodies
> of James Lomley the sonne of ould
> Dominick Lomley and Jone his wyfe
> the said James deceased the vith of
> January Anno domini 1592
> hee beinge of the age of lxxxviii
> yeares and the said Jone deceased
> the [25th] day of [September] An° 1[613]
>
> Earth goeth upō earth as moulde upon moulde
> Earth goeth upon earth all glistring in golde
> As though earth to ye earth never turne should
> yet shall earth to the earth soner then he would.

The register records the burial of James Lomely, gent. on 6th January, 1592, under the stone next before the pulpit, also of Johane Lomelyn on 25th September, 1613, in her husband's grave, right under the pulpit.

(6) A much-worn black letter inscription, 14 by 7 inches, to Francis Notingham, citizen and skinner, and his wife Mary; both died in 1563:

> here under this stone resteth ye bodies
> of ffrauncis Notyngham citizen & skinner
> of London and Mary his wyf doughter
> to Clement (?) . . . ell which ffrauncis dyed
> ye sixthe day of January a° 1563 and
> Mary dyed before hym vz ye last day of
> Decembre a° dn̄i 1563.

There is a rubbing of this brass in the collection of the Society of Antiquaries, dated 1888, at which time it was in the floor of the north aisle.

Hatton also notes the arms of Giffard; inscriptions to Edmund Martin, Esquire, 1568, Wm. Hagar, salter, 1580; and the figure of Jane Kokene, 1409.

4. *Coffin.*

At the west end of the nuns' quire is a stone coffin, with shaped head, of the 13th or 14th century.

5. *Communion Table.*

In the Chapel of the Holy Ghost is the old Communion Table from St. Martin Outwich. The top is inlaid with geometrical pattern and an eight-pointed star in the centre, the edges moulded. The four twisted legs are secured at the feet by moulded and shaped rails meeting in centre. Early 18th century.

6. *Doorcases and Doors.*

The massive *South Door* is of two leaves: the semicircular head is separated from the panels below by a continuation of the impost mouldings of the jambs; in the centre is a diminishing pilaster with an Ionic capital. The main divisions of each leaf of the door are divided into four L-shaped panels enclosing a central panel with raised moulding and a design representing an archway in perspective. The central style of the door has cut and shaped pattern and half-turned spindle ornaments.

The Doorcase, or lobby, within the south doorway. The doors are in two leaves, each with two raised and elaborately moulded panels. Above the door is a small moulding and an elliptical-headed panel filled inside and outside with a conventionalised shell ornament. In the spandrels are carvings of angels with outspread wings holding cartouches. The doors are flanked by pilasters with moulded bases and Ionic capitals, and standing on panelled pedestals; the upper portion of each pilaster is ornamented with a strap-work design and spindle ornament. The pilasters carry an entablature consisting of an archtrave and dentilled cornice with a broken segmental pediment with volutes; in the middle is a large cartouche of the Royal Stuart arms supported by two reclining angels. This pediment is said to have formed part of the old reredos. The sides and soffit of the doorcase are panelled.

West Door. The door is of two leaves with a two-centred head. On the outside there is a shaped panel on each leaf of the door, and below it on the middle-rails are raised cut and shaped designs. Above the upper rails are scrolls and other ornaments enclosing a small niche with round, scalloped head. The bottom panels are modern.

The Doorcase has doors in the three sides. The central door is of two panelled leaves; on the east face the upper panels are carved with perspective arches enriched with scale ornament, and the spandrels with arabesques. Upon each of the middle rails is a lion-head mask, and the lower panels have eared mouldings. Flanking the doorway are fluted Corinthian columns standing on panelled pedestals and supporting an entablature and a broken scrolled pediment with a carved swag ; above each column is a rampant lion holding a shaped shield, and from the middle of the pediment rises a square panel with carved drapery, and a raised inscription : "This is none other but the house of God, this is the gate of Heaven." The panel is finished with a cornice and pierced cresting, carved with a cartouche, two perspective arches and swags. Below the main entablature is a cornice supporting two cherubs with a cartouche and swags. The sides of the doorcase have each two Corinthian pilasters, corresponding to the columns on the front ; the side doors have plain raised panels. The inner sides of the central doors have two raised panels, moulded architrave, and strap work ornament over.

All these doors and doorcases are of the first half of the 17th century.

7. *Easter Sepulchre.*

See Monument 5.

8. *Font and Cover.*

The font at the west end is octagonal, of the baluster type, with a red marble shaft, cream-coloured necking and base and black marble pedestal and bowl of ovolo section. The font cover is of wood gilt. It is octagonal with upright panelled sides and slender dentilled cornice, ogee top with angle ribs enriched with bead ornament and terminating in a ball finial. This is probably the font and cover bought in 1632 for £20.

At the east end is a second font, of marble, with broken octagonal stem.

9. *Glass.*

Of the ancient painted glass now in this church the only parts which can be said to have been there before the dissolution are the roundels commemorative of Sir John Crosby, in the north-east window of the south chapel, and a few fragments used for repairing the 17th-century heraldic glass in the windows of the nuns' quire.

The glass in the Crosby window is all modern with the exception of these seven large roundels in the main lights containing heraldry proper to Sir John and his first wife, and even they are much restored. The design of all the roundels is the same, though the arms on each shield necessarily differ and the colouring, too, is varied.

The shield is set in a coloured and diapered quatrefoil, the spaces between the foils being filled with grisaille and coloured leafage, and the whole enclosed within a circular border made up of small rectangular pieces of white glass, each alternate piece bearing Sir John Crosby's merchant's mark. This mark, it will be observed, appears on the shield in one of the roundels. All the coloured parts of this Crosby glass are pot-metal, for enamel-painting in colours on glass was not practised until well on in the 16th century. The diapering of the coloured glass is of a simple character, either conventional roses or dots.

ST. HELEN, BISHOPSGATE

The arms shown on the shields are those of Crosby (*sable*, a cheveron *ermine* between three rams *argent*), the same impaling the arms of his first wife Agnes (*azure*, a fess cotised *argent*), the arms of the City of London, the merchant's mark of Sir John Crosby, the arms of the Grocers' Company, of which company Sir John was Warden in 1463, and the arms of Sir Ralph Astry (barry wavy *argent* and *azure*, a chief *gules* with three bezants therein). Sir Ralph was Mayor in 1493, and one may assume that his arms appear among the Crosby heraldry by way of compliment.

The remainder of the pre-dissolution glass in the church may be dealt with in a few words. It consists only of fragments—a piece of grisaille foliation in the base of the shield in the central main light of the easternmost window in the north wall of the nuns' quire, in the third window from the east in the same wall some fragments of 15th and early 16th-century tabernacle work, drapery, hatched grisaille made up into roundels and set in modern green glass; in the middle of the western light of the same window fragments of 15th-century ivy-leaf design on a hatched ground, and, in the middle light of the same window, pieces of early 16th-century tabernacle work surrounding a 17th-century cherub's head.

The glass in the north wall of the nuns' quire to which these fragments serve as repairs, is all of 17th-century date, and consists of roundels containing cherub-heads on a yellow ground and heraldry: in the first window from the east a shield, supported by an angel, bearing: *or*, a saltire *ermine* (perhaps the arms of Backhouse), a similar design to the last with the arms of the Leathersellers' Company, a cartouche with: *sable*, a cheveron between three couple-closes and three cinqfoils *or*, and another cartouche bearing the City arms.

There is also, in the first window from the east, a fragment of an inscription:

. . . S^r^. Martyn . . .
Knight An . . .
16 . . .

possibly referring to Sir Martin Lumley, died 1634.

The old glass in the three clerestory windows of the south transept consists of eleven shields of arms not easy to identify from the floor level. They are, mostly, in the style common to the 17th century, with the crest on a mantled helm. Some are single coats, others are impaled or quartered coats, set in circular or rectangular panels of scroll work. One is dated 1483, but the panel itself is not earlier than the 17th century.

The families commemorated comprise, among others, Green impaling Wilmot, Ward impaling Bolton (?), Naylor (?) impaling Nevill of Abergavenny, Freeman impaling Wolf (?), Joliffe impaling Boothby, Churchman, Barnardiston (?) impaling Reynardson, Reynardson alone, and Chesham. The greater part of the colour is enamel work, and the glass of which they are made is, for the most part, thin and characterless.

ST. HELEN, BISHOPSGATE

10. *Funeral Helmet.*

A made-up one in the style of a late 16th-century close helmet. It consists of the following pieces :

A. The skull (of poor outline).

B. The beevor, adapted of thin metal.

C. Visor, adapted of thin metal.

D. The chin-piece in two portions is of good work and has belonged possibly to an early 16th-century armet.

E. The front plate of the gorget.

F. The back plate.

These two latter are coarse armour, as worn by pikemen.

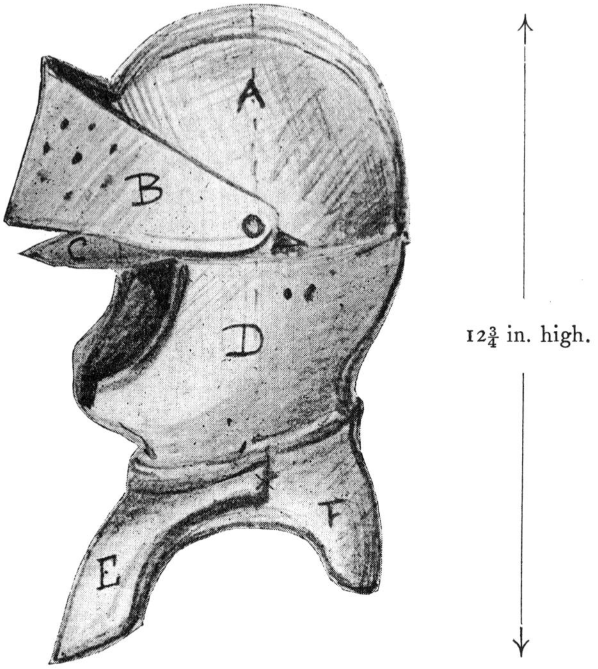
A
B
C
D
E
F
12¾ in. high.

This headpiece as a whole is of the class made for funeral purposes only, and never intended to have been worn. The thin visor and beevor work on separate pins, which would not have been the case if intended for use. The only good piece of work is the chin, which opened originally at the sides ; the holes for fixing the hinges remain. The square notch in front of chin is found in armets. The edges of the opening in the chin-pieces are turned outwards, which is the case in early pieces.

11. *Images.*

In the Chapel of St. Mary, on a carved scrolled bracket, is a seated figure of a woman in classic dress, holding a book. It probably represents one of the Muses or a Sibyl, and is of Renaissance workmanship.

12. *Niches.*

In the east wall of the Chapel of St. Mary are six ogee and cinquefoil-headed niches, four of them in two tiers on the north of the east window, and two to the south of the same ; all of them have moulded ogee labels and finials. The two northernmost have no pedestals, the others contain semi-octagonal and moulded pedestals. All are of late 14th-century date.

13. *The Organ Case.*

The organ case is of mahogany with three towers of organ pipes in front surmounted by pierced carvings and entablatures, and supported on semicircular brackets with cherub-heads and acanthus leaves. Between the brackets is a frieze of carved and pierced work. The panels between the towers are ogee-shaped on plan, and the cornice is ramped up to the centre with an ogee curve. The pipes stand upon a panelled base enriched with swags and carvings of musical instruments. The back of the organ overhangs and is supported at each end by a finely carved oak bracket consisting of a large scroll with a half-figure of a cherub issuing from it, and holding a trumpet and scroll. The upper portion of the bracket bears two-winged cherub-heads, and the lower portion consists of a winged skull with a small carved console. This appears to be the organ and case built by Thomas Griffin in 1742.* The carved brackets at the back are of mid 17th-century date re-used. The organ was formerly at the west end of the church.

14. *Piscinæ.*

In the east wall of the south transept chapels are two piscinæ of late 14th-century date with cinquefoiled arches in square heads with embattled cornices; both have shelves, and the northern retains the original drain with moulded underside.

In the nave, in the south wall, west of the screen, is a third piscina with moulded jambs and two-centred head, late 13th century, but with modern sill.

15. *Plate.*

A cup and cover paten, silver-gilt, of 1570, the cup inscribed "St. Helen's, 1570"; maker's mark: a stag's head.

A paten, silver-gilt, inscribed, "The Gift of Thomas Awdeley, Mercer, Anno Domini 1620"; maker's mark A. I.
W. T.

A pair of flagons inscribed, "The Gift of Sir Martin Lumley, Kt, and Alderman, 1632," with his arms (a fess); maker's mark: T.F.

A cup and cover paten, silver-gilt, inscribed, "Given with a Cover to the Church of St Helen's by D. W. Anō Dom. 1634." Daniel Williams, Merchant (died 1636), was otherwise a benefactor to the church.† Maker's mark: a scallop shell.

A large paten of 1638 inscribed, "In Usum Mensae Domenicæ Saint H."

A large silver bason with date mark for 1647 and maker's mark W.N. with a seed rose and three pellets below in a plain shield, and inscribed, "The Gift of Francis Bancroft Esqre—To Ye Parish Church of Saint Hellens 1728."

* J. E. Cox, *op. cit.*, pp. 152 and 155. † *Ibid.* p. 83.

ST. HELEN, BISHOPSGATE

An alms-dish of 1728, maker's mark W.D., inscribed " Pursuant to the last will of Mrs. Mary Parsons this plate is given to ye parish church of S. Hellen for ye use of ye Communion Service and to remain there so long as ye parish shall suffer ye stone that lyes over Mr. Giles Dean to remain, if removed or taken away to goe to the parish Church of S. Mary le Bow for ever."

A spoon of 1732, maker's mark F.S. (?), inscribed, " St Helena " with an irradiated I H S.

A secular cup of 1778 of urn shape with two handles and a conical cover; inscribed, " The Gift of John Smith Esqr to the Parish Church of St. Helen London for the Use of the Communion Service 1778," with a shield of arms—a saltire between four martlets, and for crest an arm in armour holding a seaxe. Maker's mark: W.H. (?).

A beadle's staff-head of bronze or brass gilt with a pedestal inscribed, " Saint Helen 1777, Regilt 1852," and an earlier seated figure of a Sibyl holding an inscribed book.

Four pewter alms-dishes.

Some of the plate from St. Martin Outwich is now at Christ Church, Stepney.

16. *Poor Box.*

The late-18th-century Poor Box is supported upon a 17th-century terminal figure of a bearded man with right arm and breast bare, holding a tall hat to receive alms. The figure grows out of an inverted square baluster with leathern ring ornament at the sides.

17. *Pulpit.*

The Jacobean Pulpit is hexagonal and stands against the south wall, just west of the Quire Screen. It is of two stages, the upper with enriched diminishing pilasters at the angles supported on trusses in the lower stage. The upper panel on each side has an architectural composition consisting of an ellipse with a keyed architrave supported by scrolls and flanked by a pair of diminishing pilasters with entablature and cresting; the lower panel in each side has a shaped inner panel. The cornice of quadrant section is carved with strap work and has in the middle of each side a cartouche with the symbols of the Evangelists and the Agnus Dei. The plain stem is of ogee form and rests on a short modern shaft. The sounding board is hexagonal, and the under side is panelled with raised mouldings, the middle panel being of circular form with keyblocks; the sides of the sounding board are treated as an entablature with the frieze enriched with bay leaves and slight scroll-like projections at the angles, bearing lion-head masks, swags, and fluting, and finished with a ball pendant at each angle. The date of the sounding board is probably *circa* 1640. The support of the sounding board forms an upright panel against the wall flanked by fluted pilasters each supporting a pair of brackets;

in the middle is a panel with bolection mouldings flanked by an inner pair of fluted pilasters supporting an entablature and segmental pediment. This portion is probably of the 18th century, except the raised and mitred panel, which is of early 17th-century character.

18. *Reredos.*

The Reredos is modern. The early 18th-century reredos was removed or destroyed in one of the restorations. It is described by Hatton (1708) as follows: "The altar-piece is painted Deal, of the Composit Order. The Inter-columns are the Commandments betn. the Lord's Prayer and Creed, done in gold Letters on Black. Over the Commandments is a Glory and these Words, *If ye love me keep my Commandments*, Joh. chap. 14. And above the Cornish, the Queen's Arms supported by two Angels."*

19. *Staircase Enclosure.*

At the south-west angle of the nuns' quire is an enclosure constructed of wood, the surface marked with channelled grooves to represent rusticated blocks of masonry. It is constructed in three stages, the lowest with plain pilasters on pedestals at the angles and a plain architrave and cornice; the middle stage is treated similarly but with rather more detail and with a three-centred arch springing from the pilasters; on the north face are two oval lunettes, the upper one having a rusticated and keyed architrave; there is one lunette upon the east face. The top stage is in the form of an attic with slender pilasters at the angles; the sides terminate against the roof. *Circa* 1700.

20. *Stalls.*

The 15th-century stalls, formerly in the nuns' quire, are now fixed in the parish chancel. There are seven stalls on the north and six on the south side, with desks in front. The moulded arms are trefoiled on plan, with the mouldings dying into the back of the seats. The edges of the divisions are moulded and have grotesque carvings above the seat level. Below the same level the divisions have in place of the moulding an attached shaft with moulded cap and base. The seats are hinged so that they may be raised, but have no misericordes. The outer faces of the backs have been fitted with early 17th-century panelling, the frieze panels having raised mouldings.

The front desks are in eight divisions to the north and six to the south, with raised moulded panels on their lower portion, while the upper frieze panels are carved and pierced with varying devices in the centre (rose, thistle, pomegranate, and fleur-de-lis). On the north side, the first three

* There is a coloured drawing of this reredos in the MS. history of the church now belonging to the parish. The pediment, etc., now surmount the south doorcase.

panels from the west appear to be modern, the styles have diminishing pilasters with moulded ornament upon them, and the cornice is dentilled. The standards have shaped beads finished with egg-and-tongue moulding and a semicircular fluted and pierced pediment. Mid-17th century.

21. *Sword-Rests.*

Lawrence.

A fine and elaborate sword-rest in wood is fixed against the pier on the south side of the parish chancel. It has an enriched moulded shelf with a segmental projection in front and supports two slightly twisted columns with wreaths of leaves and flowers carried round. The moulded bases and Corinthian caps are richly carved, and the entablature has a modilioned cornice and carved frieze. In front of the entablature is a cartouche bearing the City Arms, and above it is a square tablet with an enriched panel flanked by carved scrolls and a cartouche in front bearing the arms of Lawrence, Lord Mayor 1665 (for blazon see Monument 69). Above the tablet are two standing figures of angels supporting a third cartouche bearing the Royal Stuart Arms surmounted by a crown. This rest may be compared with the other examples in wood at St. Olave's, Southwark, at the Vintners' Hall, and the Clothworkers' Hall.

Upon the pier adjoining the lectern is a sword-rest of wrought-iron with scrolls and foliage. It incorporates four plates, two in the form of shields and two of oval shape, all painted with arms: (*a*) the Royal Hanoverian Arms surmounted by a large crown, (*b*) the City of London, (*c*) checky *or* and *gules*, on a fess *argent* three martlets *sable*, for John Thomas Thorp, Lord Mayor 1820–1821, (*d*) the Drapers' Company. On the back of (*c*) is a painting of a queen, and on the back of (*d*) the inscription: "Restored 1868."

22. *Miscellanea.*

On the south wall of the south transept behind the organ are fixed two architectural fragments: (*a*) A piece of marble with conventional design in low relief comprising a pointed scalloped shell ornament with scrolled design round it. It is late Arab (Egyptian), Moorish or Mudéjar work, and the design can be almost exactly paralleled at the Alhambra, Granada. It was found when moving the Bernard Monument to its present position. (*b*) A piece of Purbeck marble with a round sex-foiled panel in the middle enclosing a plain shield with three mortice holes for fastening a brass shield on the face. It was formerly part of the Clitherow Monument in St. Martin Outwich, and was used to repair the Pemberton Monument during its reconstruction in 1796.

At the west end of the nuns' quire are two cases containing various objects found from time to time during the alterations and restoration of the church. They include fragments of moulded staves, earthenware (mediæval and later), fragments of metal work, and several portions of mediæval slip-tiles.

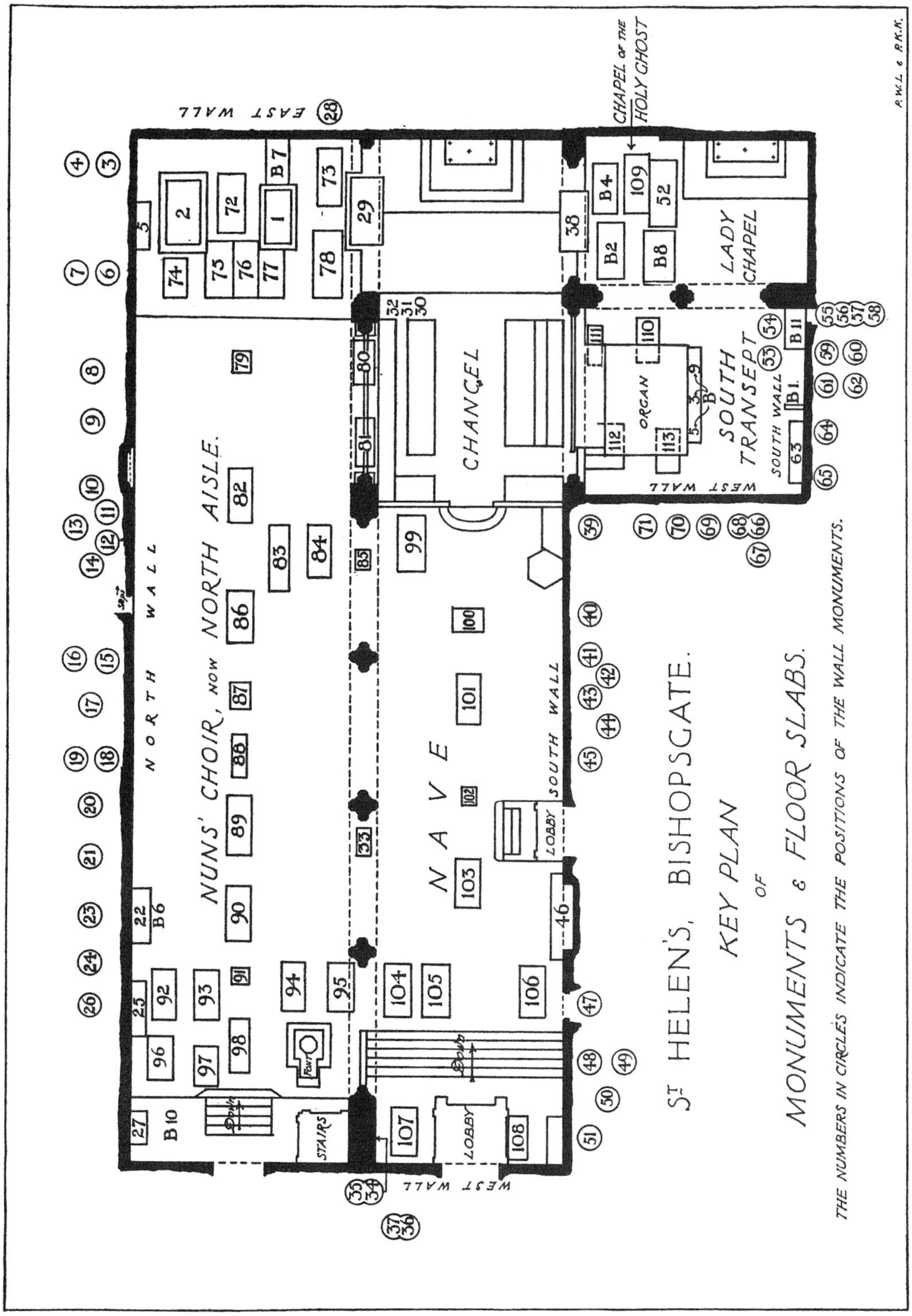
ST HELEN'S, BISHOPSGATE.
KEY PLAN
OF
MONUMENTS & FLOOR SLABS.
THE NUMBERS IN CIRCLES INDICATE THE POSITIONS OF THE WALL MONUMENTS.
EAST WALL
NORTH WALL
SOUTH WALL
WEST WALL
NUNS' CHOIR, NOW NORTH AISLE.
NAVE
CHANCEL
LADY CHAPEL
SOUTH TRANSEPT
ORGAN
CHAPEL OF THE HOLY GHOST
LOBBY
STAIRS
FONT
P.W.L. & R.K.K.

ST. HELEN, BISHOPSGATE

VII.—MONUMENTS WITHIN THE CHURCH

Starting from the east end of the nuns' quire with the two altar tombs upon a slightly raised platform.

Adelmare.

1. SIR JULIUS CÆSAR ADELMARE, 1636.

Altar tomb by Nicholas Stone,* with plain white marble sides, flat pilasters at the angles, and simple moulded base. It is surmounted by a slab of touch with three inscriptions in Latin on white marble. The top inscription takes the form of a deed with a large seal attached. Upon the seal appears in relief a shield with the following:

Arms: (*Gules*) three cinquefoils, (*argent*) a chief with three cinquefoils therein counter-coloured.

Crest: a dolphin swimming in the sea.

(For the inscriptions see opposite page.)

2. SIR THOMAS GRESHAM, 1579.

An altar tomb of white marble with fluted sides of shaped section, with enriched moulded base and capping supporting a mottled marble slab on which is cut the name, Sir Thomas Gresham, with the date of his burial, but no other inscription. Upon the north side of the tomb is an oval shield of arms flanked by a pair of cherubs with ornamental strap-work borders of fruit and flowers. Upon the south side is a shaped shield of arms with helm and mantling in high relief upon a panel with ornamental strap-work borders. At the east end is an oval shield of arms upon a panel with cut and shaped strap-work borders, enriched with fruit and flowers. At the west end is a shield of arms with helm and mantling in high relief similar to those upon the north side.

Arms:

(i) (S) (*Argent*) a cheveron (*sable*) ermined (*argent*) between three rowels *argent* (Gresham).

(ii) (S) Gresham impaling (*or*) on a bend (*vert*) three buck's heads (*argent*) (Fernely).

(iii) (E) As (ii) and (iv) (W) as (i).

Crest: A grasshopper.

On the marble slab is inscribed:

S^{R} THOMAS GRESHAM KNIGHT.

Bury^{d} Decem^{br} the 15th 1579 ∽∽

* "In 1636 I mad a tombe for Ser Julyes Ceser M^{r} of the Rooles and sett it up in St Elens Church London for [which] I had 110£." *The Notebook of Nicholas Stone*, fo. 20. See Walpole Society's publications, vol. vii. p. 74. Also see *Account Book of Nicholas Stone*, fo. 18. same vol., p. 105.

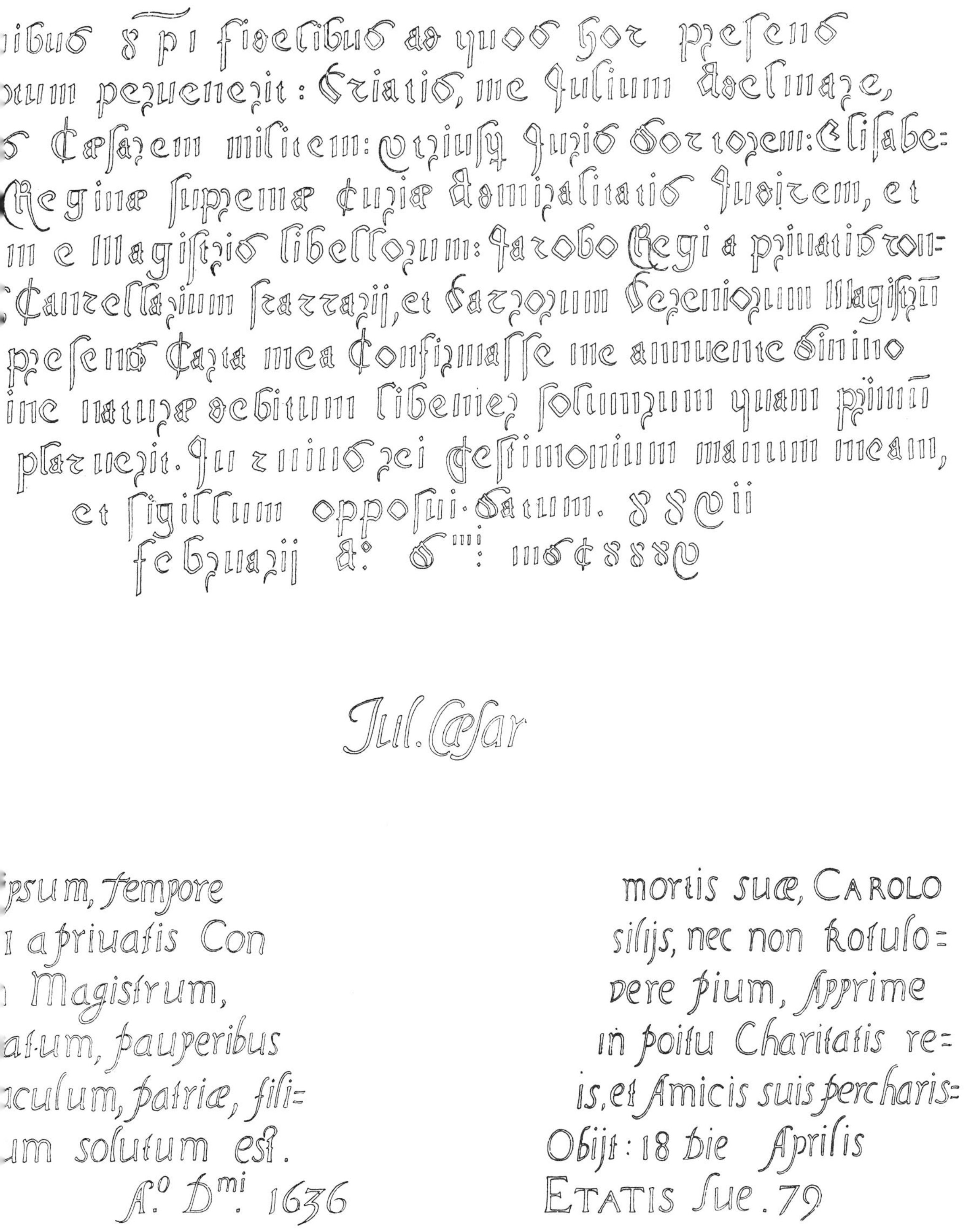
Jul. Cæsar
psum, tempore
i a priuatis Con
n Magistrum,
atum, pauperibus
aculum, patriæ, fili=
um solutum est.
A.o D.mi 1636
mortis suæ, CAROLO
silijs, nec non Rotulo=
vere pium, Apprime
in poitu Charitatis re=
is, et Amicis suis percharis=
Obijt: 18 die Aprilis
ETATIS Sue. 79

FACSIMILE OF INSCRIPTION TO SIR JULIUS CÆSAR.

ST. HELEN, BISHOPSGATE

3. ALBERICO GENTILE, 1608.

A tablet erected in 1877, the former monument being almost entirely destroyed. It apparently incorporates portions of the original work.

4. WILLIAM FINCH, 1672.

Wall-monument of marble with Ionic columns at the sides supporting an entablature and curved broken pediment with a cartouche of arms. In the middle is an inscription on black marble within an oval wreath of bay leaves. Below a projecting moulded shelf is a second inscribed panel between a pair of moulded corbels each with a cherub's head upon it. Below this again on an apron is a shield of arms and swags.

Arms:

(i) (*Argent*) a cheveron (*sable*) between three griffins passant (*sable*).
(ii) (i) impaling (*argent*) a cross engrailed (*sable*) between four pellets each charged with a pheon (*argent*).

The inscription is as follows:

Siste Gradum
Peripatetice, & paulisper contemplare,
Ornatiſsimi Microcoſmi heu! breves reliquias
Nunc in pulverem redacti olim
Guilielmi Finch, Armigeri antiquâ & data
in Agro Cantij Familia oriundi
Naturæ & Gratiæ dotibus egregie nobilitati Ad Oris Corporisq.
Venustatem acceſsit maior Animæ pulchritudo optimis virtutibus in-
signitæ Quas in Chriſtianæ Religionis testimonium et decus luculenter
usque exernit
Eximia in Deum. O. M. Pietate erga Sacros Paſtores ſummā
Reverentia, Fidelitate in Principem, Justitia in Proximum Conjugali
Paternacq Indulgentia Singulari in Familiares affectu integerrima pro
pensa in Omnes Benevolentia; Linguâ caſtus et candidus manu supra
fidem Liberalis; Nemini turpiter obloqui, aut obtrectare solitus omnibus
benefacere, inprimis Egenis absq^b*, præcinente buccina, Eleemoſynis pariter ac*
Thesauris plenus, quos probe accumulatos in Terra plurimos prudens Mercator
in Cœlo recondidit, Vitam tandem commutandis aliquandiu mercibus proſ
pere tranſactam 42 Ætatis annum emensus Jun 27. 1672
Meliori quæstu cum Morte comutavit.
Relictis & bonæ ſpei Parvulis cum dilectiſsima et
Amantiſsima Uxore quæ in perpetuam tam chari Capuis Me
moriam Monumentum hoc, constantiſsimi Amoris Pignus, extru-
endum curavit, Ipsa interim mœrore cum Illo conſepulta

Abi iam attonitus Viator, & mirare
tam probum in tam pravo seculo Virum,
aut vivere potuiſſe, aut debuiſse
MORI.

ST. HELEN, BISHOPSGATE

ESTHER FINCH FOEMINA CASTISSIMA, VIRO MORIGERA, ET CURÆ DOMESTICÆ DULCE LEVAMEN LIBERORVM (QUOS SEPTEM RELIQUIT) MATER PROVIDA, SINCERA PIETATE, ALACRI ERGA TENUIORES BENIGNITATE, LIBERA LITATE IN OMNES, MORVM DENIQUE SANCTITATE CONSPICVA. VIRI (DVM IN VIVIS ESSET) DECUS SIMUL ET SOLAMEN ; DEFVNCTI, VIDUA SVPRA QVAMDICI POTEST MOESTISSIMA. VIXIT ANNOS 41. MENSES 5. DEMP TIS DIEBUS 11. OBIIT MAII DIE 4. *ANNO SALVTIS* 1673.

5. JOHANE ALFREY, 1525.

A combined monument, squint and Easter sepulchre, in the form of a recessed altar-tomb. The base, now set very high up, owing to the lowering of the floor level, has six cinquefoiled openings in front and one on each return; a further series of mullions at the back opened into the sacristy. A moulded slab of hard stone surmounts this base, and on it rest the two side shafts of the canopied recess. This recess has a square moulded outer head surmounted by a moulded cornice covered with foliage and having the remains of a cresting of flowers; the heads of the side shafts are masked by two defaced shields. The soffit of the recess is contrived as a four-centred arch set on the splay and having cusped panelling continued down the jambs. At the back of the recess is a rectangular sinking for an inscribed plate, now missing.

The will of Johane Alfrey, widow, 1525 (*P.C.C.*, 5 Porch) refers specifically to the remaking of this monument and Easter sepulchre. She desires to be buried in the "quere under a tumbe in the walle standing before the image of Saint Helyn whereuppon the Sepulcre of our Lord hath ben yerely used to be sett. And for the same cause specially I will that the said tumbe be newe made by myn executors . . . a stone to be laide upon the grave of my late husbonde William Ledys making mencion who lyeth buried under the same stone . . . a table conteyning thre ymages, that is to say the ymage of the Trinitie to be in the myddes of the same table and the ymage of our Lady to be on the right side of the same Trinitie and the ymage of saint Kateryn to be on the left side of the same Trinitie and that in the same table be well and workmanly wrought and paynted an ymage of a gentilwoman kneling holding hir handes joyntly togiders and loking upon the said ymages with an oracion to be written in letters upon the same table and the same table to be fastened upon the walle bitwene my said tumbe and the ymage of Saint Helyn." Johane was wife first of William Ledys and secondly of Thomas Alfrey of Lancing, Sussex. The identity of the existing monument with that mentioned in the will is rendered certain by the record by Hatton of two coats-of-arms on an old monument in this position—(*a*) a fess between three eagles displayed, the arms of Leeds, and (*b*) a cheveron between three anulets.

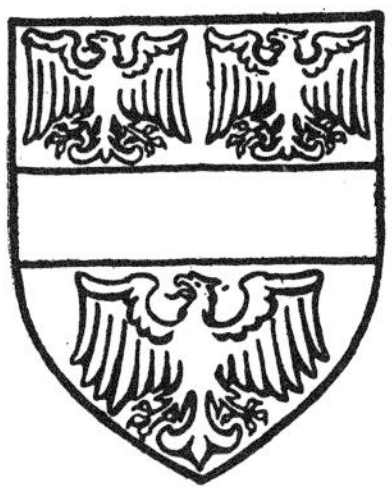

Leeds.

Bond.

6. WILLIAM BOND, 1576.

A small mural monument of two bays divided and flanked by Corinthian columns resting on a panelled and inscribed base of quadrant section and supporting an entablature and a broken pediment with a round cartouche in the middle, enclosing a shield of arms. In the recesses between the columns are kneeling figures of a man and six sons (on the left) and his wife and one daughter (on the right) with a desk on each side of the middle column; above the figures are a shield and lozenge of arms.

Arms:

(i) *Argent* on a cheveron *sable* three bezants. A crescent for difference. Crest: A seated lion.
(ii) (i) impaling *gules* a cheveron *argent* between three birds *argent(?)* with three lozenges *gules* on the cheveron.
(iii) The impaled coat of (ii).

Upon the front of the base, upon the left-hand side, is inscribed:

FLOS MERCATORVM, QVOS TERRA BRITANA CREAVIT,
ÉCCE, SVB HOC TVMVLO GVLIELMVS BONDVS HVMATVR.
ILLE MARI MVLTVM PASSVS PER SAXA, PER VNDAS
DITAVIT PATRIAS PEREGRINIS MERCIBVS ORAS.
MAGNANIMVM GRÆCI MIRANTVR IASONA VATES
AVREA DE GELIDO RETVLIT QVIA VELLERA PHASI.

Upon the right-hand side:

GRAECIA DOCTA TACE GRAII CONCEDITE VATES:
HIC JACET ARGOLICO MERCATOR IASONE MAIOR.
VELLERA MVLTA TVLIT MAGIS AVREA VELLERE PHRYXI
ET FRETA MVLTA SCIDIT MAGIS ARDVA PHASIDOS VNDIS.
HEI MIHI QVOD NVLLO MORS EST SVPERABILIS AVRO
FLOS MERCATORVM, GULIELMVS BONDVS HUMATVR.

Beneath the Sarcophagus upon the left-hand side:

HEERE LIETHE THE BODIE OF WILLM̄ BONDE ALDERMAN
SOMTIME SHREVE OF LONDON A MARCHANT ADVENTVRER

On the right-hand side:

MOSTE FAMOVS IN HIS AGE FOR HIS GREATE ADVEN
TVRES BOTHE BY SEA AND LANDE OBIIT 30 MAY 1576.

7. PETER GAUSSEN, 1788, and others.

Above (5) is a plain rectangular inscribed tablet, recessed at the sides, with a moulded cornice and a shaped apron with a shield of arms and foliage.

Above the cornice is a pyramidal slab with figures in high relief of a woman (probably Charity) holding a medallion portrait of the deceased and with three children below. Twined about the figures is a broad ribbon.

Arms: *Sable* a lion (?) passant *or* (?) on a chief *or* (?) three . . . impaling a defaced coat.

The inscription runs:

THIS MONUMENT WAS ERECTED TO THE MEMORY OF

PETER GAUSSEN ESQ.

HE CLOSED A LIFE OF BENEVOLENCE
BY A DEATH OF PATIENCE AND RESIGNATION
THE 20TH NOV:R 1788, AGED 66 YEARS.

Here are likewise deposited the remains of

PETER GAUSSEN Esq who died 17.th Septr. 1759,
Aged 82 Years.
And IANE GAUSSEN Wife of the last mentioned
who died 4th Iany 1747, Aged 71 Years, Uncle and Aunt
to the first mentioned PETER GAUSSEN.
Likewise ANNA MARIA GAUSSEN who died the 24th Iune, 1767,
Aged 6 Years and 6 Months.
PAUL GAUSSEN who died 17th Iany 1774, Aged 16 Years.
PETER GAUSSEN who died 28th Octr 1781, Aged 25 Years.
Children of the first mentioned PETER GAUSSEN Esq.
ANNA MARIA GAUSSEN Widow of PETER GAUSSEN Esqr
Obt December 6th 1804 in the 70th Year of her Age.

8. MARTIN BOND, 1643.

A wall monument flanked by Corinthian columns resting on carved trussed corbels and supporting separate entablatures and a broken segmental pediment with an achievement of arms in the middle. Between the columns is a rectangular panel with a camp scene in high relief. In the middle is the armed figure of the deceased seated in the entrance of a tent; at the sides are sentries armed as musketeers, and to the left is a horse and groom; below the panel is an enriched apron with an inscribed tablet and shield of arms; a third shield of arms hangs at the back of the tent.

Arms:

(i) *Argent*, a cheveron *sable* with three bezants thereon.
(ii) The Merchant Venturers' Company.
(iii) As (i).

The inscription is as follows :

MEMORIÆ SACRVM

NEERE THIS PLACE RESTETH $\overset{E}{Y}$ BODY OF $\overset{E}{Y}$ WORTHY CITTIZEN & SOLDER
MARTIN BOND ESQ SOÑ OF WILL BOND SHERIFE & ALDERMAN OF LONDON
HE WAS CAPTAINE IN $\overset{E}{Y}$ YEARE 1588 AT $\overset{E}{Y}$ CAMPE AT TILBURY & AFTER REMAINED
CHEIFE CAPTAINE OF $\overset{E}{Y}$ TRAINED BANDES OF THIS CITTY VNTIL HIS DEATH
HE WAS A MARCHANT ADVENTVER & FREE OF $\overset{E}{Y}$ COMPANY OF HABERDASHER,
HE LIVED TO THE AGE OF 85 YEARES AND DYED IN MAY 1643
HIS PYETY PRVDENCE COVRAGE AND CHARITY, HAVE LEFT
BEHINDE HIM A NEVER DYEING MONVMENT

Quam Prudens hic Miles erat quam Nobile Rectus,
Nouerunt Princeps Patria Castra Duces
Ciui quanta fuit Pietas, quam larga Manusq
Pauperis agnoscunt viscera Templa Togœ,
Miles hic et ciuis qualem Vix millibus Unum
Sæcla referre queant nec meminisse Parem

PATRVO BENE MERITO GVLIELMVS BOND ARMIGER POSVIT.

9. HENRY PETER KUHFF, 1796.

A plain inscribed tablet with a marble border carried on a small pair of corbels and surmounted by a simple moulded cornice and a black marble pyramidal slab with an urn in front of it.

NEAR THIS SPOT
ARE DEPOSITED THE REMAINS
OF
HENRY PETER KUHFF ESQUIRE,
WHO DEPARTED THIS LIFE
OCTOBER THE 10TH 1796
IN THE 70TH YEAR OF HIS AGE.
OF
PETER KUHFF HIS SON
WHO DIED
JANUARY THE 10TH 1786,
IN HIS 7TH YEAR.
OF
FREDERICK CHARLES KUHFF ESQUIRE,
WHO DIED
MARCH THE 11TH 1792
AGED 50 YEARS.

ST. HELEN, BISHOPSGATE

10. VALENTINE MORTOFT, 1641.

Mortoft.

A wall monument with an inscribed tablet of black marble, with gilt lettering, in the middle and a moulded border flanked by a pair of Corinthian columns resting on trusses and supporting an entablature with a segmental broken pediment, and an achievement of arms. The apron has an inscribed tablet and a scrolled enrichment at the base.

Arms :

(i) *Sable*, a couched stag looking backward with a moor-cock rising between its antlers *argent* impaling (dexter) Glover and (sinister) Hammersley.

(ii) *Azure*, a fess embattled and counter-embattled *ermine* between three crescents *argent* (Glover, first wife).

(iii) *Sable*, a couched stag looking backwards *argent* (Mortoft without the moor-cock).

(iv) *Gules*, three rams' heads cut off at the neck *or* (Hammersley, second wife).

(v) Mortoft (as iii) impaling Glover.

(vi) Mortoft (as iii) impaling Hammersley.

The inscriptions are :

I ſhall ſee God in my fleſh

NEERE VNTO THIS PLACE LYETH BURYED THE BODY OF VALENTINE MORTOFT ESQ. HAVEING LIVED COMFORTABLY W^TH TWO WIVES: THE FIRST ELLEN GLOVER, BY WHOME HEE HAD WILLIAM, WHO WAS LIVEING AT HIS DEATH. HIS SECŌD WIFE MARGARET DAVGHTER OF SIR HVGH HAM̃ERSLY K^T & ALDERMAN OF LONDON, BY HER HEE HAD ISSVE FOVR SONS, AND THREE DAVGHTERS OF W^CH HE LEFT LIVEING ONE SON & ONE DAUGHTER

HEE FINISHED THE COVRSE OF 68 YEARES AND YEILDED VP HIS SPIRIT TO GOD SEPT. 16. 1641. BEQVEATHING HIS BODY TO Y^E EARTH TO WAYT FOR A GLORIOUS RESVRRECTION.

The memoriall of the just shall be had in Everlasting Remembrance

ST. HELEN, BISHOPSGATE

11. ELIZABETH THOMPSON, 1828.

12. SAMUEL WINTER, 1837.

13. HENRY WHITE, 1702–3.

A shaped tablet or cartouche with scroll-work and cherubs' heads on either side surmounted by a coat-of-arms.

Arms: *Gules*, an annulet *or* all within a border *sable* charged with eight stars *or*, a crescent for difference.
Inscription:

Here lies
Interred the Body of

HENRY WHITE

Late of BILBAO Merchant
who Departed this life
the first day of Ianuary
Anno Dom̃: 170$\frac{2}{3}$
Ætatis Suæ 29
et filius et ffrater erat

14. ANN JENNINGS, 1773.

A plain inscribed tablet surmounted by a simple moulded capping and an urn; beneath the tablet is a shaped apron with palm branches.

In a Vault Adjoining
Lies the Remains of

ANN the wife of

JOHN JENNINGS

of this Pariſh
Who Departed this Life
The 9th. of March 1773
Aged 27 Years

She was an Affectionate Wiſe
A Tender Mother a ſincere friend
And a good Christian
Her Loſs to her Disconsolate Husband is
Irreparable

15. A newly erected memorial to the men who fell in the Great War [1914–18].

ST. HELEN, BISHOPSGATE

16. JOHN SMITH, 1783.

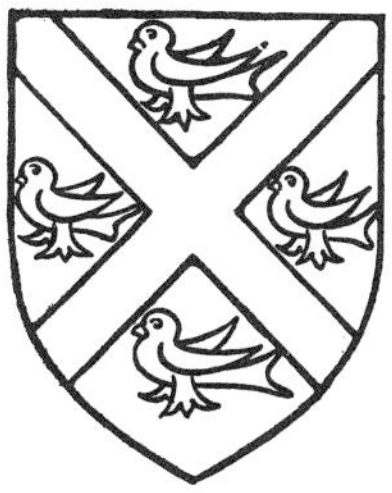

Smith.

A plain oblong inscribed tablet resting on corbels and surmounted by a simple cornice and pediment and a shield of arms; below the tablet is a moulded shelf and a shaped apron.

Arms: *Azure* a saltire *or* between four martlets *or*.

In Memory of
JOHN SMITH E^{SQR}
of this Pariſh who died
June 29TH 1783 Aged
80
By
Strict Probity
Sincerety and Benevolence
he endeared himself to
ALL
who knew him:
But more especially to the
Poor. and Needy.
by kind Condeſcenſion and boundleſs
CHARITY

Reader!
" Go and do thou likewiſe "

17. ELIZABETH HUTCHINSON, 1799.

A plain inscribed tablet flanked by narrow pilasters and surmounted by a simple cornice and an urn.

SACRED
TO THE MEMORY OF
MRS ELIZABETH URSULA HUTCHINSON
WIFE OF JAMES HUTCHINSON ESQ^{RE}
OF THIS PARISH
WHO DIED JULY 6TH 1799 AGED 73 YEARS

The tablet commemorates other members of the family after 1800.

18. FRANCIS BANCROFT, 1727.

A modern inscription. The original monument now rests beneath the floor of the church, in accordance with the instructions of the deceased, that it should remain for one hundred years and then be placed underground.

The achievement of arms is no doubt part of the original monument, as it incorporates part of a moulded cornice which forms no part of the present design. An engraving showing the complete monument is included in J. T. Smith's *Antiquities of London.*

Arms: *Or* a bend *azure* between six crosslets *azure* with three wheat sheaves *or* on the bend.

Crest: A wheat sheaf between two wings *or.*

IN MEMORY OF
MR FRANCIS BANCROFT
WHO BEQUEATHED THE
BULK OF HIS PROPERTY
IN LONDON AND MIDDLESEX
ON TRUST TO THE WORSHIPFUL
COMPANY OF DRAPERS, TO
BE APPLIED BY THEM IN
THE CAUSE OF CHARITY
AND EDUCATION. HE DIED
MARCH XIX 1727. AGED 75

19. GEORGE KELLUM, 1732.

Above the monument to Francis Bancroft is a plain mural tablet recessed at the sides and having a cornice and segmental pediment above, and a slightly moulded shelf and a shaped apron below.

Near this Place lies interr'd the Body of
Major General GEORGE KELLUM, Third Son
of GEORGE KELLUM Esqr of this Parish.
He had the Honour to serve his Country under
the best of Princes, King WILLIAM the Third,
of Glorious Memory:
And after his Decease under the victorious
IOHN Duke of MARLBOROUGH
And was Colonel of an English Regiment
of Horse.
He died in the Communion of the Church of
CHRIST, and rests in hope of a bleſsed
Resurrection: Through the alone Merits of
his Saviour IESUS CHRIST
Born September the 26th, 1659:
Died December the 23^{d}, 1732:
Aged, 73.

ST. HELEN, BISHOPSGATE

20. ANN ROBERTSON, 1750.

A plain inscribed tablet slightly raised on an equally plain background.

IN MEMORY OF
ANN ROBERTSON WIFE OF FRANCIS ROBERTSON
WHO DIED 4TH OCTR 1750, AGED 31.
FRANCIS ROBERTSON, DIED 21ST JANY 1787, AGED 73.
JANE ROBERTSON, SECOND WIFE OF FRANCIS ROBERTSON,
DIED 5TH JANY 1795, AGED 77.

(And others after 1800)

21. CHARLES BURDETT, 1737.

A plain tablet having a cornice, segmental pediment, and urn above, with a shaped apron and a cartouche of arms below.

Arms: *Azure* two bends *argent* each charged with three martlets *gules* impaling *gules* three demi-lions *or* (?)

Near this Place,
Is buried CHARLES BURDETT
Who died the 25th of *October* 1737.
Aged 85
And also MARY BURDETT
his wife,
Who died the 3d of *March* 1758,
Aged 91.
Thomas Burdett their Son,
has erected this Marble to
the ever honoured, and
beloved Memory of his
worthy Parents.

22. HUGH PEMBERTON, 1500. (Formerly in St. Martin Outwich. See also under Brasses.)

Consists of an altar tomb, canopy, and wall panel all of Purbeck or Sussex marble. The altar tomb has a panelled front with three square quatrefoiled panels enclosing blank shields, and four upright panels each divided into two lights; the ends have similar panels; the slab has a moulded edge recessed for brass fillets. The canopy rests on two free piers and two shafted responds against the wall; the piers are buttressed and have shallow niches with crocketted spires and pinnacles; the front of the canopy is richly panelled and has three ogee crocketted arches springing from intermediate pendants and having cusped segmental sub-arches; there is a similar arch at each end of the canopy. The moulded cornice is enriched with roses and square flowers, and is finished with a cresting of 'Tudor flowers.' The soffit has a richly panelled vault. The wall panel at the back has brasses and indents of brasses, partly cut away.

Arms :

(i) (*Argent*) a cheveron (*sable*) between three buckets (*sable*) banded (*or*) impaling checky on a fess three martlets.

(ii) The old arms of the Merchant Taylors' Company. The inscription is a late addition. Part of the original inscription is given by Hatton.*

23. ALEXANDER MACDOUGALL, 1855. (Modern Brass.)

24. GEORGE NIBBS, 1796.

Plain white marble tablet.

In Memory of
GEORGE NIBBS *ESQ*R.
from the Island of TORTOLA.
Barister at Law
of the Inner Temple,
who died January 15th. 1796,
Aged 23 Years.
lies Intere'd near this Place.

25. A modern base with a Bethersden marble slab, just beneath the monument to John Robinson.

26. JOHN ROBINSON, 1599.

A handsome wall monument of two bays flanked by Corinthian columns resting on a deep panel and inscribed base of quadrant section and supporting an entablature and an enriched cartouche of arms. Each bay has a round arch with carved spandrels and tympanum with a shield of arms ; below the arches are kneeling figures of a man and nine sons and his wife and seven daughters with a prayer desk in the middle. Beneath the curved base is a shaped apron with a round panel enclosing a lozenge of arms.

Arms :

(i) (*Vert*) a cheveron (*or*) between three roebucks *or* with three cinquefoils (*gules*) on the cheveron (Robinson).

(ii) and (iii) Robinson impaling (*argent*) a cheveron (*sable*) between three crosslets (*sable*) (Anderson).

(iv) Anderson.

* Hatton, *op. cit.*, ii, p. 356.

Upon the base on the left-hand side:

WITHIN THIS MONVMENT LYE THE EARTHLY PARTS OF IHON ROBINSON MARCHANT OF Ÿ STAPLE OF ENGLAND FREE OF Ÿ COPANY OF MARCHANT TALORS, AND SOMETYMES ALDERMAN OF LONDŌ, AND CHRISTIAN HIS WIFE ELDEST DAVGHTER OF THO: ANDERSON GROCER THEY SPENT TOGETHER 36 YEARES IN HOLY WEDLOCK AND WERE HAPPY BESIDES OTHER WORLDLY BLESSINGS IN NYNE SONNES AND SEAVEN DAVGHTERS. SHE CHANGED HER MORTALL HABITATION FOR A HEAVENLY ON THE *24* OF APRILL. *1592.* HER HVSBAND FOLLOWING HER ON THE *19* OF FEBRUARY *1599.* BOTH MVCH BELOVED IN THEIRE LIVES, AND MOARE LAMENTED AT THEIRE DEATHES ESPECIALLY BY THE POORE TO WHOME THEIRE GOOD DEEDES (BEING ALIVE) BEGOTT MANY PRAYERS AND NOW (BEING DEAD) MANY TEARES: THE GLASSE OF HIS LIFE HELD THREESCORE AND TEN YEARES, AND THEN RAN OVT. TO LIVE LONG AND HAPPY IS AN HONOR, BVT TO DYE HAPPY A GREATER GLORY, BOETH THEIS ASPIRD TO BOETH HEAVEN (NO DOUBT) HATH THEIRE SOVLES, AND THIS HOWSE OF STONE THEIRE BODYES WHERE THEY SLEEPE IN PEACE, TILL THE SOMONS OF A GLORIOVS RESVRRECTION WAKENS THEM.

27. Against the north wall upon the raised platform at the west entrance a small altar with chamfered slab given by William Robinson, 1633, inscribed in a panel in front:

THE GIFT OF
MR WILLIAM
ROBINSON ✧
MERCER . 1633

28. SIR ANDREW JUDD, 1558.

Judd.

A small painted wall monument upon the east wall of the nuns' quire; it is of two bays divided and flanked by Corinthian columns, resting on panelled and enriched pedestals and supporting an entablature on which is a centre-piece with an achievement of arms. Each bay has a round arch with carved spandrels and a mask at the apex; below the arches are kneeling figures of a man and four sons and wife and one daughter, with a prayer desk on each side of the middle column. Between the pedestals are inscribed panels.

Arms: Quarterly 1 and 4 *gules* a fess raguly (*argent*) between three boars' heads cut off at the neck (*argent*) 2 and 3 *or* three lions *gules.*

Crest: A boar's head.

On the left-hand panel:

To RVSSIA AND MUSSOVA
To SPAYNE GYNNY WITHOVTE FABLE
TRAVELD HE BY LAND AND SEA
BOTHE MAYRE OF LONDON AND STAPLE
THE COMMENWELTHE HE NORISHED
SO WORTHELIE IN ALL HIS DAIES
THAT ECH STATE FVLLWELL HIM LOVED
TO HIS PERPETVALL PRAYES

On the right-hand panel:

THREE WYVES HE HAD ONE WAS MARY
FOWER SVNES ONE MAYDE HAD HE BY HER
ANNYS HAD NONE BY HIM TRVLY
BY DAME MARY HAD ONE DOWGHTIER
THVS IN THE MONTH OF SEPTEMBER
A THOWSANDE FYVE HVNDERD FYFTEY
AND EYGHT DIED THIS WORTHIE STAPLAR
WORSHIPYNGE HIS POSTERYTYE

Under the left-hand panel:

S.R ANDREW

Under the right-hand panel:

JUDD KN.T

Pickering.

29. SIR WILLIAM PICKERING, 1574.

Beneath the first arch of the arcade between the nuns' quire and the parish quire is a large monument of marble, consisting of a panelled base supporting a moulded sarcophagus with a recumbent effigy in Elizabethan armour on a rush mattress. The canopy is in two bays with round arches and coffered soffits and is finished with an entablature, ball-finials and pierced cresting; the solid ends are panelled, as are the pilasters at the angles and between the bays. The canopy rests on three pairs of Corinthian columns supporting separate entablatures, and between the pairs of columns at the ends are panelled walls, each pierced by a round-headed opening with carved spandrels and transom. From the middle of the canopy rises a fluted pedestal supporting an elaborately carved circular cartouche with an achievement of arms on both faces. Round the monument is a wrought-iron rail with buttressed standards having twisted and ball-topped pinnacles. For inscription see No. 30.

Arms: *Gules* a cheveron between three fleurs-de-lis *or*.
Crest: A fleur-de-lis *or*.

ST. HELEN, BISHOPSGATE

30. WILLIAM PICKERING, 1542, and his son, 1574.

At the east end of the north arcade adjoining the above-mentioned monument an inscribed tablet with a moulded border flanked by panelled pilasters bearing heads carved in relief, two to each pilaster. Above and below the tablet are a pair of scrolls separated above by a small square of coloured marble and below by a roundel, the whole supported by a pair of carved and moulded corbels.

Crest: A fleur-de-lis.

QVIESCIT HIC GVLIELMVS PIKERINGVS PATER, EQVESTRIS ORDINIS VIR, MILES MARESCHALLVS. QVI OBIIT XIX MAII ANNO SALVTIS A CHRISTO M.D.XLII.
IACET HIC ETIAM GVLIELMVS PIKERINGVS FILIVS MILES, CORPORIS ANIMIQ, BONIS INSIGNITER ORNATVS, LITERIS EXCVLTVS, ET RELIGIONI SINCERVS. SEX LINGVAS EXACTE PERCALLVIT QVATVOR PRINCIPIBVS SUMMA CVM LAVDE INSERVIVIT: HENRICO SCILICET OCTAVO MILITARI VIRTUTE: EDWARDO SEXTO LEGATIONE GALLICA: REGINÆ MARIÆ NEGOTIATIONE GERMANICA: ELIZABETHÆ PRINCIPI OMNIVM ILLVSTRISSIMÆ SVMMIS OFFICIIS DEVOTISSIMVS. OBIIT LONDINI IN ÆDIBVS PIKERINGIIS ÆTATE LVIII. ANNO GRATIAE MDLXXIIII. IANVARII QUARTO.

CVIVS MEMORIÆ THOMAS HENNEAGIVS MILES CAMERÆ REGIÆ THESAVRARIVS, IOHANNES ASTLEY ARMIGER IOCALIVM MAGISTER, DRVGO DRVREIVS MILES, ET THOMAS WOTTONVS ARMIGER TESTAMENTI SVI EXECVTORES, MONVMENTVM HOC POSVERE.

31. JOHN STANDISH, 1686.

Above the tablet to William Pickering is another of slightly convex section with fruit and scroll-work, surmounted by a winged cherub's head and an urn with drapery beneath, the whole supported upon a corbel of slight projection with a shield carved upon it, but no arms.

IOHANNES STANDISH S.t.p.
pétriburgim Agro Northamp.
Natus Colleg. S^t petri apud cantabrig
Trigenta annos plus̃ minũs, socius
Rector de Therfeild in agro
Hartford. nec non Serenifs Reg

Carolo 2do et Jacobo 2do a sacris
Mortalitatis Exuvias
Deposuit 2do calend.
Januar: Ann: Dom: milefs^{mo}
Sccentifs^{mo} Octuagefs^{mo} Sexto
Ætatis . 53

32. JOHN WILLIAMS, 1831.

Kirwin.

33. WILLIAM KIRWIN, 1594.

Beneath the third arch of the arcade, between the nuns' quire and the parish nave, a small altar tomb with panelled sides bearing incised figures of children, two shields and a lozenge of arms, carved pilasters at the angles and slab forming the cornice of the entablature. It is enclosed within a plain wrought-iron railing. Monument repaired and restored 1868.

Arms:
- (i) Fretty on a chief three fleurs-de-lis (Kirwin).
- (ii) The Masons' Company.
- (iii) Kirwin impaling a chief with three griffins' (?) heads raised therein.

Crest: A hand holding a fleur-de-lis.

Upon the south side of the altar tomb is the following inscription:

HERE	LYETH THE BODIE OF WILLIAM KERWIN OF THIS CITTIE OF LON	DON
FREE	MASON WHOE DEPARTED THIS LYFE THE 26TH DAYE OF DECEMBER AN̊ DŌ	1594

(The words at each end are upon the pilasters.)

In smaller lettering below the architrave moulding and between the pilasters on either side:

MAGDALENE JACET [V]IRTVS POST FATA SVPSTES: CORPVS HVMO TECTVM CHRISTO VENIENTE RESVRGET
CONIVGIONE FIDE RELLIGIOQE MANET . VT MENTIS CONSORS ASTRA SVPREMA COLAT

Upon the east end is an inscription recording:

Repaired and restored by the Parish, 1868.

Upon the north side, arranged similarly to those on the south side:

AND	H[E]ERE ALSOE LYETH THE BODIE OF MAGDALEN KIRWIN HIS WIFE BY WHOME HE	HAD
ISSVE	III SONNES AND II DAVGHTERS SHEE DECEASED THE XXIIITH OF AVGVST	1592

ÆDIBVS ATTA LIOIS LONDINVM QVI DECORAVI : ME DVCE SVRGEBANT ALIJS REGALIA TECTA
EXIGVAM TRIBVVNT HANC MIHI FATA DOMV̄ ME DVCE CONFICITVR OSSIBVS VRNA MEIS

At the bottom :

BEIMIN KIRWIN Y^E SONNE OF WILLIAM KIRWIN DECEASED Y^E 21TH OF IULY ANº. DOMN. 1621 WHOE HAD ISHVE 7 SONNE[S] AND 5 DAVGHTERS WHEREOF 5 OF THEM LYETH HEERE IN THIS VAVLT.

At the west end of the monument, on the frieze :

CHRISTVS MIHI VITA,
MORS MIHI LVCRVM

Below the architrave moulding :

NOS QVOS CERTVS AMOR PRIMIS CONIVNXIT AB A[N]NIS
IVNXIT IDEM TVMVLVS IVNXIT IDEMQVE POLVS

34. ROBERT DINGLEY, 1741.

Near the west door of the parish nave, a plain inscribed tablet of white marble upon a black marble background, and surmounted by a draped skull. Beneath the tablet is a shield.

Arms: Barry of four, in chief a molet, between two roundels a scutcheon charged with a crown encircling two sceptres saltire-wise.

In a Vault in the Churchyard
Lyeth the Body
of ROBERT DINGLEY
Late of this Parifh Jeweller.
He Behaved
As a Son a Hufband and a Parent
With an uncommon Greatnefs of Mind
He dyed 30 March 1741. Aged 63.
In the fame Vault refteth
SUSANNAH His Wife
Whofe Virtue and Piety
Were Exemplary
She dyed 4 Oct. 1747. Aged 67.
They had 19 Children 6 Survived them
REBECCA SUSANNA ROBERT CHARLES
CATHARINE and FRANCES
This Monument was Erected
By their Son ROBERT
As an Inftance
Of his Gratitude and Affection.
alfo to the Memory of
HENRY & REBECCA ELKIN,
Parents of the above named SUSA: DINGLEY

35. FRANCES BAUMER, 1832.

36. HESTER JAMES, 1828.

37. RICHARD JAMES, 1800.

Small oval tablet surmounted by an urn.

Sacred
to the memory of
RICHARD JAMES, Son of
Richard and *Hester James*
of this City died 2nd of Novr 1800
aged 1 Year and 9 Months
and of
THOMAS JAMES the second Son
died 12th of June 1801
aged 1 Year and 1 Month
Of such is the kingdom of God.

38. SIR JOHN CROSBY, 1476, and AGNES, his first wife.

Under the first arch of the arcade between the parish quire and the Chapel of the Holy Ghost, an altar tomb of Purbeck or Sussex Marble with a moulded slab and panelled sides with three panels on each side, divided by pairs of buttresses and one panel at each end, all elaborately cusped and bearing a shield of arms in the middle of each panel. Upon the slab are two recumbent effigies in alabaster, the man in armour with a cloak, thrown back, and a collar of suns and roses, and at his feet a griffon, the woman with a butterfly head-dress and elaborate necklace, her feet resting on two dogs.

The inscription on a brass fillet on the edge of the moulded slab has now entirely gone, but Hatton* records a portion of it, as remaining in 1708, and the full inscription is preserved by Weever :†

"Orate pro animabus Johannis Crosby Militis Ald. atque tempore vite Majoris Staple ville Caleis et Agnetis Uxoris sue ac Thome, Richardi, Johannis, Johannis, Margarete et Johanne liberorum ejusdem Johannis Crosby militis. Ille obiit 1475 et illa 1466 Quorum animabus propitietur Deus."

Arms :

(i) (*Sable*) a cheveron ermine between three rams passant (*argent*) (Crosby) impaling (*azure*) a fess cotised (*argent*).
(ii) Crosby.
(iii) The impaled coat of (i).
(iv) At west end, the Grocers' Company.
(v) to (vii) As (i) to (iii).
(viii) At east end, the staple of Calais.

* Hatton, *New View of London*, i, p. 276.

† Weever, *Ancient Funeral Monuments* (ed. 1631), p. 421.

ST. HELEN, BISHOPSGATE

39. REV. JAMES BLENKARNE, 1836.

40. REV. JOHN EDMUND COX, 1890.
Author of *Annals of St. Helen's, Bishopsgate.*

41. CHARLES MATTHEW CLODE, 1893.
Master of the Merchant Taylors' Company.

42. JANE ELIZABETH BLENKARNE, 1840.

43. JOHN BATHURST DEANE, 1873.
First rector of the united parishes of St. Martin Outwich, and St. Helen.

44. JAMES FLETCHER, 1907.

45. RICHARD STAPER, 1608 (formerly in St. Martin Outwich).

Staper.

A large wall monument in two arched bays with panelled pilasters at the sides and a corbel in the middle; the spandrels and the tympana are carved and have two shields of arms; in the recesses are kneeling figures of a man and five sons and a woman with four daughters. The monument is flanked by Corinthian columns standing on an inscribed base of quadrant section and supporting an entablature with an achievement of arms within a circular cartouche, and ornamental strap-work. Above the cartouche is a cornice supporting the hull of a ship.

Arms: *Argent* a voided cross *sable* between four stars *sable.*
Crest: A seated lion gardant.

On the sarcophagus, on the left-hand side:

HERE RESTETH THE BODIE OF THE
WORSHIPFVL RICHARD STAPER ELECTID
ALDERMAN OF THIS CITTYE ANNO 1594 HEE
WAS THE GREATEST MERCHANT IN HIS
TYME THE CHEIFEST ACTOR IN DISCOVERI, OF
THE TRADES OF TVRKEY, AND EAST
INDIA, A MAN HVMBLE IN PROSPERITY,
PAYNEFVL AND EVER READY IN THE
AFFAYRES PUBLIQVE AND DISCREETELY

On the right-hand side:

CAREFVL OF HIS PRIVATE A LIBERAL
HOWSEKEEPER, BOWNTIFVL TO THE POORE,
AN VPRIGHT DEALER IN THE WORLD, AND
A DIVOVT ASPIRER AFTER THE WORLD TO
COME MVCH BLEST IN HIS PROSPERITY, AND
HAPPY IN HIS AND THEIR ALLYAVANCES. HE
DYED THE LAST IUNE ANNO DOMINE 1608
INTRAVIT VT EXIRET.

ST. HELEN, BISHOPSGATE

Spencer.

46. SIR JOHN SPENCER, 1609.

A very large and magnificent monument against the south wall of the nave, originally under the north arch of the south transept but removed to its present position in 1867. It consists of a panelled altar tomb on which are recumbent effigies of a man and wife, the former in armour with a long cloak and ruff. At the feet of the woman's figure is a kneeling figure of a daughter at prayer-desk and facing east. On either side of the tomb is a large obelisk with ball finial and spike and standing on a panelled pedestal. Behind the effigies is a wall canopy with two round arches with coffered soffits having cherub-head keystones and supporting an entablature with the cornice brought forward on four shaped brackets. The back of the arched recesses has carved enrichment, two inscribed tablets and two shields of arms and in the middle spandrel a cartouche of arms. Above the cornice is a centre-piece with carved pilasters and an achievement of arms; flanking the centre-piece are cartouches with shields of arms.

Arms :

(i) (*Argent*) two gimel bars *sable* between three spread-eagles *sable* (Spencer).
(ii) The same.
(iii) Quarterly, 1, *sable* a leopard *argent ;* 2, *sable* three roses *argent ;* 3, *azure* a cheveron *or* between three falcons' heads razed *or ;* 4, *gules* three pales *or* within a border *or* charged with roundels *sable*.
(iv) As (i).
(v) (i) impaling (iii).
(vi) As (iii).

Crests : (*a*) a falcon rising ; (*b*) a lion's head razed.

In the left-hand recess behind the recumbent effigies :

HIC SITVS EST IOANNES SPENCER
EQVES AVRATVS, CIVIS, & SENATOR
LONDINENSIS, EIVSDEMQ CIVITATIS
PRÆTOR ANNO DN̄I MDXCIIII
QVI EX ALICIA BROMFELDIA
VXORE VNICAM RELIQVIT FILIAM
ELIZABETH GVILIELMO BARONI
COMPTON ENVPTAM, OBIIT 3°
DIE MARTII ANNO SALVTIS MDCIX

In the right-hand recess :

SOCERO BENE MERITO
GVILIELMVS BARO COMPTON
GENER POSVIT

An inscription at the foot of the male effigy records the fact that the tomb originally stood in the northern arch of the south transept, and was removed to its present position, restored and repaired in 1867 by Charles, 3rd Marquis of Northampton.

47. THE REV. JOHN ALFRED LUMB AIREY, 1909 (over vestry door).

48. FANNY GAMBLE, 1907.

49. ALICE ESCOTT, 1837.

50. RICHARD BACKWELL, 1731.

White marble tablet with sunk inscribed panel, pediment and cartouche of arms; shaped apron with three shields of arms.

Arms:

(i) *Argent* on a cheveron *sable* three covered cups *or*.
(ii) (i) Impaling *sable* a cross engrailed *or* (?)
(iii) (i) Impaling a cross *or* between four fleurs-de-lis *or* with a roundel *gules* (?) on the cross.
(iv) The impaled coat of (iii) impaling *gules* three crescents *or* and a border *ermine* (?)

Crest: A demi-bull rising out of a mural crown.

H. S. E.
RICHARDUS BACKWELL ARMIGER
(EDVARDI BACKWELL HUJUS OLIM
CIVITATIS ALDERMANNI FILIUS)
HEU! MAXIME DEFLENDUS
PATRIÆ ADMODUM ET AMICIS
(HAUD ÆQUE SIBI)
UTILIS VIXIT.
OBIIT APRILIS DIE 26. A.D. 1731. ÆTAT. 67.
PATRIS DILECTISSIMI
MEMORIÆ
HOC MARMOR DICAVIT
RICHARDUS BACKWELL
FILIUS

51. ABIGAIL LAWRENCE, 1682.

A mural tablet resting upon a plain marble altar tomb and consisting of a plain tablet recessed at sides, flanked by scrolls of palm leaves and having a spreading moulded base; the architrave at the top slopes back in a bold cavetto to a heavily scalloped shelf supporting a large fluted urn.

In Memory
Of Dame ABIGAIL LAWRENCE
Late Wife of S^{R}. IOHN LAWRENCE K$^{t}_{n}$ & alderman heere Interr^{ed}
was this tombe Erected
Shee was the tender Mother of ten Children
the nine first being all daughters
shee suckled at her owne breasts
They all liued to be of age
her last a ſon died an Infant
Shee liued a married wife thirty nine years
three and twenty whereof
Shee was an Exemplary matron of this Cittie
dying in the 59th. year of her age
being the 6 Iune
1682.

52. JOHN OTESWICH, late 14th century (formerly in St. Martin Outwich *).

Modern base with recumbent effigies in alabaster, the man in gown buttoned at neck and belted at waist, long anelace or short sword and under-garment with tight buttoned sleeves; woman in sideless coat-hardie, cloak and veiled head-dress; angels at heads of both figures, man's feet on lion, woman's feet on dog.

The inscription is modern. The old inscription had disappeared in Hatton's time (1708), but he records a coat-of-arms as then existing on the tomb—two bars with two molets (?) in chief and a scallop in base†.

53. NATHANIEL SIMPSON, 1849 (from St. Martin Outwich).

54. JOHN TUFNELL, 1686.

Upon the east wall of the south transept an oval tablet with a moulded border surmounted by a keystone and pedestal with shield of arms below.

Arms: Quarterly, 1 and 4 *azure* a fess *or* between three ostrich feathers *or* with three choughs *sable* on the fess; 2 and 3 *gules* a cross botony *or*, each point of the cross charged with 3 scallops *sable*.

* John Oteswich founded a chantry in St. Martin's Church under licence of Edward III, 1331 (*Hustings Roll*, 60, 95).

† *Op. cit.*, ii, 356. The arms were a late addition on a renaissance cartouche. See illustration in R. Wilkinson's *Antique Remains from St. Martin Outwich*, 1797, Plate IV.

ST. HELEN, BISHOPSGATE

H.P.S.E.

JOHANNES TUFNELL

Filius Natu Maximus JOHANNIS TUFNELL *Arm.*

Eximiæ Spei Adolefcentulus
Formâ pariter et Ingenie præftans ;
Quem
(Ineunte jam Sexto Ætatis Anno)
Et nimia Virtus
Et Fatorum Invidia (heu femper deflenda)
In Cœlum evexere
iv.º Cal. Nov. A.D. MDCLXXXVI.

Durum . . . fed levius fit patientiâ,
Quicquid corrigere eft Nefas

South wall of Transept.

55. REV. JOHN ROSE, 1821 (from St. Martin Outwich).

56. THOMAS CLUTTERBUCK, 1714 (from St. Martin Outwich).

A small-shaped tablet with palm leaves and surmounted by a cartouche of arms flanked by cherubs' heads.

Arms: *Azure* a lion rampant *or* on a chief (*sable* ?) three scallops *argent*.

Near this place lies
the Body of
THOMAS CLUTTERBUCK late
of ye Parifh of KINGSTANLY in ye
County of GLOUCESTER Gent:
who died the 13TH MAY 1714
In the 26TH year of his Age

Alfo

Here Lies ye Body of
JASPER CLUTTERBUCK
Late MERCHT of LONDON
who died 23d JANUARY
1697 In the 63 year
of his Age

57. BEAUMONT ATKINSON, 1847 (from St. Martin Outwich).

58. HANNAH STANLEY and MARY SMITH, the wives of CHARLES GOODMAN (from St. Martin Outwich).

A plain tablet with a moulded shelf and shaped apron surmounted by a cornice and cartouche of arms.

Arms: Parted palewise *ermine* and *sable* a double-headed eagle *or*, on a quarter *sable* a martlet *or* (Goodman).

In a Vault contiguous to this
PILLAR lyes Interred the Bodyes
of HANNAH the daughter of
MR JOHN STANLEY and MARY
the daughter of MR ALLYN SMITH
Both ye wives of CHARLES GOODMAN
late of this PARISH Gent.
The Former dyed JULY 14TH 1708. *Aged* 32 *years*
The Latter MARCH 27TH 1713. *Aged* 34 *years*

And alſo CHARLES a Son by y^e ſaid MARY
who dyed November 24th 1714 aged 2 Years
And 10 Months

59. MARY TEASDALE, 1804 (from St. Martin Outwich).

60. WILLIAM JONES, 1882. (Inscription below recording presentation of window.)

61. Lt.-Col. JAMES CRUICKSHANK GRANT, 1826 (from St. Martin Outwich).

62. BARBARA GOULD SIMPSON, 1827 (from St. Martin Outwich).

63. WALTER BERNARD, 1746.

A large monument in the south transept, consisting of a plain inscribed base on which are two urns and a sarcophagus with a fluted top. On the sarcophagus is a pyramidal centre-piece with an achievement of arms and flanked by Ionic columns supporting entablatures with continuous cornice and finished with an urn and two burning lamps.

Arms: A muzzled bear rampant impaling a fleur-de-lis.

Crest: A demi-bear rampant and muzzled.

In a Vault near this place are Depofited the Remains of
WALTER BERNARD. Esqr
Alderman & late Sheriff of this City;
in both which Stations He acted to the General Satisfaction
of his Fellow Citizens,
He was a Sincere Christian,
a Faithfull Husband, a kind Master, and a true Friend
and as the whole Conduct of his Life
was agreeable to the principales of true Religion & Virtue
so his Death was universally Lamented
He dyed May the : 4 : 1746 Aged : 51.

64. ELIZABETH ELLIS, 1835 (from St. Martin Outwich).

65. THOMAS LANGHAM, 1700 (from St. Martin Outwich).

Langham.

An inscribed tablet flanked by Corinthian pilasters with separate entablatures and an achievement of arms between them. Below the tablet is a moulded shelf with two corbels and a cartouche beneath it.

Arms:
(i) (*Argent*) three bears' heads razed (*sable*) muzzled (*or*).
(ii) (*Argent*) a cheveron (*sable*) between three birds (*sable*) impaling (i).

Near this place are interr'd
the Bodies of
THOMAS LANGHAM
Citizen of LONDON
who died Decemb^{r} 3^{d} 1700;
And of ELEANOR his wife
who died Decemb^{r} 2^{d} 1694
And of REBEKAH their only Child
who was married to
BENIAMIN ROKEBY of LONDON Merch^{t}.
& had Ifsue by him one fon
LANGHAM ROKEBY & two daughters
REBEKAH & ELIZABETH
fhe died December 21th 1692

Non, nifi per mortem patet iter ad Aftra
Benjamin Rokeby Efq
dyed the 3^{d} *of February* 173$\frac{2}{3}$ *Aged* 89

66. THOMAS GREENAWAY, 1829.

67. JOHN MILES, 1814.

68. GERVASH RERESBY, 1704.

Upon west wall of south transept a draped tablet flanked by a pair of winged cherub-heads and surmounted by an achievement of arms, the whole resting upon an enriched corbel.

Arms: *Gules* on a bend *argent* three crosses paty *sable*.

Crest: A goat (?) passant.

Hic jacet

Quod Mortale erat GERVASH RERESBY

Antiquiſsima ejusdem nominis familiâ
Eboracenſi oriundi
Qui cum triginta plus annos in Hiſpania
fide indelibatâ ſummoque honore
Vixiſset
In Angliam tandem
rediit
atque animā mente inconcuſsa
Salvatori reddidit
An° Dom̃: MDCCiv

Hoc patri optimo
Filius poſuit unicus

MERCY *JESU.*

Chambrelan.

69. RACHEL CHAMBRELAN, 1687.

A large mural monument in two tiers, the upper consisting of an inscription-tablet recessed at sides, flanked by a pair of cherubs surmounted by an entablature, above which rises an urn upon a moulded base, flanked by swags of fruit and foliage and a pair of lamps. Beneath a heavy cabled shelf is a second inscription-tablet with capping and base moulding, flanked by wreaths and cherub-heads, and below a corbel enriched with a pair of cherub-heads, drapery with a pendant of fruit and flowers.

Arms: *Gules* within an orle of cinqfoils *or* a scutcheon *argent* (Chamberlain), impaling *ermine* a cross raguly *gules* a quarter *sable* ermined *argent* (Lawrence).

ST. HELEN, BISHOPSGATE

M. S.
CHARLES CHAMBRELAN Esq;
Alderman of this City;
in testimony of his true affection
and sorrow for their deaths
hath consecrated this Monument;
to the memory of his dearly beloved Wife
RACHEL
(the daughter of S^{r} JO: LAWRENCE K^{t}
Lord Mayor of London, 1665.)
who dyed August the 21st 1687
soon after the delivery of her 10th child.
and of his fourth Daughter *HESTER*
who dyed the 9th of June 1687,
at the Age of 6 Years 8 Months
Both whose Bodies are here deposited in a Vault
near this Place;
(belonging to his Ancestors,)
In expectation of a joyful Resurrection
at the last day.

Upon the apron:

M. S.
In the same Vault with his dear Wife and Daughter
(and with like hopes of a joyful Resurrection together)
Lyeth the Body of *CHARLES CHAMBRELAN* Esq; Alderman of this City.
who departed this Life Jan^{ry} 29th 1704, Aged 65 Years:
having no where left behind him either a Merchant better accomplished;
or a Gentleman more compleatly adorn'd with all sorts of usefull Knowledge.
In memory of her most affectionate & entirely beloved Father, *ABIGALL*
his sorrowful Daughter & sole Executrix (the wife of *LEMYNG REBOW Esq;*)
caused this Monument to be enlarg'd.

70. THOMAS ROWLAND ALSTON, 1844.

71. HENRY WILLIAM WARD, 1826.

VIII.—FLOOR SLABS WITHIN THE CHURCH

72. WILLIAM DRAX, 1669.

Epitaph

On the lamented death of his honoured friend William Dra[x]
Esq, who exchanged this life for immortality Decemb 17
1669 in the 63 yeare of HIS Age

To thy deare memory blest soule İ paie
This humble tribute though in such away.
As reather doth proclaime my want of skill.
Than any want of loue of heart, or will.
True to thy trust, none in our memory.
Can charge the more or lefs with treuchery.
Bringe forth the ꝑson, Rich, poore, old, or Younge.
That can iustly say he ever did them wronge.
In others weal or woe thy heart
Would simputhies and take its part.
Oh whats more like the Deity.
Than Blefsed hoary piety
A soule fitted for heauen when glorio(us) (g)race
Triumphs with him, in his sure restinge (pla)ce
But is he dead can I beleeue
That he should die and we should liue
Methinks we may the knot vntie
Better to liue fitter to dye.
Now death I see doth wisely chuse.
The gold but doth the drofs refuse.
Weepe not as without hope, cry not alafs
Hees better where he is than where he was
Hearke, is not that his voice : doth not he say
Heauens meanest mansion is worth this Globe of clay
Who so doth liue, and doe and die like thee
His fame shall last to all (eter)nity

Achievement of arms at top.

Arms : Checky on a chief three marigolds (?) impaling a stag's head caboshed.

Crest : a demi-dragon rampant holding a scroll.

ST. HELEN, BISHOPSGATE

73. WILLIAM FINCH, 1672.

GVILIELMI FINCH NON ITA
PRIDEM MERCATORIS LON
DINENSIS NECNON ESTHER
CASTISSIMA CONJVGIS QVOD RE
LIQUUM EST SISTE PARVM VIA
TOR ET SVSPICE MARMOR EX ADVER
SO POSITVM DOCEBIT QVID DE TA
LO VIRO SENTIENDVM ET QVID DE
TALI FŒMINA ABI VIATOR & PRO
PRIÆ MORTIS MEMOR QVA [.]
LAVDE DIGNA [I - - C - SI DVIO I.M.III]

Arms at head of slab: (*Argent*), a cheveron (*sable*) between 3 griffons (*sable*).

74. EDWARD BERKELEY, 1669.

E[DVARD]VS BERKLEY
OBIJ[T] [8] MAIJ
1669

Arms at head of slab: (*Gules*) a cheveron (*argent*), between six crosses formy (*argent*) with five martlets on the cheveron impaling parted bendwise two piles counter coloured.

75. GEORGE FINCH, 1710.

Here lyeth Interrd the Body
of GEORGE FINCH of Valentine
in Efsex Efq^r^ who Dyed the 5
of October *1710* aged 48 who
was Son to WILLIAM FINCH of
this Parifh Efq^r^ & Married to
CONSTANCE the Daughter of
NATHANIL HORNEBY Citizen
of London by whome he had five
Sons & one Daughter where of
JAMES & HENRY Dyed young & ly
Buried near this Place the Reft
Survived him.

Achievement of arms above. Arms: (*Argent*), a cheveron (*sable*) between three griffons (*sable*). Crest: A griffon.

ST. HELEN, BISHOPSGATE

76. JANE GAUSSEN.

Here Lyeth Interred the Body of
M^RS^ IANE GAUSSEN late wife of
PETER GAUSSEN Efq^r^ of this Parifh
Merchant; who departed this Life
the 4th day of Ianuary 1747
Aged 71 Years.
Alfo the Body of PETER GAUSSEN
Efq^r^ Hufband of the aforefaid who
Died Sepr 17th 1759 Aged 82 Years
ANN MARIA GAUSSEN Obit 24 June 1767
Æt Six Years 7 Months & 3 Days.
PAUL GAUSSEN. Obit Jany 17th 1774
Aged 16 Years.
Grand Nephew of the above
PETER GAUSSEN Esqr.
and Brother to ANN MARIA.
Mr PETER GAUSSEN. Iun^r^. Obiit Octr 28th 1781 Æt. - -

Achievement of arms above. Arms: (*Azure*) on a mount (*vert*) a lamb (*argent*) on a chief (*argent*) three bees (*proper*).

Crest: a hive of bees.

77. MRS. MAGDALEN BERCHERE.

Here lyeth Interr'd the Body
of M^RS^ MAGDALENE BERCHERE
Wife of
JAMES LEWIS BERCHERE Efq^r^
of this Parifh who departed this Life
the 23^d^ Decemb^r^ 1750, Aged 77 Years.
And alfo the Body of the above faid
JAMES LEWIS BERCHERE, ESQ^R^
who departed this Life the 3^d^ May
1753 Aged 83 Years.

Enriched cartouche of arms above. Arms: A moor's head cut off at the neck between three pierced molets of six points impaling quarterly 1st and 4th. On a castle a running beast (? greyhound), 2nd and 3rd three bars wavy. Motto: MEMORIA PII ETERNA.

ST. HELEN, BISHOPSGATE

78. JAMES STANIER, 1663.

H. S. L.
IACOBVS STANIER huiusce
Civitatis Mercator ſatis Insignis
Denatus
X^bris XVI cIↄIↄcLxiii cum vixisſet An Lix
Nec non
THOMASINA VXOR EJUS Quæ obijt
—^bris [cIↄ I]ↄ ↄcLxxvi
Ætat Sua lx[ii]
Conjugale Foedus quam Pijssime
inter ſe Coluere
Annos circiter xxv
quibus Procreati ſunt iv Filii ac
totidem Filiæ

IACOBUS SAMVEL IACOBUS DAVID	&	ABIGAIL THOMASINA IANA REBECCA

ſors intermittit Vitam non Eripit
Veniet iterum qui Nos in Lucem
Reponat Dies

Coat-of-arms: (*Azure*) a cheveron between three horse-bits (*argent*) impaling a cheveron between . . . .

79. Entrance to a Vault.

80. Pew
e into M
NARDS

81. CLARKE, 1773.

A slab commemorating two members of the Clarke family who died in 1773 and 1779 respectively. The slab is half covered by a screen.

82. GEORGE BRIGGS, 1663.

IN OBITUM GEORGIJ BRIGGS [A]RMIGERI
QUI OBIIT 21 DIE IANUARIJ 1663

Belliger hicce jacet, vox cœlo sola locuta eſt
Dux es cœleſtis, nates, uterq deo
Merecator quondam, nulli pietas secundus
Pallida mors merces viribus arma rapit
Indi te plorant, plorat charisſima conjux
Quis lachrymas alter caſa doloris meſt

Arms: A crown between three roundels impaling a fess between three formy crosses with three roundels on the fess.

ST. HELEN, BISHOPSGATE

83. HENRY RAPER, 1674.

HENERY RAPER ESQ[R] CITIZ[EN]
AND GROCER OF LONDON DEC
EASED Y[E] 17TH OF IANVAR 1674
IN THE 68 YEARE OF HIS AGE
WHERE WHITH HIM SELFE LYES
INTERD AND FOWER OF HIS
GRAND CHILDREN BY ELIZABE[TH]
HIS DAVGHTER ELIZABETH
BENIAMIN HENRY AND ANN
COLES Obyt 1663 1665
1667 1668
Eliz[a] 1675 Eliz[a] 167—
& Benj Colef 8th March
1679
80
Sarah Coles Aged 1 year
5 months Dyed y[e] 27th Iune 1681
Hannah Coles Daughter of Benj
Coles Aged 6 Yeares & 20 Days
Departed Her life the 17 of Aprill
1682

Shield of arms above: Quarterly of six (charges defaced)

84. SIR MARTIN LUMLEY, 1634.

HERE LY[ETH] S[IR] [MARTIN]
LVMLEY K[NI]G[HT]
[S]OME TIME LOR[D] M[AYOR]
OF [LON]DON. . . . .
THIS LY[FE] [16 . .]

85. MP. TP. Vault Stone.

ST. HELEN, BISHOPSGATE

86. ELIZABETH DALE, 1764.

Here
lieth Interr'd
ELIZABETH Daughter of
JOHN and MARY DALE
who died the 29th Day of May 1764
Aged two Years and 5 Months

Likewiſe

JOHN Son of the above
JOHN and MARY DALE
who died the 2^{d} Day of June 1764
Aged 1 Year and 1 Month
Likewiſe here lieth Interr'd the Body
of MR JOHN DALE
Father to the abovemention'd Children
who Departed this life on the
7th Day of October 1767
Aged 38 Years

87. JOSEPH PORTAL, 1820.

88. THOMAS EDWARDS, 1716, and JANE his wife, 1720.

HIC IVXTA

CO . . . . R RELIQ
[TH]OM[AS] EDWARD[S]
E[T]
IANE VXORIS [SUAE]
QV[I] OBIIT . . .
HAEC. XIII. DIE. APRILI[S] AD. [MD]CC . . .
ILLE XXVII. DIE FEBRV[A]RII. A.D. MD[C]C . . .
M. . M.
P. N P. I. I. N.
OMNES EODEM CO[GIMVR]

ST. HELEN, BISHOPSGATE

89. THOMAS BURDETT, 1772.

Hoc sub Marmore
Sepultus jacet
THOMAS BURDETT Armiger
Qui in Urbe Londinenſi
Per Annos prope 48
Mercaturam laudate honeſteque
exercuit.
Summa quoq Benevolentia Morumq Suavitate
Æſtimationem omnium quibuſcum ibidem degebat unde
Sibi facile comparavit
Sed Podagra. variiſque Morbis satis vehementer diuque
conflictatus
Animam efflavit
3 : Feb : Ann : Dom : 1772
Ætat : 78
In cvjvs Memoriam
Soror ſua Domina Otger Vidva
Mœrens Posvit.
Hic etiam Sepultus Jacet
Carolus Burdett D.D.
Obijt Decemb 1ſt 1772
Ætat 74.

90. GEORGE HARRISON, 1745.

Here Lieth Interr'd the Body of
Mr. GEORGE HARRISON ∽
of this Par[is]h who Departed this
Life December the 5th 1745 ∽
Aged 41. Years.

91. VAULT STONE [Name defaced.]

92 MRS MARY PAYNE, 1747.

Here Reſts the mortal Remains of
MRS MARY PAYNE the beloved wife of
MR THOMAS PAYNE of this Pariſh
who Departed this life Octor 7th 1747
Aged 46 Years
as Alſo ALICE PAYNE Daughter of
MR THOS & MRS MARY PAYNE obijt : June
22d 1746, Aged 9 Years and 4 Months
THOS PAYNE ſon of MR THOS & MRS MARY
PAYNE Obijt ; Augſt 5th 1753. Aged
11 Years & 2 Months.

Silent Grave ; to thee I truſt
These Precious Piles of Lovely duſt
Keep them safely ; Sacred Tomb
Till a Father, asks for Room.

Here alſo lieth the Body of
MR. THOMAS PAYNE, Huſband of the
above-ſaid MRS MARY PAYNE wh[o]
Departed this life Ma[rc]h . . 1766
Aged 64 Years having been an
Inhabitant of this Pariſh 30 Years.
And [alſo] here lieth the Body of
MRS MARGARET PAYNE
Widow of the aboveſaid MR THOMAS PAYNE Gent
who departed this life Novbr the 13th 1777
AGED 68 YEARS

93. JOHN MORGAN, 1809.

94. GEORGE KELLUM, 1672.

Here Lyes the Bodye of
George Kellum Esq of this
Parish whoe deceased the 30
Of Aprill A° 1672 Being then
aged 48 yeare . and here
alsoe Lyes interred seuerall
of his Children
Here alſo lies the Body of
his Wife Katherine Kellum
who died ye 14 of Octobr 1703

Achievement of arms above. Arms: (*Gules*) a crowned double leopard rampant (*argent*) with one head. Crest: A crowned leopard's head.

95. KATHARINE KELLUM, 1717.

Here lies the Body of
KATHERINE KELLUM *Spinſter* eldeſt
Daughter of GEO KELLUM Eſqr of
this *Pariſh* who died April the *16.*
1717. *Aged 70* YEARS

Reſt *Virtuous* Maid
Till *time* ſhall be no *More*
Then GOD this *Body*
Glorious will *Reſtore.*

Inscription to others added after 1800.

Achievement of arms above. Arms: a crowned double leopard rampant with one head within a border impaling a bend. Crest: A crowned leopard's head.

ST. HELEN, BISHOPSGATE

96. SARAH TRYON, 1686.

Here Lyeth Interr'd
the body of Mrs
SARAH TRYON
one of ye Daughters of
MOSES TRYON of Harring-worth
in ye County of Northampton Efq
who departed this life ye 12th
day of February
Anno Dnĩ. 1686
Ætatis suæ 84

Lozenge of arms above: (*Azure*) an embattled fesse (*or*) between six stars (*or*).

97. JAMES TAYLOR, 1761.

Here lies Interred the Bod[y of]
Masr JAMES TAYLOR.
Son of NICHOLAS TAYLOR Efqr
of the Island of St Chriftophers
who died April 17th 1761 Aged 12 Years
Alfo ALEXANDER DOUGLAS Efqr
who died Auguft the 31ft 1797
In the 67th Year of his Age.

(And others after 1800.)

98. THOMAS CHAMBERLIN, 16 . .

UNDERN[EATH] THIS STONE
LYETH INTERRED YE BODY
OF THO[MAS CHA]MBERLIN
PURVIOU[R TO HIS] PRESENT
MAJESTIE [WHO DE]CEASED
MAY THE 3D 16[ ]
AGED 27 YEARE[S]

HERE ALSO LYETH INTERRED
YE BODY OF MARY HIS WIFE
WHO DYED YE 24TH OF SEPT 16[86]
AGED 39 YEARS

ST. HELEN, BISHOPSGATE

99. MARY BACKWELL, 1670. And others.

HERE LIES
MARY THE SECOND WIFE OF EDWARD BACKWELL EſQ
LATE ALDERMAN OF THIS CITY
WHO DIED JUNE 4 1670
BY WHOM HE HAD THREE SONS AND THREE DAUGHTERS
RICHARD BARNABY LEIGH
MARY ANNE AND JANE

HERE ALSO LIES
MARY THE WIFE OF THE SAID RICHARD BACKWELL EſQ
WHO DIED JAN 19. 1712.
AND LEFT THREE SONS AND TWO DAUGHTERS
RICHARD BARNABY DENCOME
MARY AND SUSANNA.

AS ALSO
BARNABY BACKWELL EſQ
SON OF THE ABOVE RICHARD BACKWELL [EſQ]
WHO DIED MARCH 25 1723

AND
RICHARD BACKWELL EſQ THE FATHER
WHO DIED APRIL 26 1731. EI. LXVII
TO WHOSE MEMORIES
THIS STONE IS DEDICATED
BY
RICHARD BACKWELL [TH . . . .]
MDCCXXXI

Achievement of arms above. Arms: (*Argent*) on a cheveron (*sable*) three covered cups (*or*). Crest: A demi-horse [?] rampant rising from a mural crown.

100. SAMUEL STONE, 1816.

101. VAULT OF THOMAS TRUMBLE, 1811.

102. JOANE DEBOUSY, 1649.

IOANE DEBOVSII WIFE OF FREDERICK
DEBOVSIJ. CITTIZEN & HABERDASHER
OF LONDON WAS HERE BVRIED THE
25TH DAYE OF OCTOBER 1649

The iuſt shall be had in
euerlasting remembrance.

103. Mrs. MARGARET GOSLING, 1809.

104. JOHN BROWN, 1746.

Here Lies Interr'd the Body of
[J]ohn Brown Esqr who Departed
[t]his Life March the 2^{d} 1746 Aged
65 Years.
Alſo John Charles Burges
who died the 22^{d} of Novr 1756
Aged 5 Months and 5 Days
Likewise the Body of Margaret Brown
Relict of the above John Brown Esq
who died the 19th March 1757. Aged 6 .
And al[s]o Mrs Margaret Burges
Daughter of the above John a[nd]
Margaret Brown who died th[e]
. . . March 1761 Aged 30

105. GEORGE KELLUM, 1732.

The Honble Major General
GEORGE KELLUM

Achievement of arms above as No. 94.

106. HENRY DURLEY.

The Entrance
of Henry . Durley Esqr
Vault
Ian^{y} the 10th 1716

107 Undecipherable.

108. JOHN JOURDAIN, 1706.

Here [Lyeth Interr'd the Body of]
[John J]ourdain of Rochelle
who [depa]rted ye life ye 9TH Octob^{R}
1706 In ye 77TH year of his Age
& Gideon ye grandſon of the
Aboveſaid departed this life ye 7TH [of]
august [170]8 In ye 16TH [year of his Age]
[Also . . . . . . wife of]
Lewis Jourdain & Mother of
the Abovesaid Gideon depart^{d}
this life y^{e} 3^{d} of Ianvary 1710
[in] the 49th year of Her Age

ST. HELEN, BISHOPSGATE

109. REGINA WOOLFE, 1691/2.

Here lyeth y^e body of REGIN(A)
WOOLFE, late daughter of IOHN
WOOLFE of *London* Mer^ct &
REGINA his wife who was
Borne y^e 1 Feb^r $16\frac{90}{91}$ & departed
Y^e 19 of y^e same month
Allso LVCIE WOOLFE their other
Daughter who was borne the 4th
February 1689 & departed this
Life the 2 . . .^th day of Ianuary 1691
AND REGINA WOOLFE . . .
Mother of the Two Children
Above who Departed this li(fe)
The 28th day of Ianuary $169\frac{1}{2}$
Aged 37 years.

110. Name hidden under organ.

111. Surname hidden under organ.

HESTER HIS WIFE & 4 SONNES
ABRAHAM THOMAS CHARLES
& RICHARD.

(And one after 1800.)

112. JOHN TUFNELL, 1686. (Removed from St. Martin Outwich.)

Within this Vault Lyeth Interr'd y^e Body of
IOHN TUFNELL Efq^r who Departed this life
(remainder hidden under organ.)

Achievement of arms above. Arms: (*Azure*) a fess (*argent*) between three ostrich feathers (*argent*), with three martlets (*sable*) on the fess impaling on a pile three gloves. No crest.

113. MARY GEORGE, 1777.

Here under lieth the Body [of]
MARY the Wife of
HENRY GEORGE of this Parifh
who Died the 23^d of Sepr 1777
Aged 30 Years
MR HENRY GEORGE
Died 14 January 1801
Aged 89 Years

IX.—MONUMENTS IN THE CHURCHYARD

114. JOSEPH LEM, 1686.

Copied from an MS. History of St. Helen's; the slab is now nearly illegible.

In a Vault under this Stone lyeth buried the body
Of Joseph Lem Citizen of London who departed
this life the 21st o^{f} August 1686 in ye 56th year of his Age
who had issue by his first wife five children. One
sonn and four daughters, and by Ann his second wife
Two sonns and nine daughters, of which sixteen
Children, Eleven died young, and were here buried
before him, the five that survived were Deborah by his
first wife, and Elizabeth, Joseph, Mary and Ann
by Ann his relict.
Here also lyeth the body of Ann Lem, relict of
Joseph Lem, who departed this life the 4th of
November 1701, in the 56th year of her Age.
Here also lyeth the body of Anne Lem, daughter of
the said Joseph and Ann Lem, who departed this
life the 12th of March 1707 in the 26th year of her Age.
Here also lyeth the body of Elizabeth Spurstowe
relict of Henry Spurstowe Esq who als lyeth
buried in this Church, and daughter of the said
Joseph and Ann Lem, who departed this life
the 27th of November 1709 in the 40th year
of her Age
Here also lyeth the body of Mary Clapham
daughter of William Clapham of Eltham in the
County of Kent Gent, by Mary his wife and
daughter of the said Joseph and Ann Lem
who departed this life the 21st of June 1712
in the 9th year of her age
Here also lyeth the body of Joseph Lem
Only surviving son of Joseph and Ann Lem
who died the 3^{d} August 1727 in the
56th year of his Age.

A table-tomb with a shield of arms. (*Argent*) on a bend (*gules*) three lions passant (*or*).

ST. HELEN, BISHOPSGATE

115. GEORGE LOW, 1783.

In Memory of
MR GEORGE LOW Upwards of 60 Years
an Inhabitant of this Pariſh
who departed this Life the 13th
of June 17[8]3 Aged 69 Years
Alſo the Body of M^RS^ MARY LOW
Wife of the aboveſaid MR GEORGE LOW
who departed this Life the 1st of Feby 1761
Aged 37 Years
Likewiſe Five of their Children
who died in their Infancy
And Two Children of the aboveſaid
MR GEORGE LOW by a Second Marriage
Also the Body of
MR GEORGE ARCHDALE LOW
Late of Joiner's Hall
Upper Thames Street Packer
Son of the above MR GEORGE LOW
who departed this life on the . . .
August 1816 etc. etc.

Eight lines more.

Upon the south side of the above Monument is another inscription :

IN MEMORY OF *M^RS^ ELIZ^TH^ HOUSTON*
WIFE OF *MR THOS HOUSTON* OF THIS PARISH
WHO DIED 4TH JULY 1788 AGED 59 YEARS
ALSO THE [ABOVE NAMED] *MR THOS HOUSTON*
WHO DIED [15TH NOV^R^ 1796] AGED 64 YEARS
LIKEWISE [. . . MANC .] HOUSTON
WIFE OF M^R^ S[AM] HOUSTON
[ ] OF THE ABOVENAMED
[ ] ELIZ HOUSTON

The rest is illegible.
Also an inscription upon the western end of the same monument.

X.—MONUMENTS WHICH HAVE DISAPPEARED

The undermentioned monuments, recorded by Stow as existing in the church at the end of the 16th century, have now disappeared :

Thomas Langton	Chaplain (in the quire)	1350
Adam Frances	Mayor	[1354]
Elizabeth, wife of William Vennar	Alderman & Sheriff	1401
John Swinflat		1420
Nicholas Marshall	Alderman & Ironmonger	1474
Joan, wife of John Cocken, Esquire		1509
Marie, wife of Sir Lewis Orrell, Knight		—
Henry Sommer and Katherine his wife		—
Walter Huntington, Esquire		—
John Gower	Steward of St. Helen's	1512
Sir William Sanctlo, father and son		—
Eleanor, daughter of Sir Thomas Butler, Lord Sudley		—
John Southworth		—
Nicholas Harpsfield, Esquire		—
Thomas Sanderford or Sommerford	Alderman	—
Alexander Cheyney		—
Walter Dawbeney		—
George, son of Hugh Fastolph		—
Robert Liade		—
William Hollis	Mayor	1540
John Fauconbridge, Esquire		1545
– – – Hacket	Gentleman of the King's Chapel	—
William Skegges	Sergeant poulter	—
Richard, son of Sir Thomas Gresham		1564

The following names of persons buried here are added by Strype :

Elizabeth Greystock, widow, late wife of Sir John Vavasor (buried on the N. side of the Lady Chapel)	1509
Robert Knollys, Gent. Usher of the Privy Chamber	1420 [*sic.*]
Rafe Machin (buried before the Trinity)	1488

He also mentions a gravestone near the Spencer monument to Abraham Orelius, Preacher of the French Church.

In the possession of the Merchant Taylors' Company is a drawing of a floor-slab, inlaid with marble, to Edward Skeggs, 1592, bearing his incised effigy, with an achievement and four shields of arms (see plate 120).

BIBLIOGRAPHICAL NOTE

THE reader is directed to the following general works, which contain information relative to St. Helen's Church and Priory:—

The Victoria County History. London. Vol. I.

Londina Illustrata. 1819. By Robert Wilkinson.

Londinium Redivivum. 1803. J. P. Malcolm.

Antiquities of London. 1791. J. T. Smith.

Views of London Churches. 1736–39. West and Toms.

New View of London. 1707. Hatton.

Ancient Funeral Monuments. 1631. John Weever.

Survey of the Cities of London and Westminster. 1598. John Stow. (Also subsequent editions, edited by Strype.)

The following works are either exclusively devoted to the subject or are of special importance in this connection:—

Annals of St. Helen's, Bishopsgate. 1876. Rev. J. E. Cox.

Registers of St. Helen's, Bishopsgate.

The Last Ten Years of the Priory of St. Helen, Bishopsgate. *Trans. London and Middlesex Archæological Society*. Vol. II. 1865. Rev. Thos. Hugo

History of the Worshipful Company of Leathersellers. 1871. W. H. Black.

A Survey of the Priory of St. Helen. *Archæologia*, XVI. By W. H. Black.

Notices of St. Helen's, Bishopsgate. *Trans. London and Middlesex Archæological Society*. Vol. I. Rev. Thos. Hugo.

MSS.—The Gardner Collection of London drawings. The portions relating to St. Helen's Church and the monastic buildings are now in the possession of the Merchant Taylors' and Leathersellers' Companies. The latter Company has also an extensive collection of drawings of its own.

The Crace Collection. British Museum.

Muniments of the Dean and Chapter of St. Paul's Cathedral.

INDEX TO NAMES

PLATE 1

SOUTH EAST VIEW OF THE NUNNERY OF ST HELEN, BISHOPSGATE STREET

FROM WILKINSON'S *LONDINA ILLUSTRATA*

PLATE 2

NUNS' FRATER FROM THE SOUTH-WEST. FROM A DRAWING BY FREDERICK NASH

LEATHERSELLERS' OLD HALL. FROM A DRAWING BY FREDERICK NASH

PLATE 4

THE CHURCH of ST. HELENS and LEATHER SELLERS HALL With the Cornhill Military Association

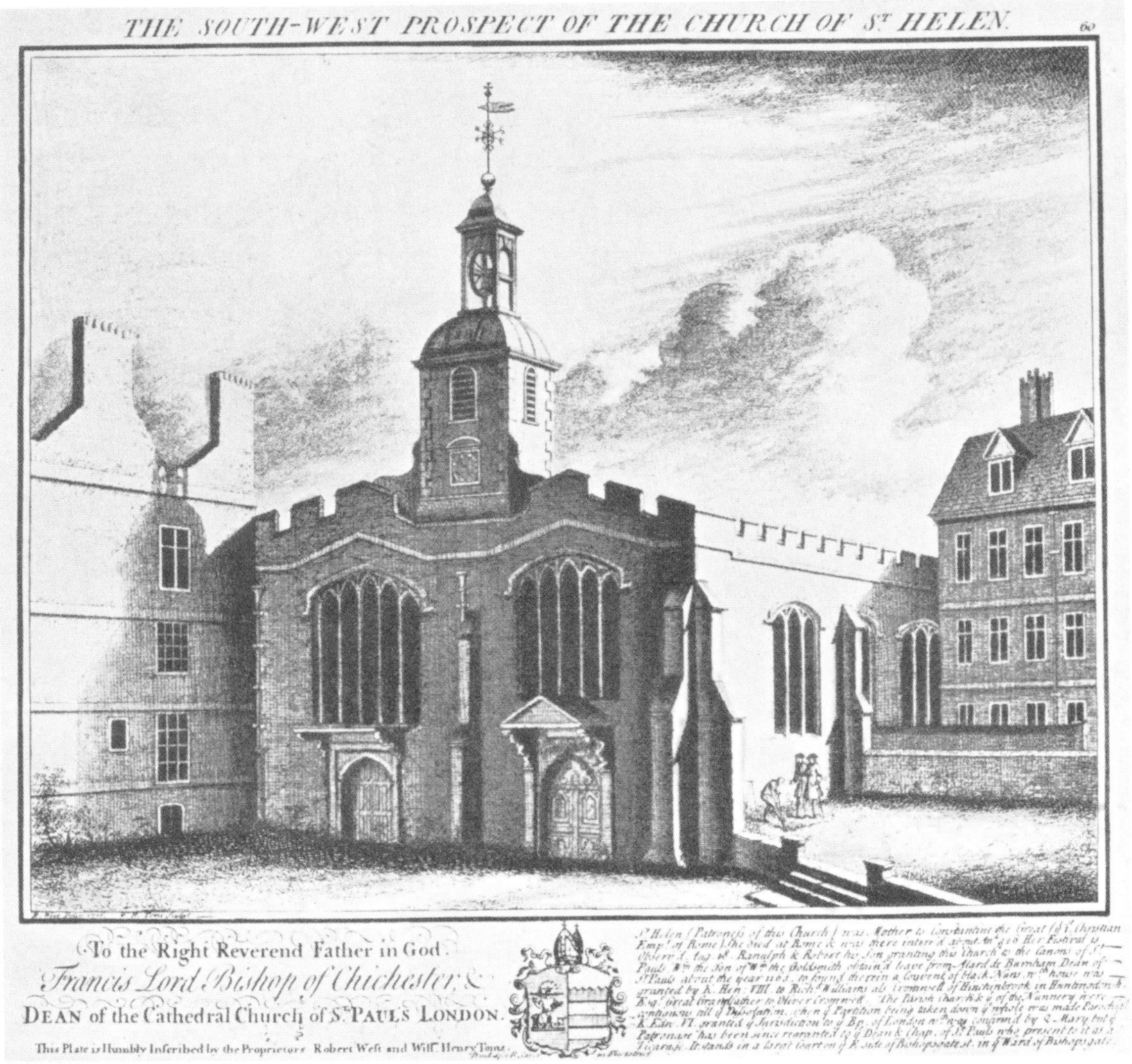
THE SOUTH-WEST PROSPECT OF THE CHURCH OF ST. HELEN.
60
To the Right Reverend Father in God
Francis Lord Bishop of Chichester, &
DEAN of the Cathedral Church of St. PAULS LONDON.
This Plate is Humbly Inscribed by the Proprietors Robert West and Willm. Henry Toms.

PLATE 6

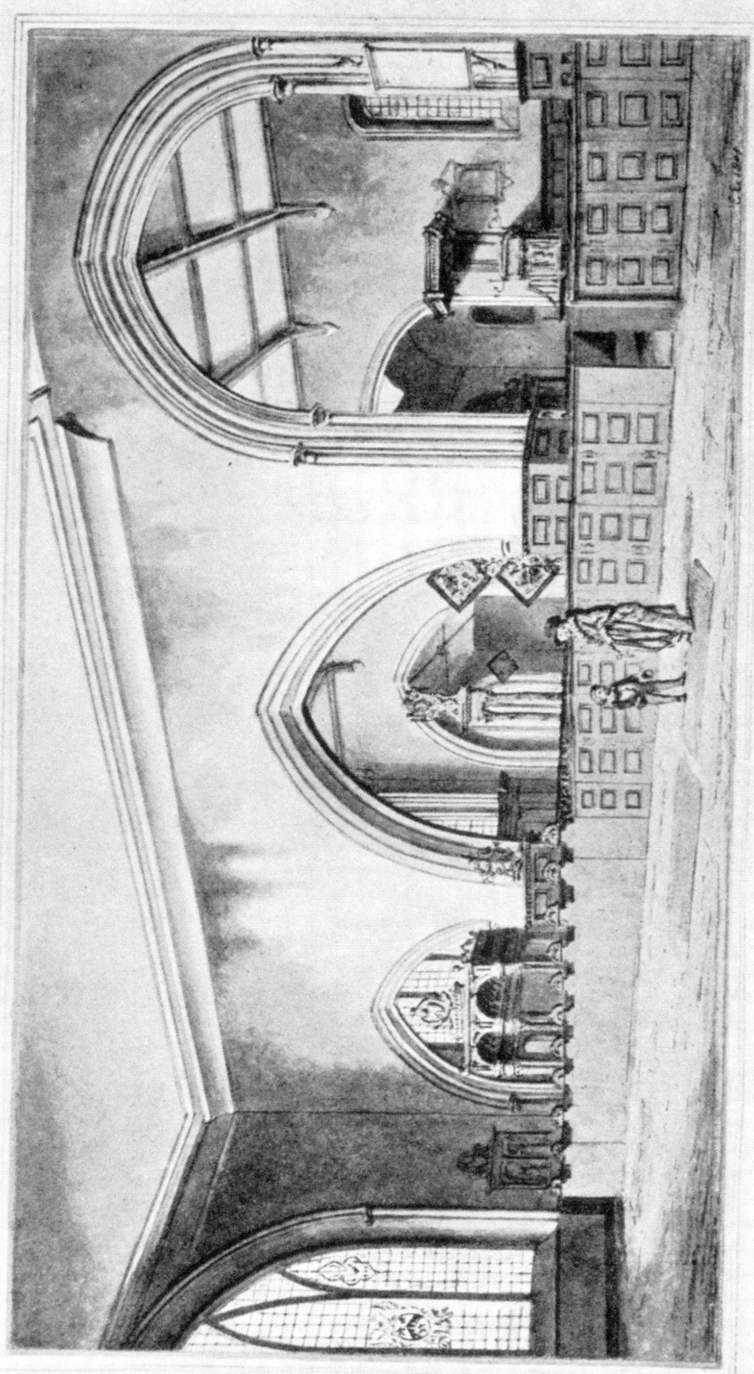

INTERIOR ST HELENS A.D. 1805

Inside of S.t Helen's

FROM MALCOLM'S *LONDINIUM REDIVIVUM*

THE CRYPT OF THE ANTIENT NUNNERY OF ST HELEN, BISHOPSGATE STREET, LONDON;

THE UNDERCROFT OF THE NUNS' DORTER
FROM WILKINSON'S *LONDINA ILLUSTRATA*

PLATE 9

I. THE CHAPTER HOUSE LOOKING EAST
II. THE SACRISTY LOOKING WEST
III. THE DORTER UNDERCROFT LOOKING SOUTH

PLATE 10

THE WEST FRONT

THE SOUTH-WEST DOOR

S·HELENA

THE SOUTH DOOR

(*a*) EXTERIOR, NORTH WALL, NUNS' QUIRE

(*b*) CORBEL IN SACRISTY

EXTERIOR, NORTH WALL OF NUNS' QUIRE
(REMAINS OF SACRISTY)

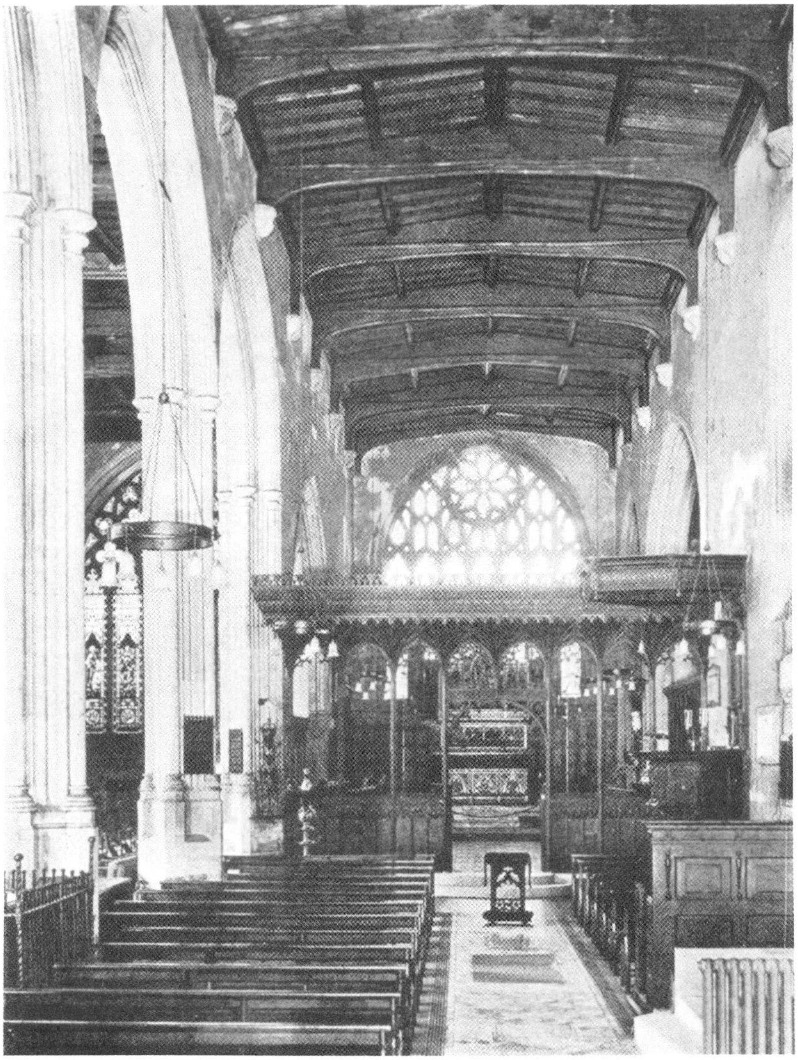

THE PARISH NAVE LOOKING EAST

THE ARCADE BETWEEN THE NAVE AND THE
NUNS' QUIRE, LOOKING SOUTH-WEST

THE ARCADE BETWEEN THE NAVE AND THE NUNS' QUIRE, LOOKING SOUTH-EAST

DETAILS OF ARCADE BETWEEN NAVE AND NUNS' QUIRE

NORTH WALL OF THE NUNS' QUIRE,
LOOKING WEST

PLATE 20

CHURCH *of* S^T^ HELE

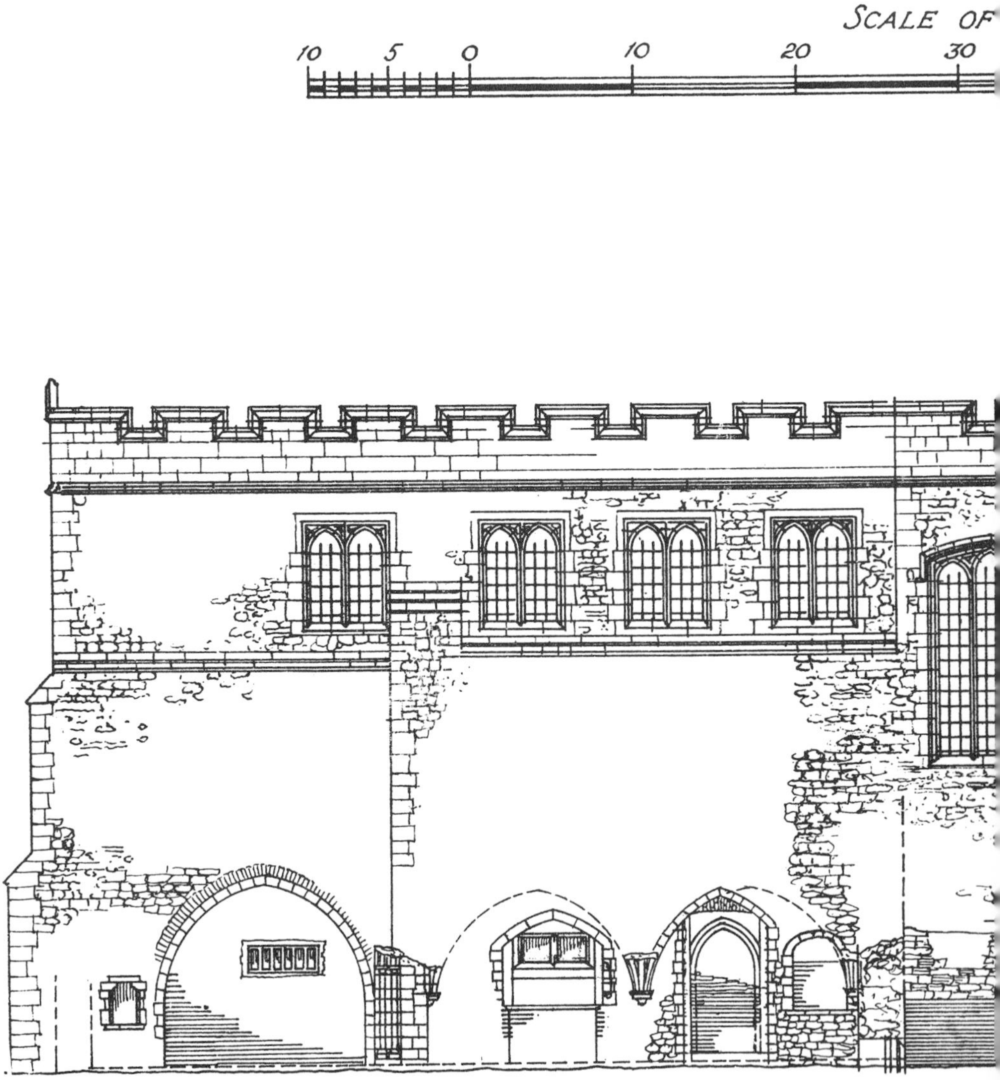
SCALE OF
10 5 0 10 20 30

N

BISHOPSGATE.

50
60
70

ATION.

PLATES 21 & 22

CHURCH *of*

10 5 0 10

SOUTH ELEVATION OF NAVE

ELEN, BISHOPSGATE.

E OF FEET

30 40 50 4 70

P.W.L

SOUTH ELEVATION OF TRANSEPT &c

PLATE 23

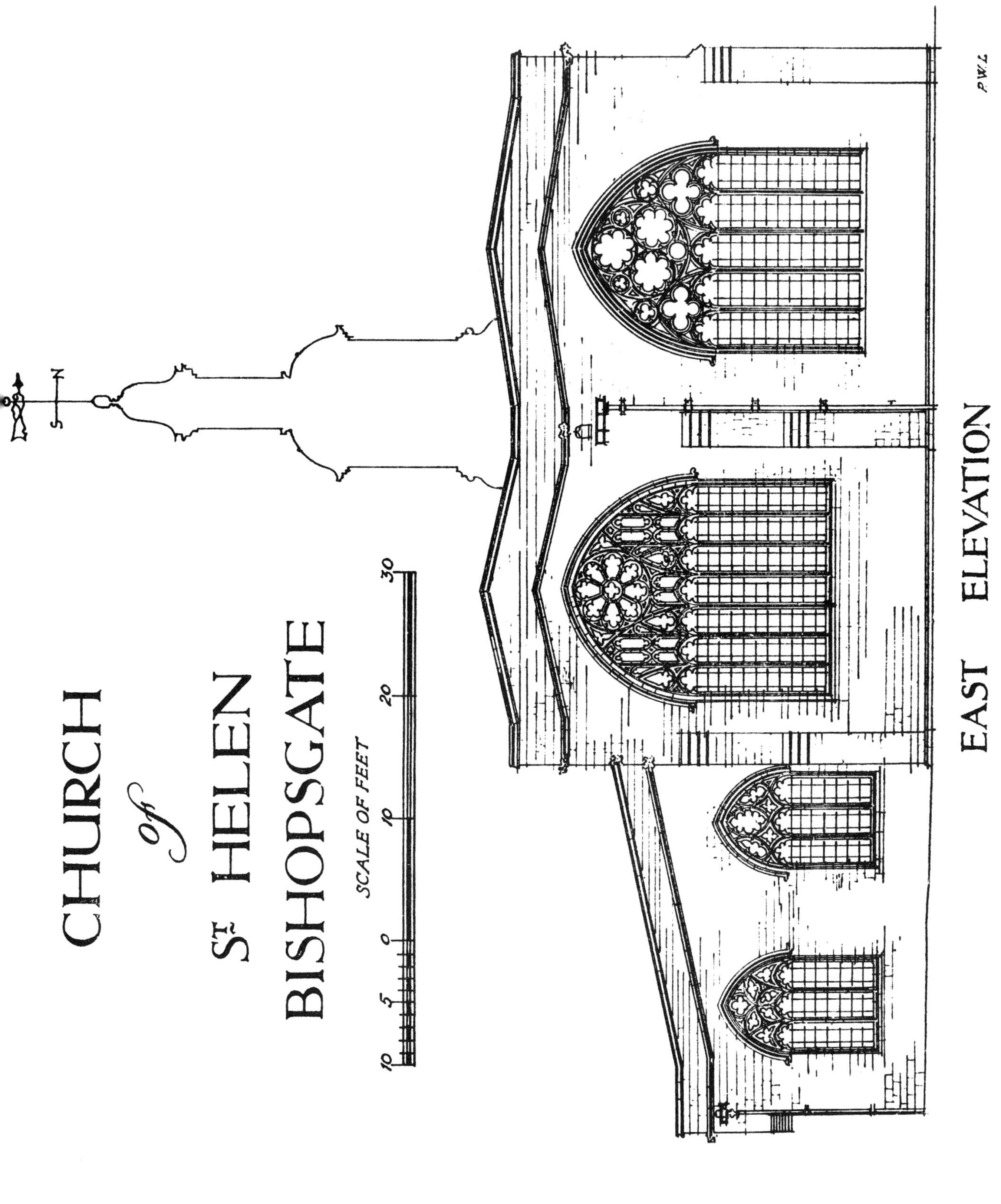
CHURCH of St HELEN BISHOPSGATE
SCALE OF FEET
10 5 0 10 20 30
EAST ELEVATION
P.W.L.

CHURCH
of
St HELEN
BISHOPSGATE
SCALE OF FEET
10 5 0 10 20

WEST ELEVATION

P.W.L

PLATE 25

CHURCH of
10 5 0 10
W E
NAVE
SECTI

ELEN, BISHOPSGATE.

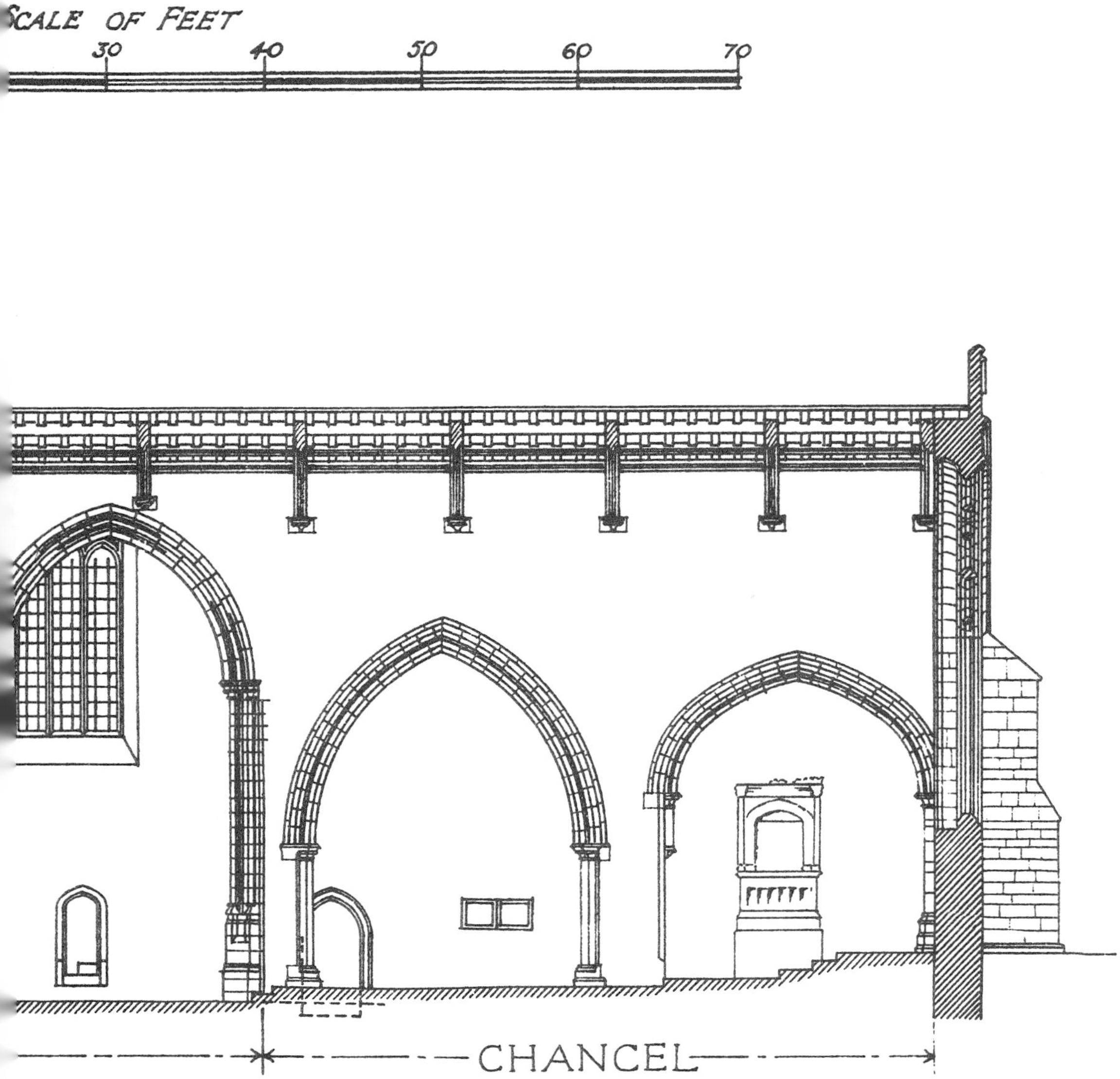

SCALE OF FEET
30
40
50
60
70
CHANCEL

ING NORTH

P.K.K.

PLATE 26

CHURCH *of* S^T^ HE

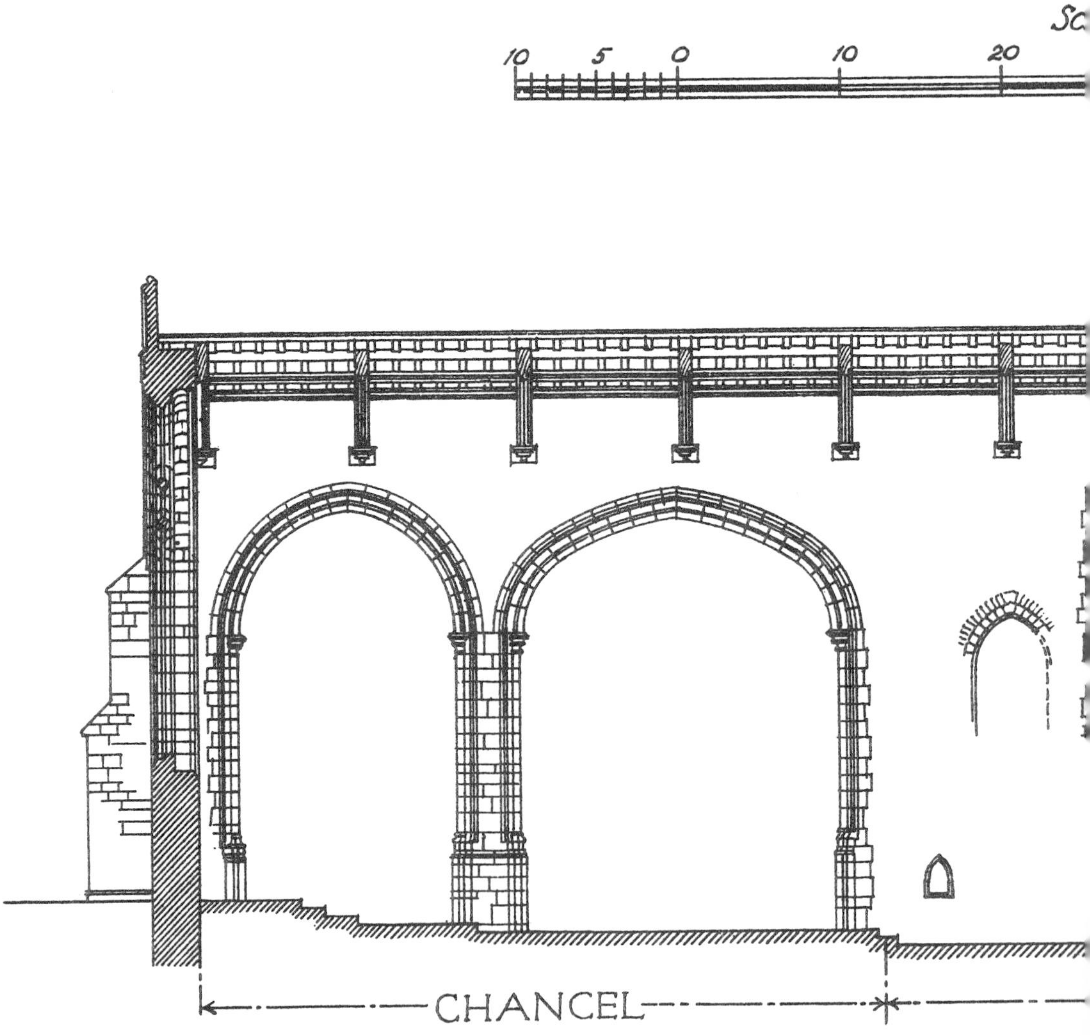
Sc
10 5 0 10 20
CHANCEL

SECT

N, BISHOPSGATE.

ET
40
50
60
70

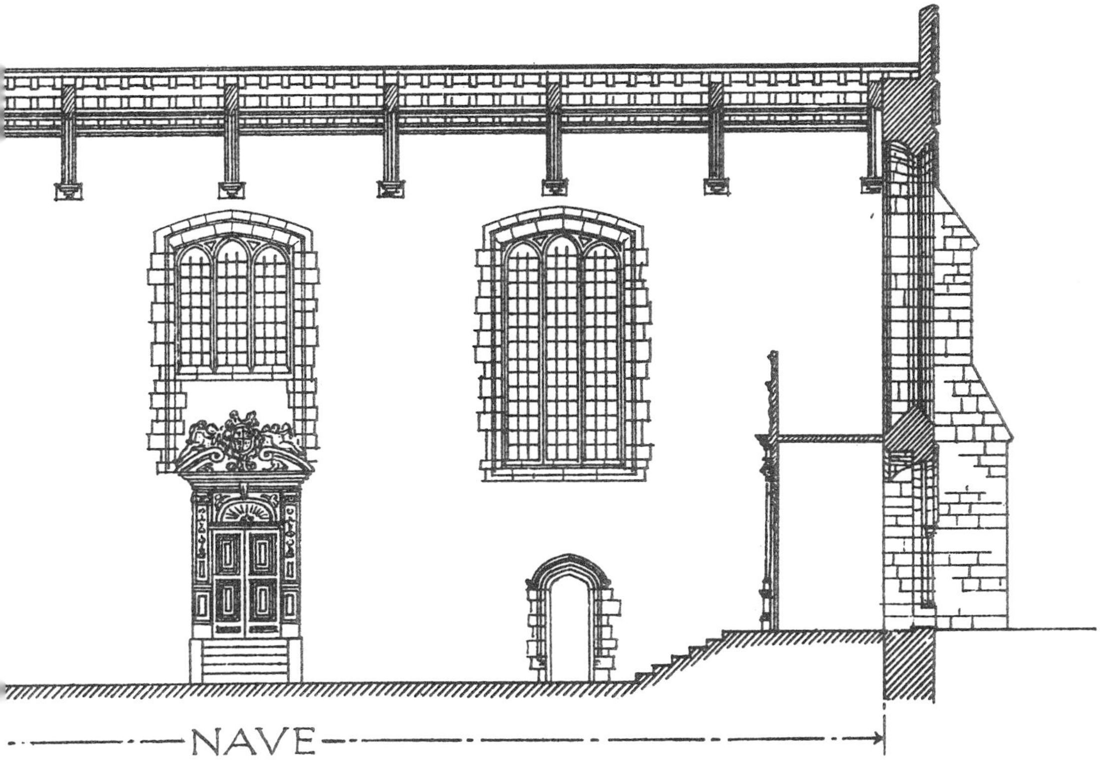
NAVE

ING SOUTH

CHURCH *of* St. HELEN, BISHOPSGATE.

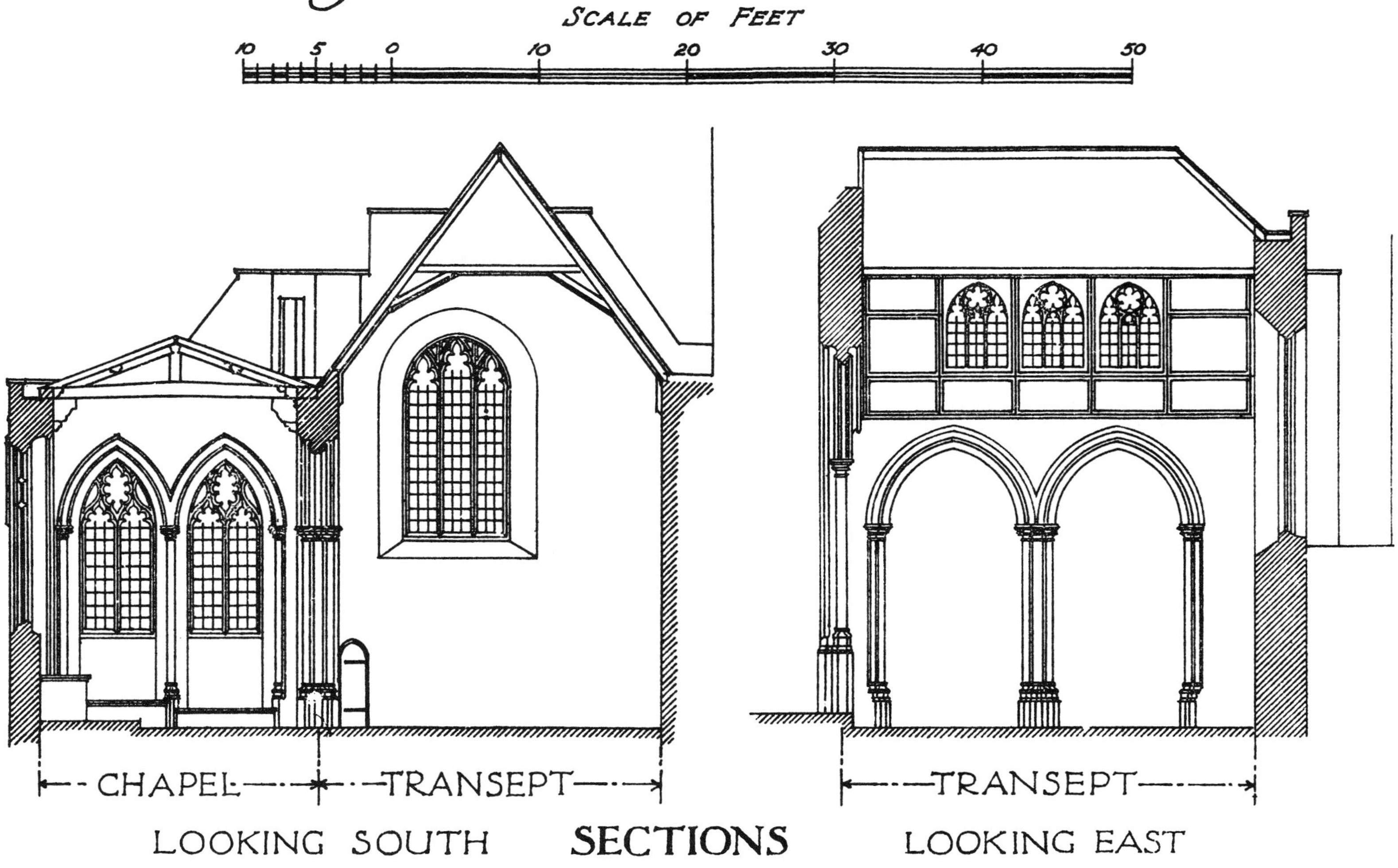
SCALE OF FEET
10 5 0 10 20 30 40 50
CHAPEL
TRANSEPT
LOOKING SOUTH
TRANSEPT
LOOKING EAST

SECTIONS

CHURCH *of* S^T HELEN, BISHOPSGATE.

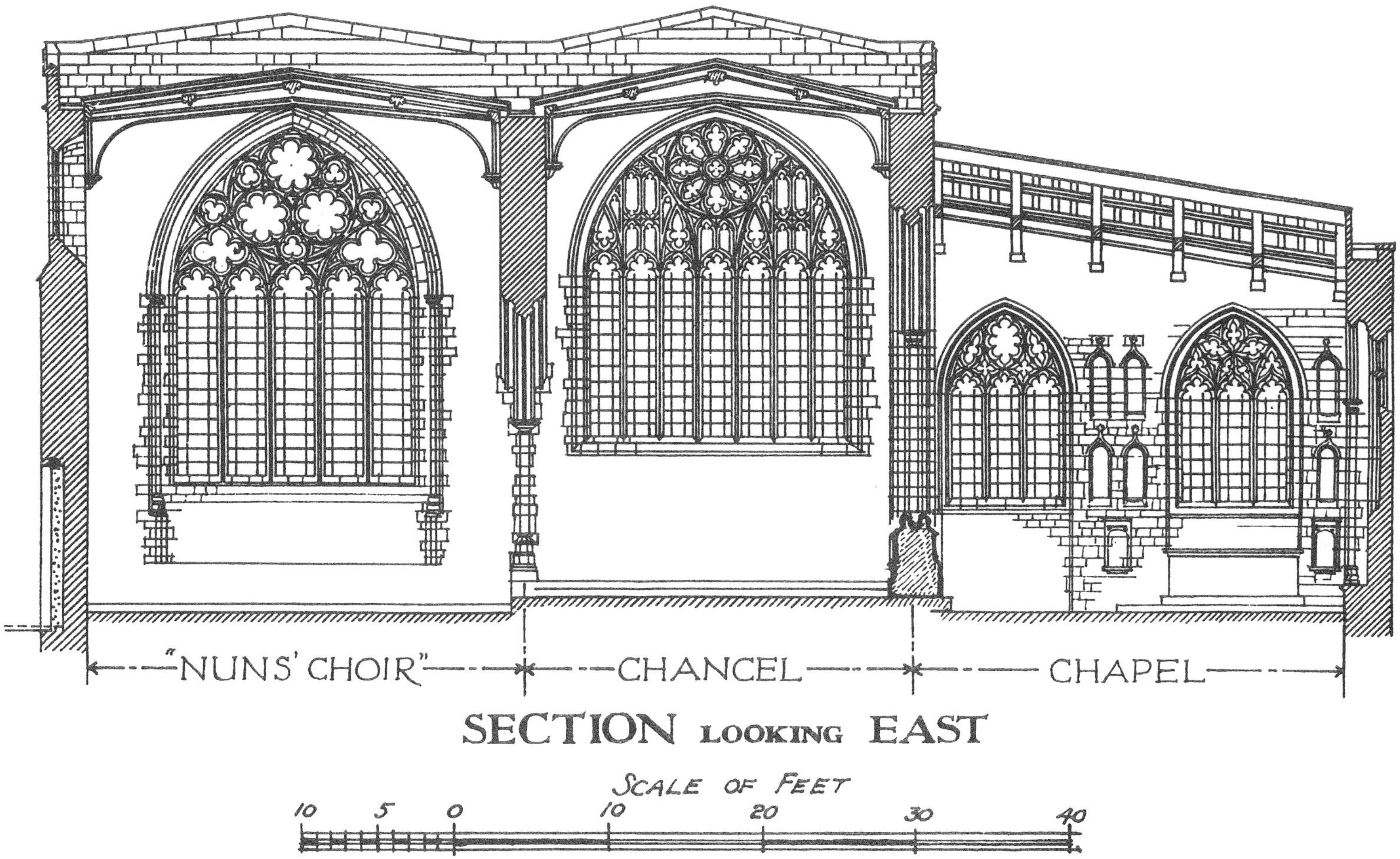
"NUNS' CHOIR"
CHANCEL
CHAPEL
SCALE OF FEET
10 5 0 10 20 30 40

SECTION LOOKING EAST

PLATE 28

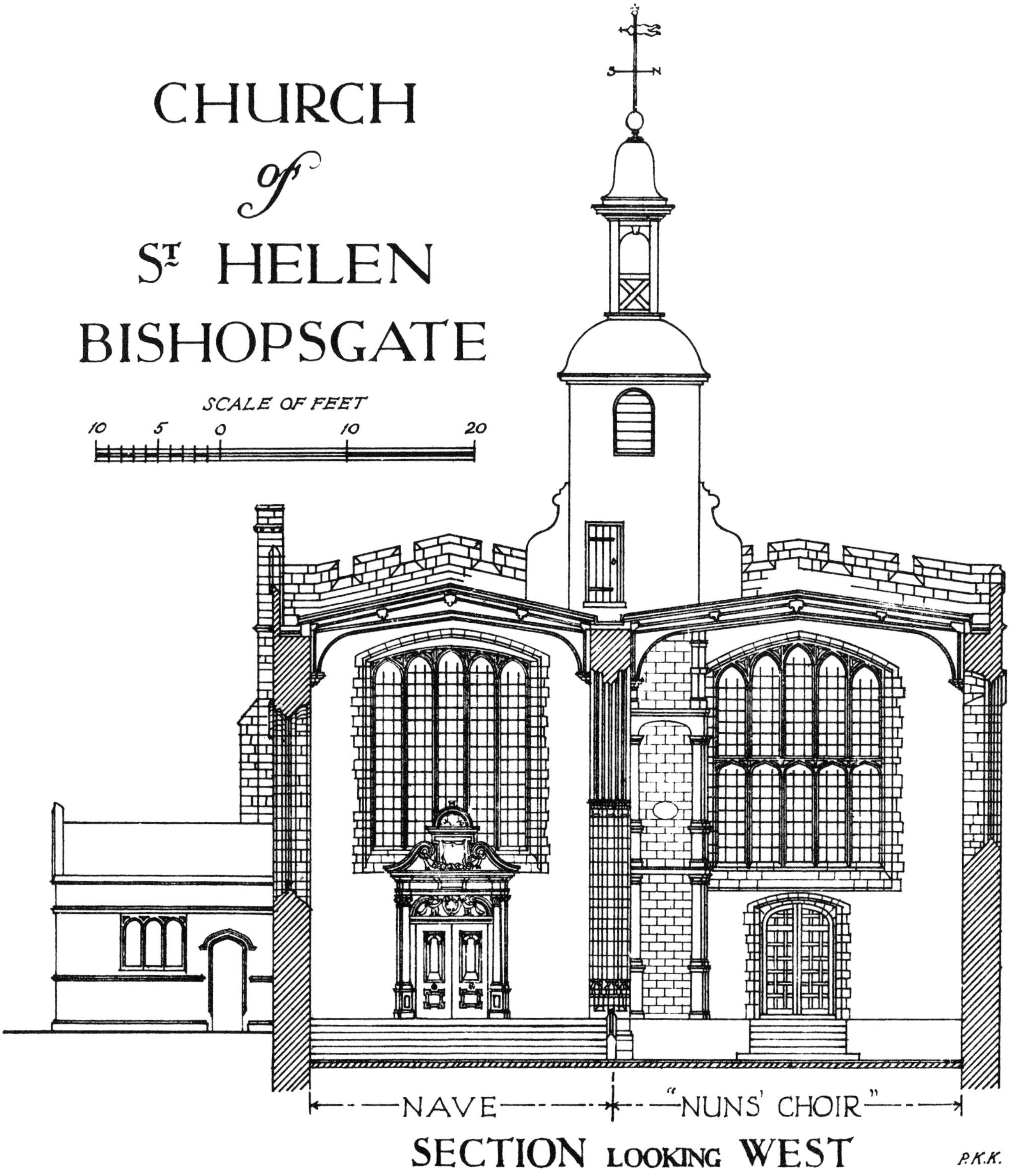
CHURCH
of
St HELEN
BISHOPSGATE
SCALE OF FEET
10 5 0 10 20
S N
NAVE
"NUNS' CHOIR"
SECTION LOOKING WEST
P.K.K.

CIVILIAN AND HIS WIFE, *c.* 1465.

Orate p aīa dnī Nich̄i Wotton quondam Rector istius ecclie Et
Baccallarij legis qui obiit Septimo die mensis Aprilis Anno
dnī millmo CCCC° lxxxij° Cuius Anime propicietur deus Amen

NICHOLAS WOTTON, L.L.B., RECTOR OF ST. MARTIN, OUTWICH, 1482.

Hic iacet Thomas Wylliams Generos' et Margareta uxor eius qui quidem
Thomas obiit xvij die mensis Januarii A° dni M° CCCC lxxxxv Et predicta
Margareta obiit die mensis Anno dni M° CCCC
quorum

THOMAS WYLLIAMS, 1495, AND MARGARET HIS WIFE.

JOHN LEVENTHORP, 1510.

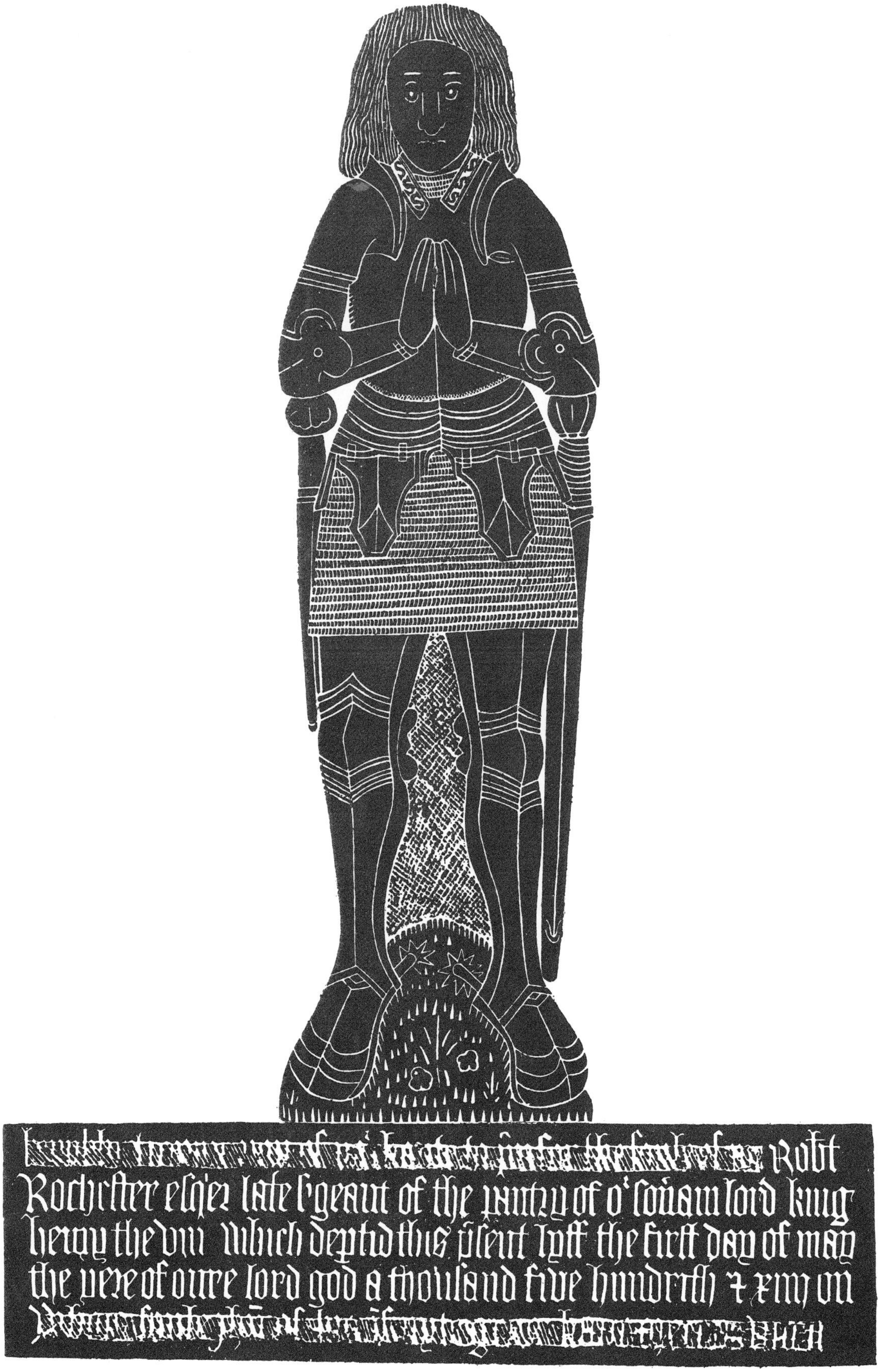
Robt
Rochester esqier late sergeaunt of the pantry of o' souerain lord king
henry the viii which deptid this psent lyff the first day of may
the yere of oure lord god a thousand five hundreth & xiiij on

ROBERT ROCHESTER, 1514.

A LADY IN HERALDIC MANTLE, *c.* 1535.

Scale, Two Inches to a Foot
Scale, One Inch to a Foot

THE BRASS SHOWN IN PLATE 35 SHOWING ORIGINAL SLAB

f 28
f 3.7
Scale, One Inch to a Foot.

(a)

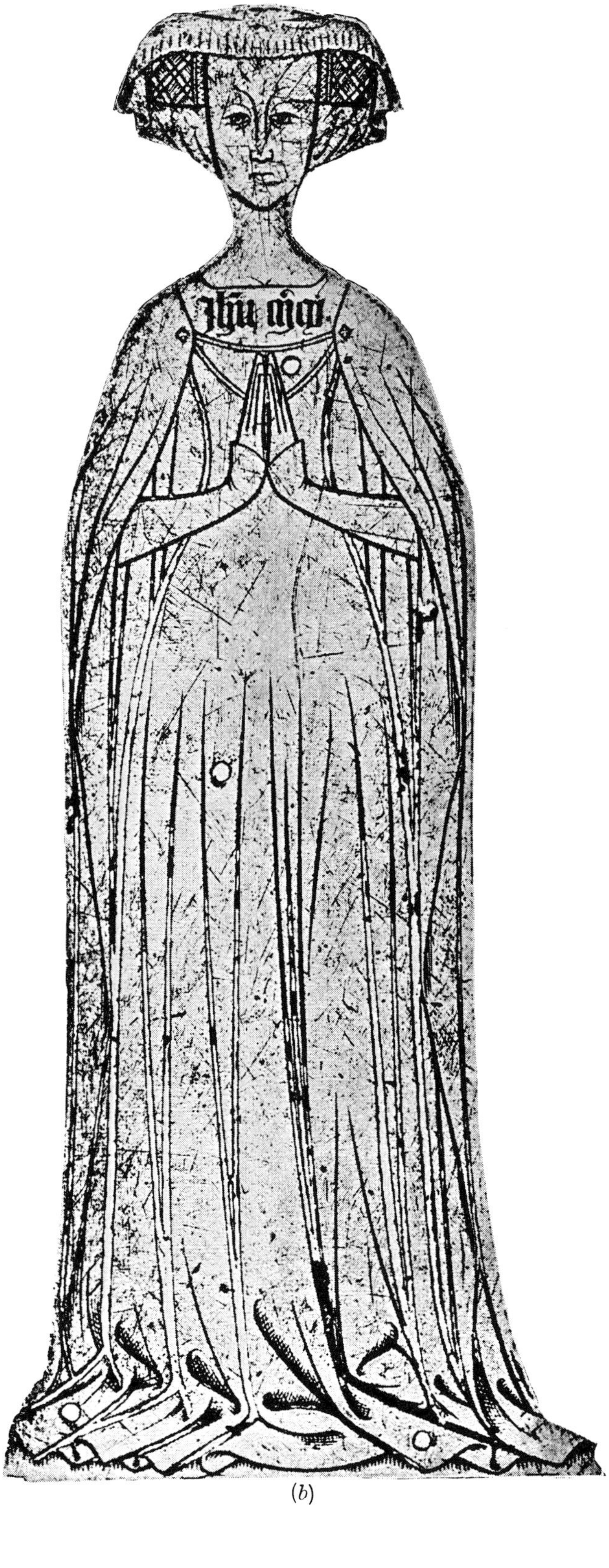
Jhu mci

(b)

LADY c. 1420 (NOW LOST)
(a) SHOWING ORIGINAL SLAB
(b) FIGURE FROM RUBBING

THOMAS BENOLT AND HIS TWO WIVES, 1534,
IN ORIGINAL SLAB

Scale two Inches to a Foot.

THOMAS BENOLT AND HIS TWO WIVES

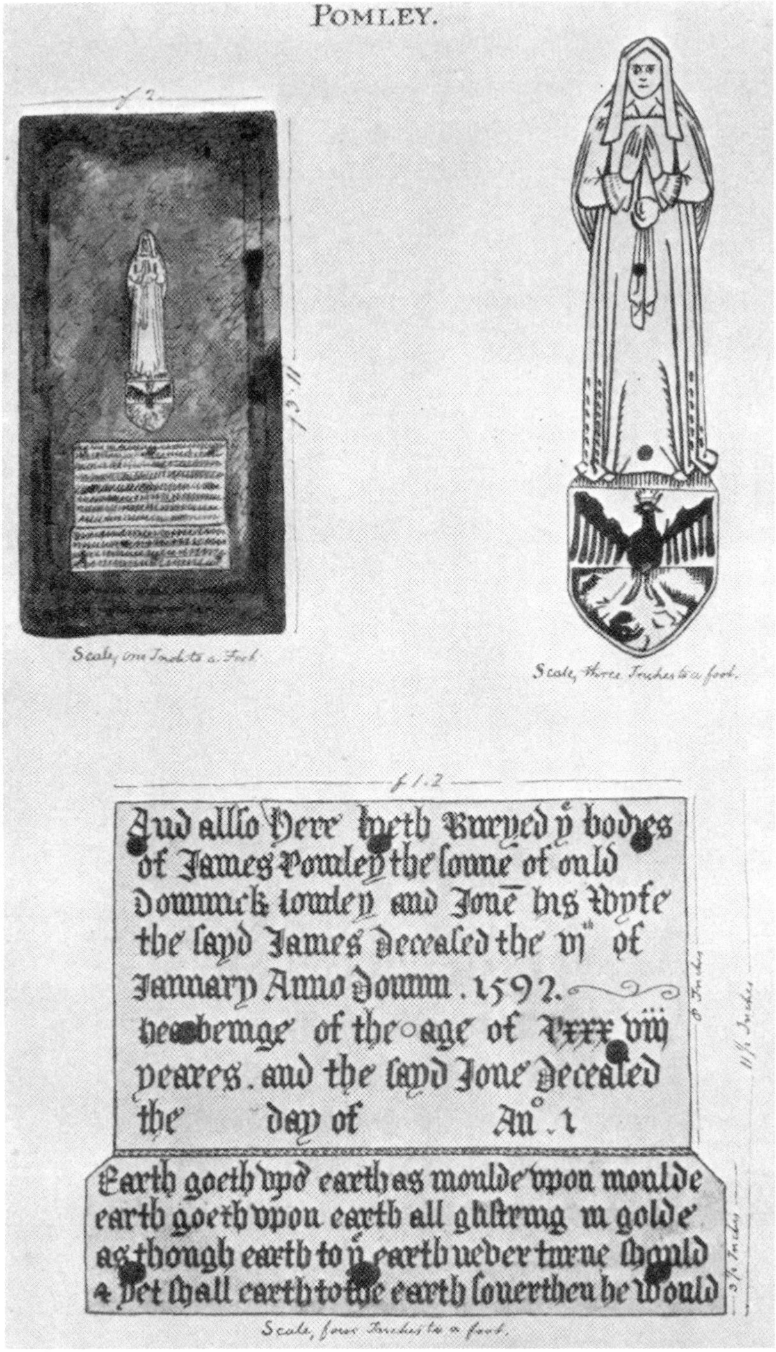
POMLEY.
Scale, three Inches to a foot.
And allso Here lyeth buryed y bodyes
of James Pomley the sonne of ould
Dominick lomley and Jone his wyfe
the sayd James deceased the vj of
January Anno domini . 1592.
he beinge of the age of xxx viij
yeares . and the sayd Jone deceased
the day of An. 1
Earth goeth upon earth as moulde upon moulde
earth goeth upon earth all glistring in golde
as though earth to y earth never turne should
& yet shall earth to the earth sooner then he would
Scale, four Inches to a foot.

A LADY *c.* 1540, WITH ADDED INSCRIPTION TO JAMES LOMLEY, 1592

THE COMMUNION TABLE

THE SOUTH DOOR CASE

PLATE 43

PEDIMENT AND FIGURES ABOVE SOUTH DOOR CASE

Entablature 11⅞"
Cornice
Architrave
Cap.
Neck Mould
Pilaster 6'-0⅜"
Band
Base
Cap
Panel
Pedestal 5'-10"
Base
Side Elevation
Front Elevation
Scale of Inches 12 0 1 2 3 4 5 6 7 8 9 10 Feet
— E. R. B. Harriss —
MENS ET DELT

THE SOUTH DOOR CASE.

THE SOUTH-WEST DOOR CASE

THE FONT

PLATE 47

FONT AND COVER

SCALE OF FEET

0 1 2 FT

JUNE 1922 P.K. KIPPS

PLATE 48

FONT AT EAST END

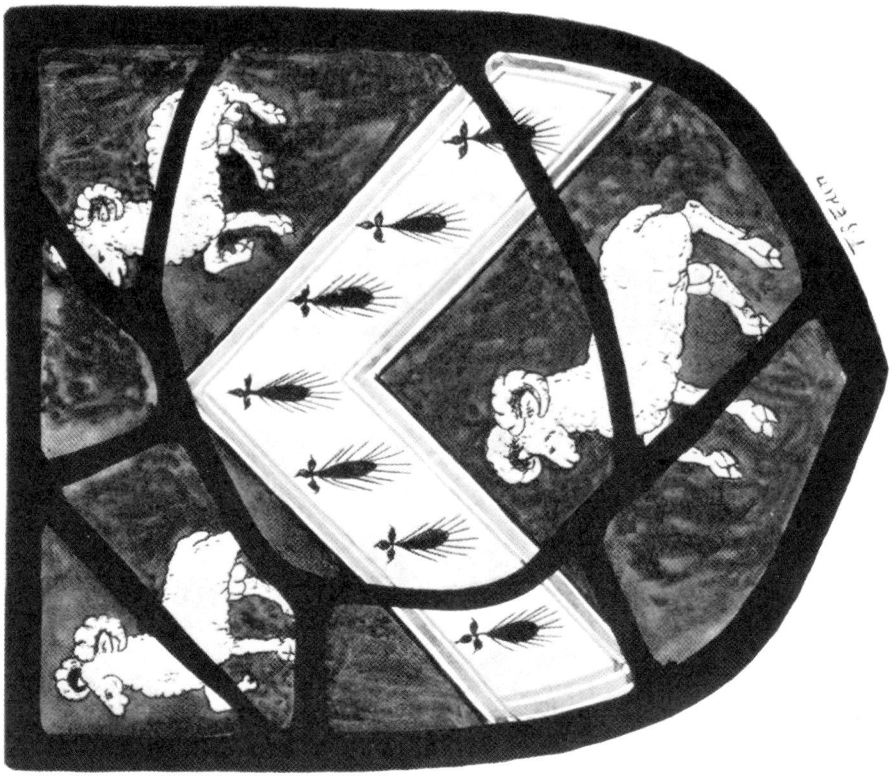

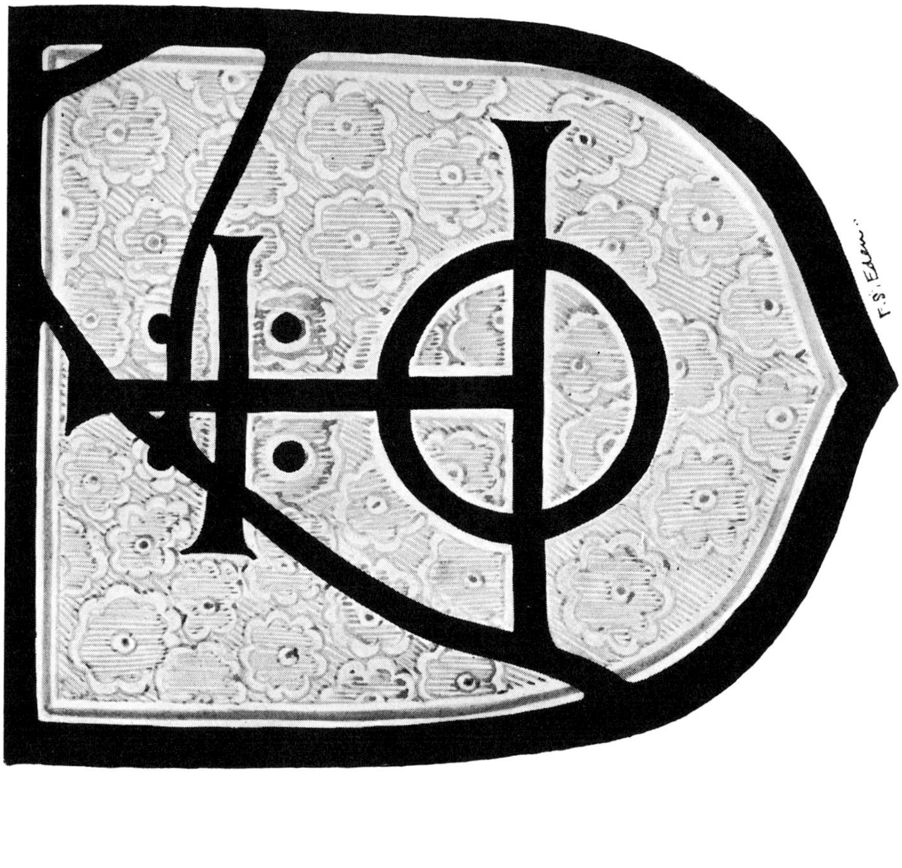

PAINTED GLASS IN SOUTH CHAPEL
MERCHANT'S MARK AND ARMS OF
SIR JOHN CROSBY

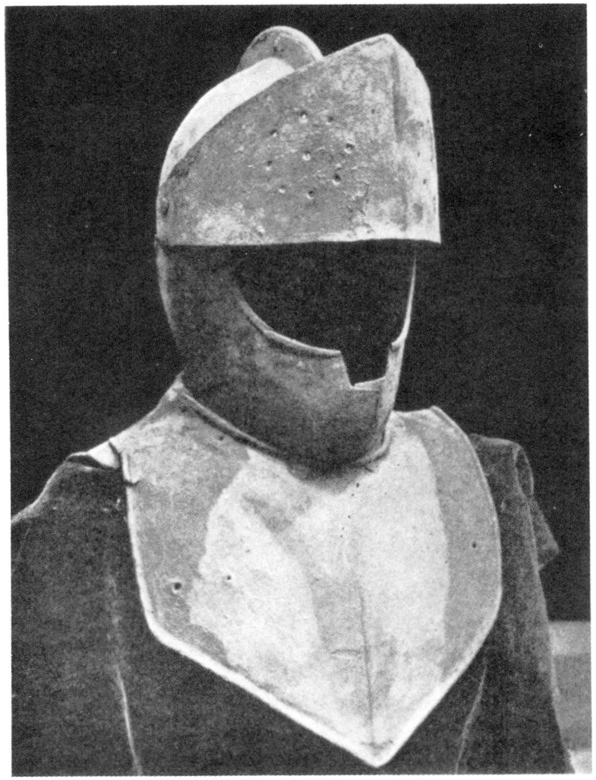

FUNERAL HELM

CONSOLE AT BACK OF ORGAN CASE

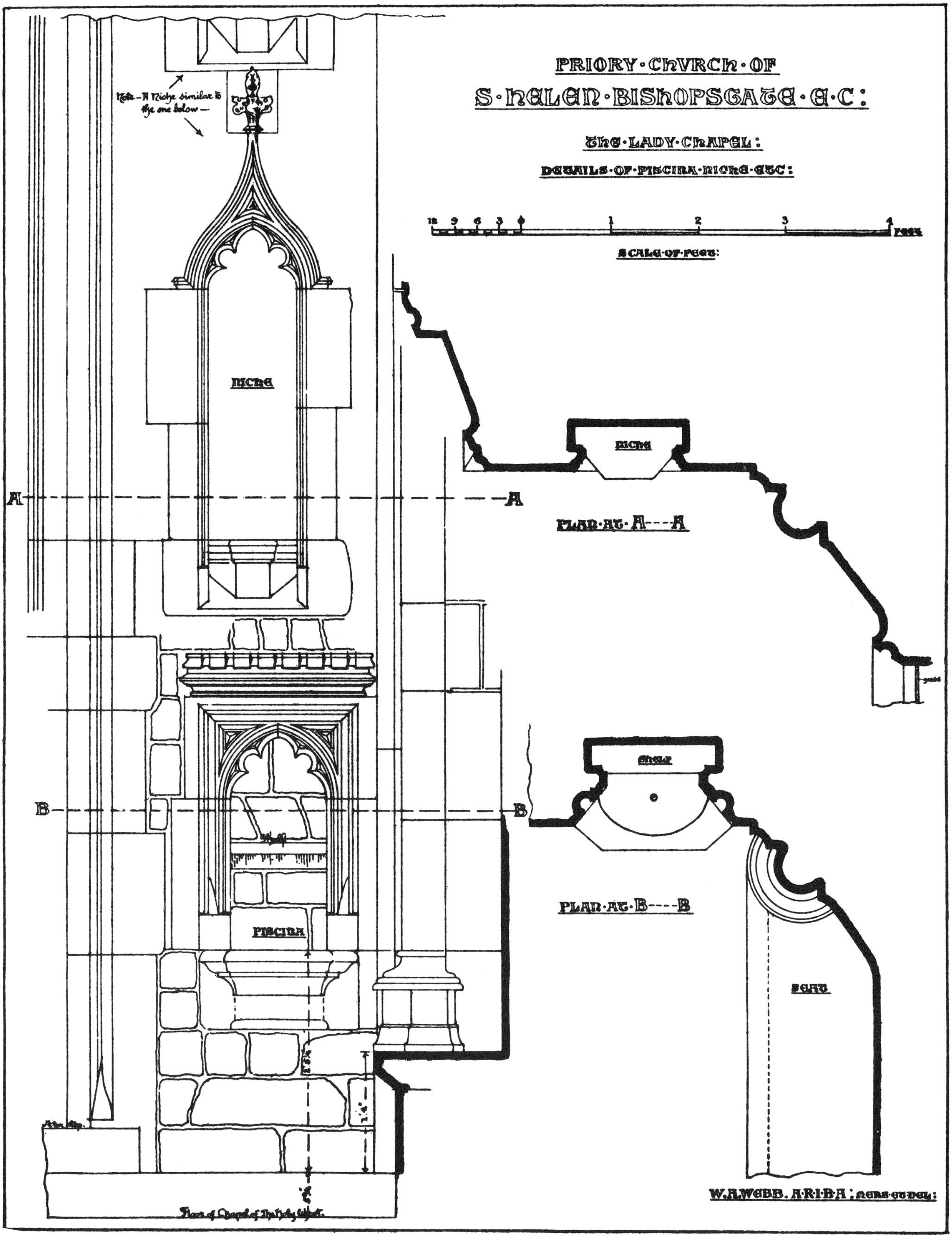
PRIORY·CHURCH·OF
S·HELEN·BISHOPSGATE·E·C:
THE·LADY·CHAPEL:
DETAILS·OF·PISCINA·NICHE·ETC:
SCALE·OF·FEET:
Note — A Niche similar to the one below —
NICHE
PLAN·AT·A---A
SHELF
PISCINA
PLAN·AT·B----B
SEAT
Floor of Chapel of The Holy Ghost
W.A.WEBB. A·R·I·B·A; MENS·ET·DEL:

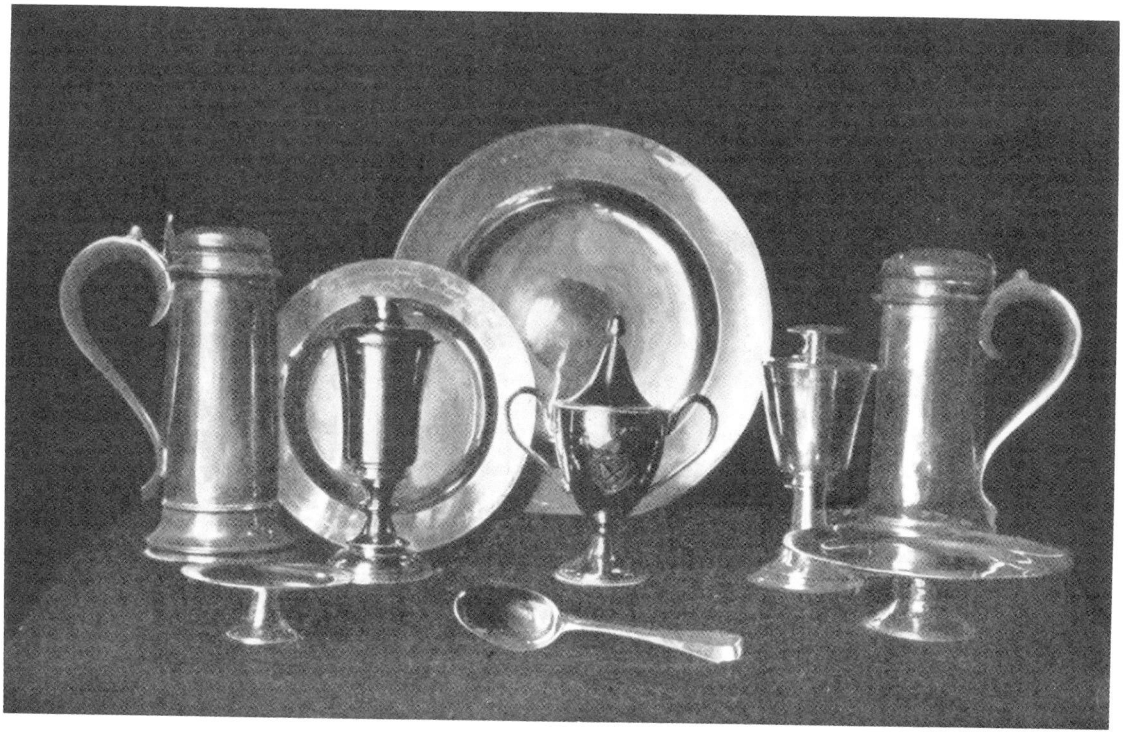

CHURCH PLATE

ALMS DISHES

FRAGMENT FOUND IN THE
BERNARD MONUMENT

POOR BOX

THE PULPIT

DETAIL OF PULPIT PANELS

PLATE 56

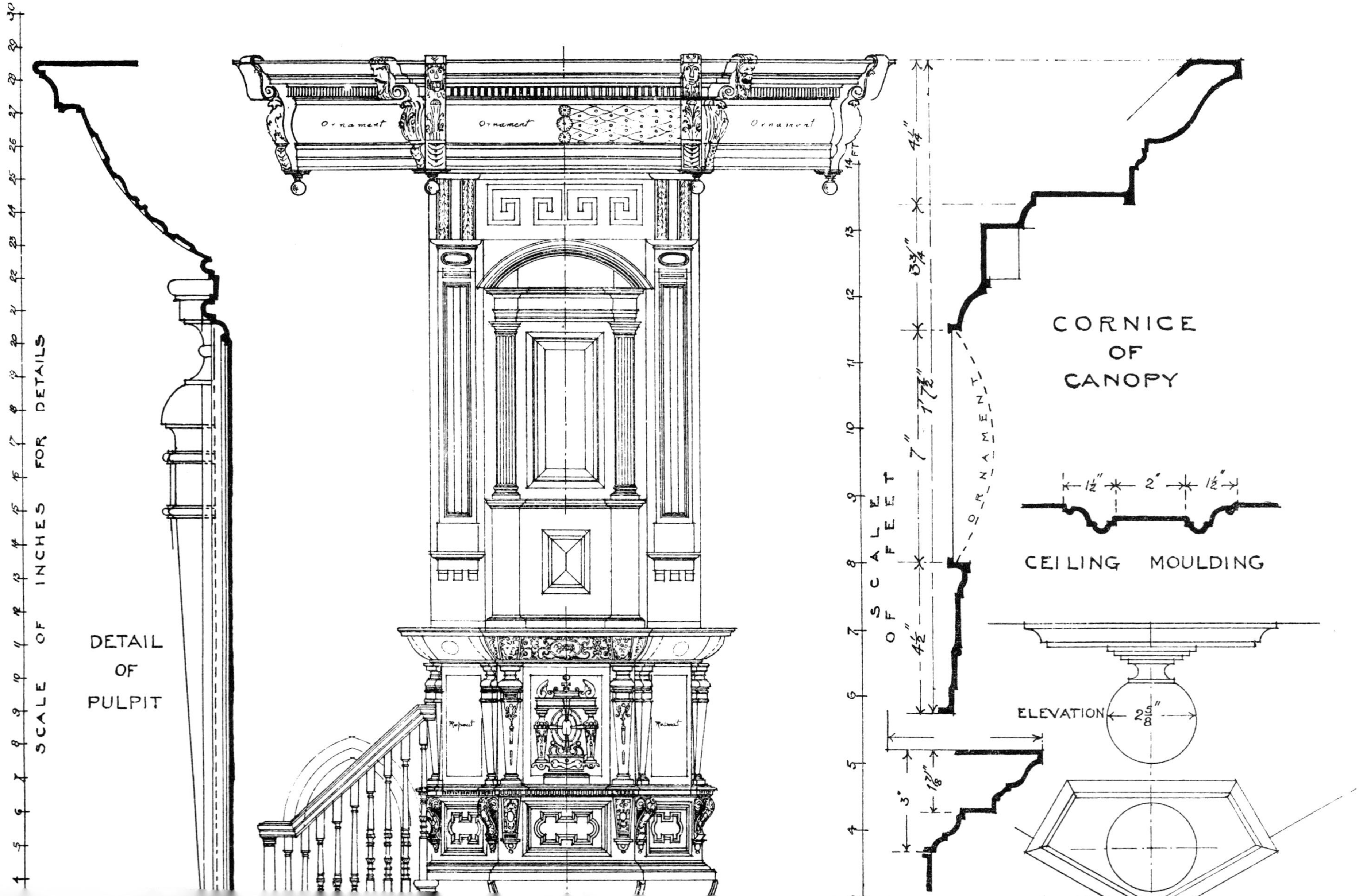
SCALE OF INCHES FOR DETAILS
DETAIL OF PULPIT
Ornament
Ornament
Ornament
Repeat
Repeat
14 FT
SCALE OF FEET
4¼"
3¾"
7"
17½"
4½"
ORNAMENT
CORNICE OF CANOPY
1½"
2"
1½"
CEILING MOULDING
ELEVATION
2⅝"
3"
1⅞"

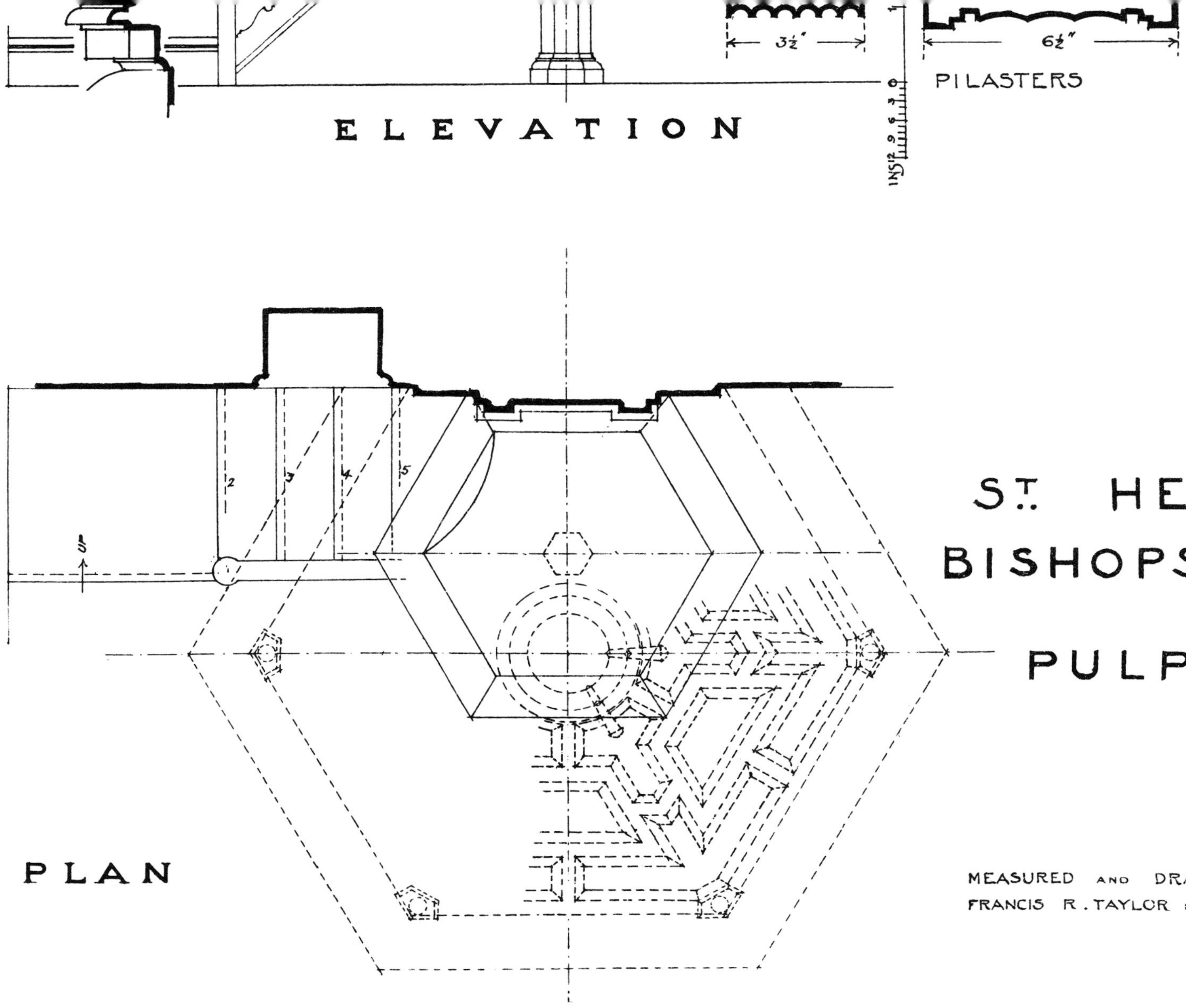

ELEVATION
3½″
6½″
PILASTERS
INS 12 9 6 3 0
2
3
4
5
PLAN

ST. HELEN'S BISHOPSGATE PULPIT

MEASURED AND DRAWN BY
FRANCIS R. TAYLOR LICENTIATE R.I.B.A.
192[illegible]

PLATE 57

WROUGHT-IRON
SWORD REST

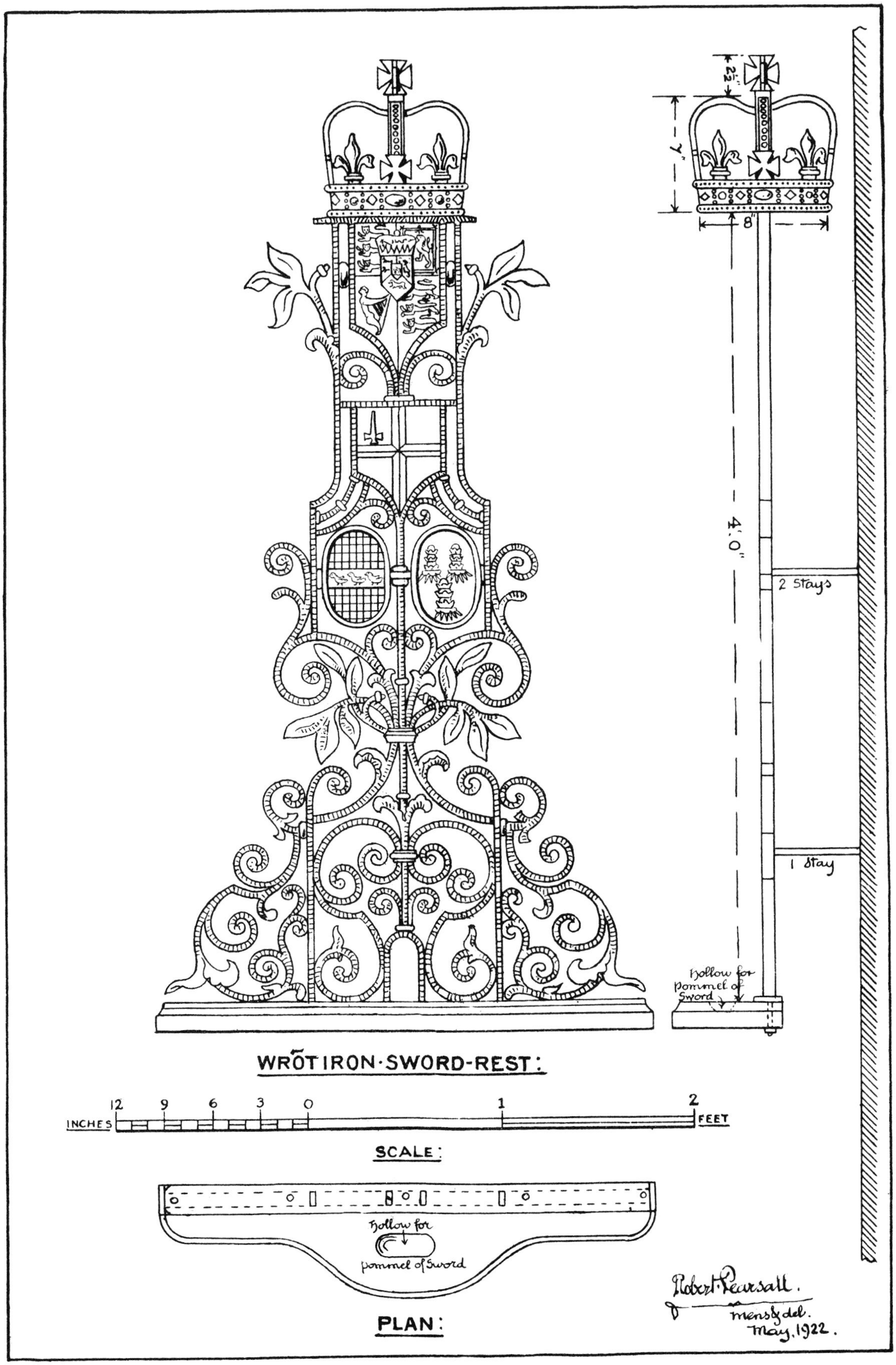
2½"
7"
8"
4'.0"
2 Stays
1 Stay
Hollow for pommel of Sword
WROT IRON·SWORD·REST:
12 9 6 3 0 1 2
INCHES
FEET
SCALE:
Hollow for pommel of Sword
PLAN:
Robert Pearsall.
mens & del.
May, 1922.

THE WOODEN SWORD REST

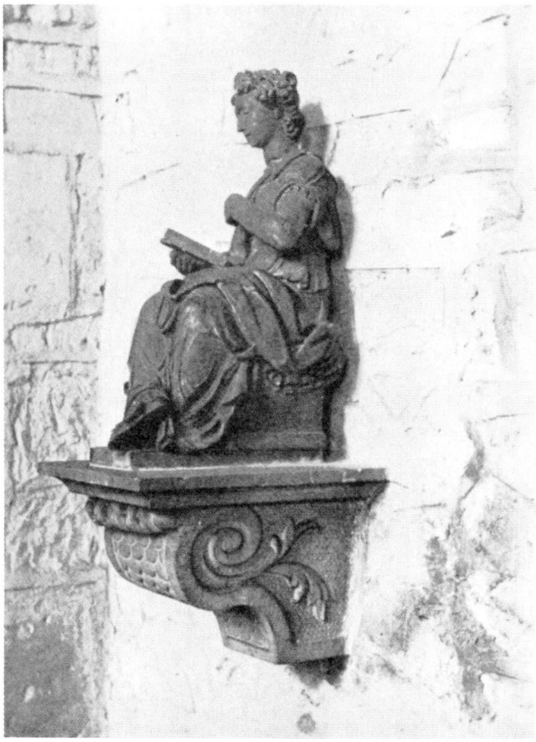

FIGURE IN LADY CHAPEL

STALLS FROM THE NUNS' QUIRE

MONUMENTS IN THE N.E. CORNER
OF THE NUNS' QUIRE

PLATE 62

SIR THOMAS GRESHAM, 1579

COAT OF ARMS, GRESHAM MONUMENT

TOMB of SIR THOMAS GRESHAM.

A.D. 1579.

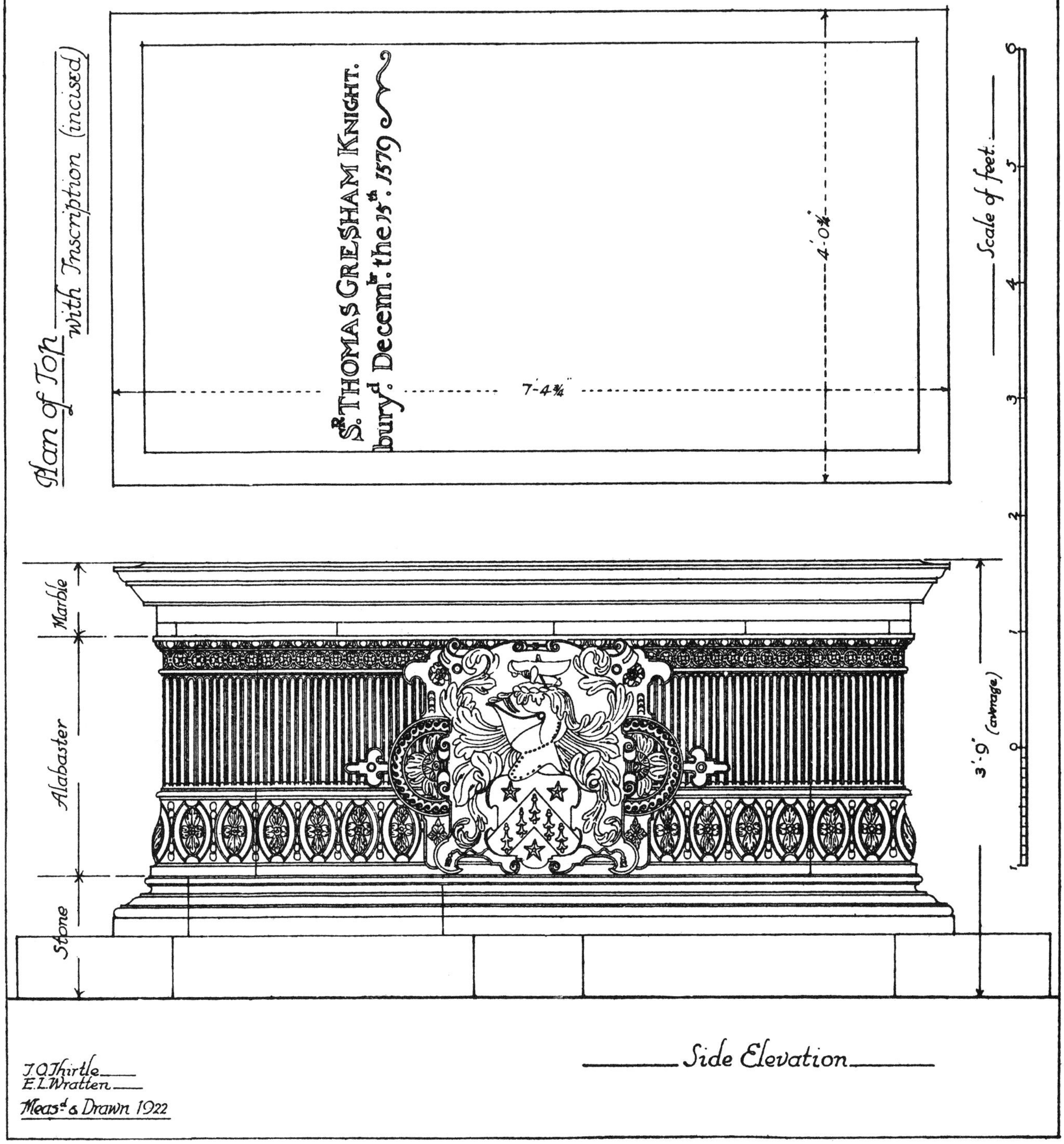
Plan of Top with Inscription (incised)
S^R. THOMAS GRESHAM KNIGHT.
bury^d. Decem^br. the 15th. 1579
4'-0¼"
7'-4¾"
Scale of feet.
Marble
Alabaster
Stone
3'-9" (average)
Side Elevation
J.O. Thirtle
E.L. Wratten
Meas^d & Drawn 1922

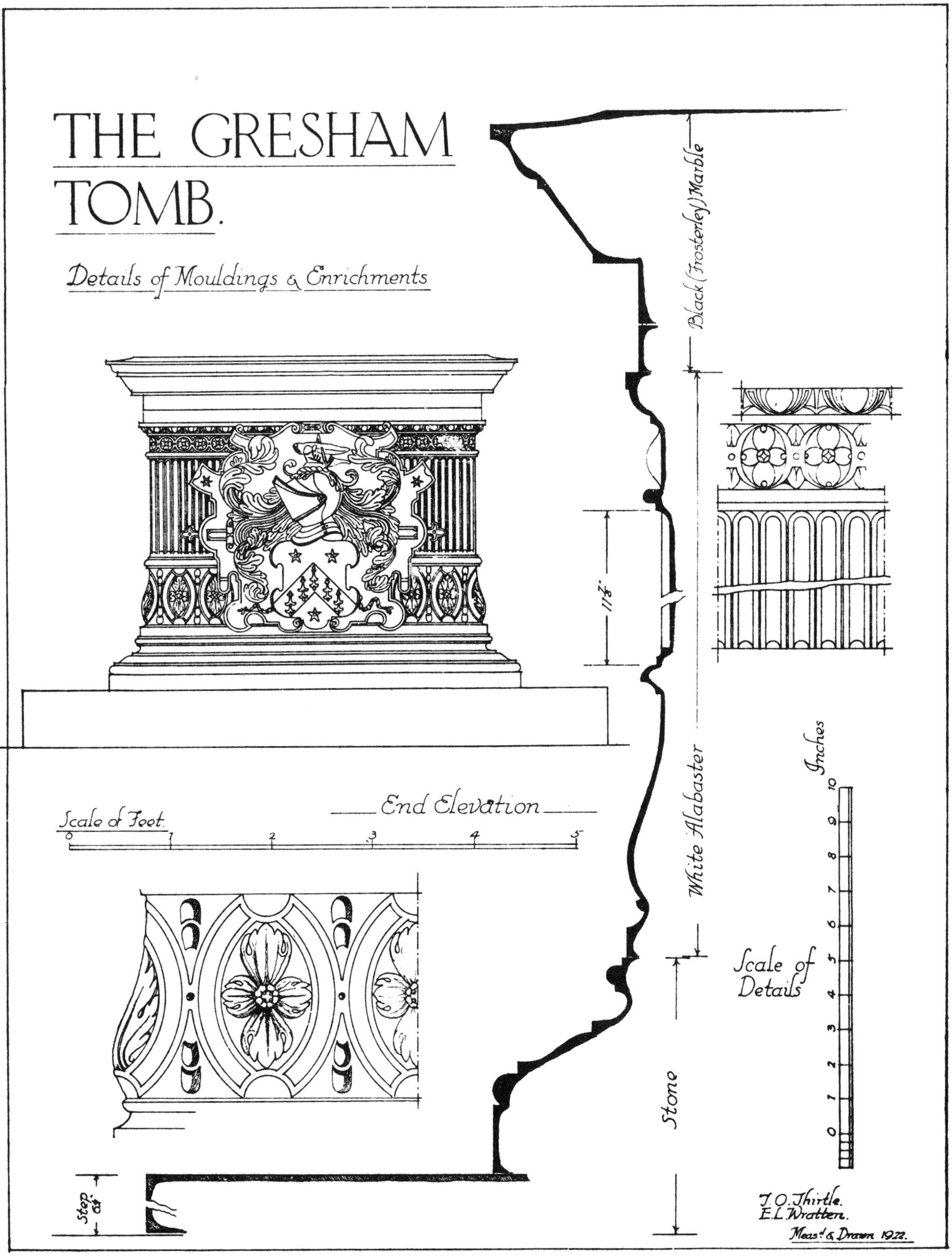
THE GRESHAM TOMB.
Details of Mouldings & Enrichments
End Elevation
Scale of Feet
0 1 2 3 4 5
Black (Frosterley) Marble
White Alabaster
Stone
11⅞"
Step 6¾"
Inches
Scale of Details
0 1 2 3 4 5 6 7 8 9 10
J. O. Thirtle.
E. L. Wratten.
Meas^d & Drawn 1922.

WILLIAM FINCH, 1672

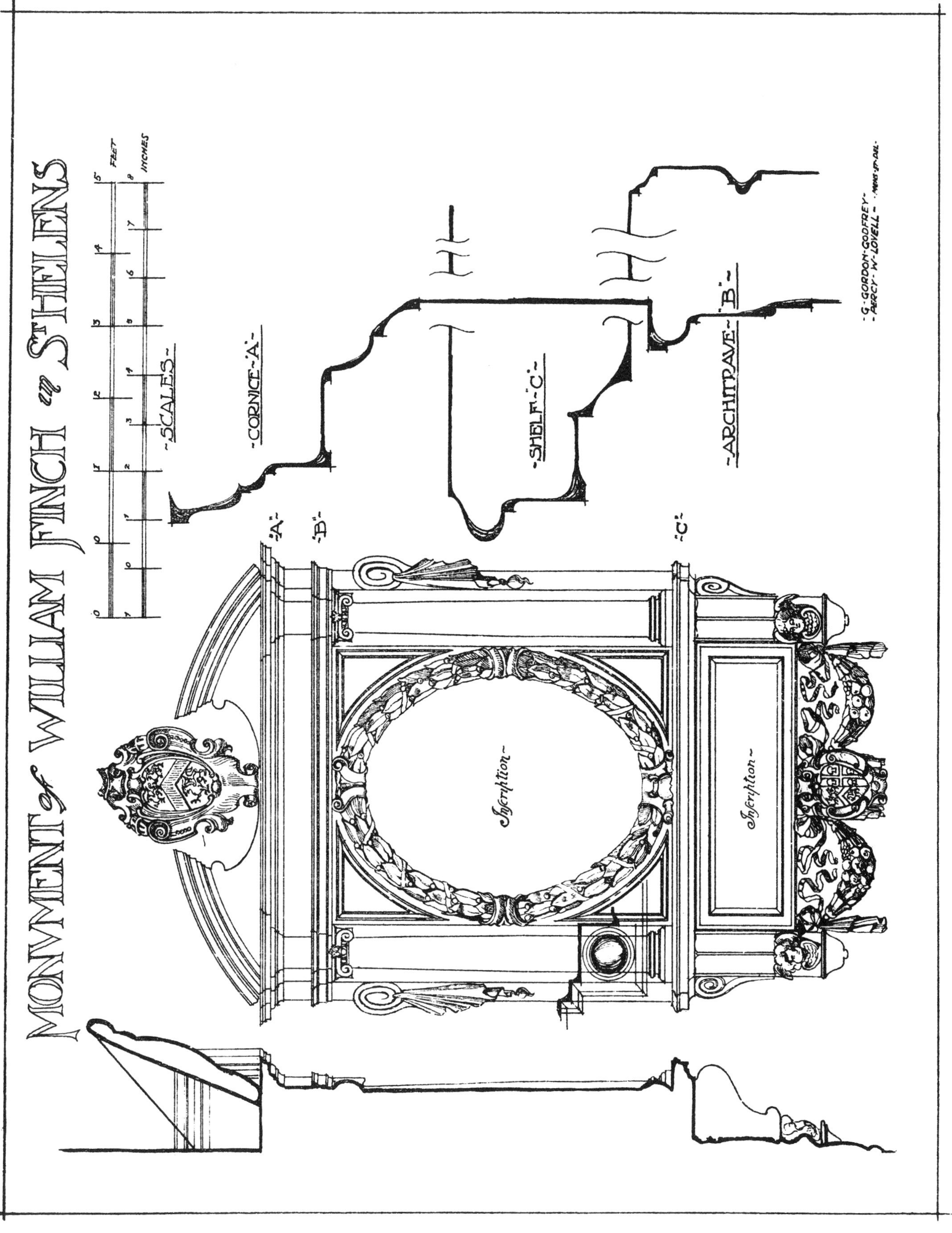
MONVMENT of WILLIAM FINCH in St HELENS
-SCALES-
FEET
INCHES
-CORNICE-'A'-
-SHELF-'C'-
-ARCHITRAVE-'B'-
'A'
'B'
'C'
Inscription
Inscription
-G. GORDON-GODFREY-
-PERCY-W-LOVELL-
MENS ET DEL

S. HELENS, BISHOPSGATE.
NUNS' SQUINT & EASTER TABERNACLE.

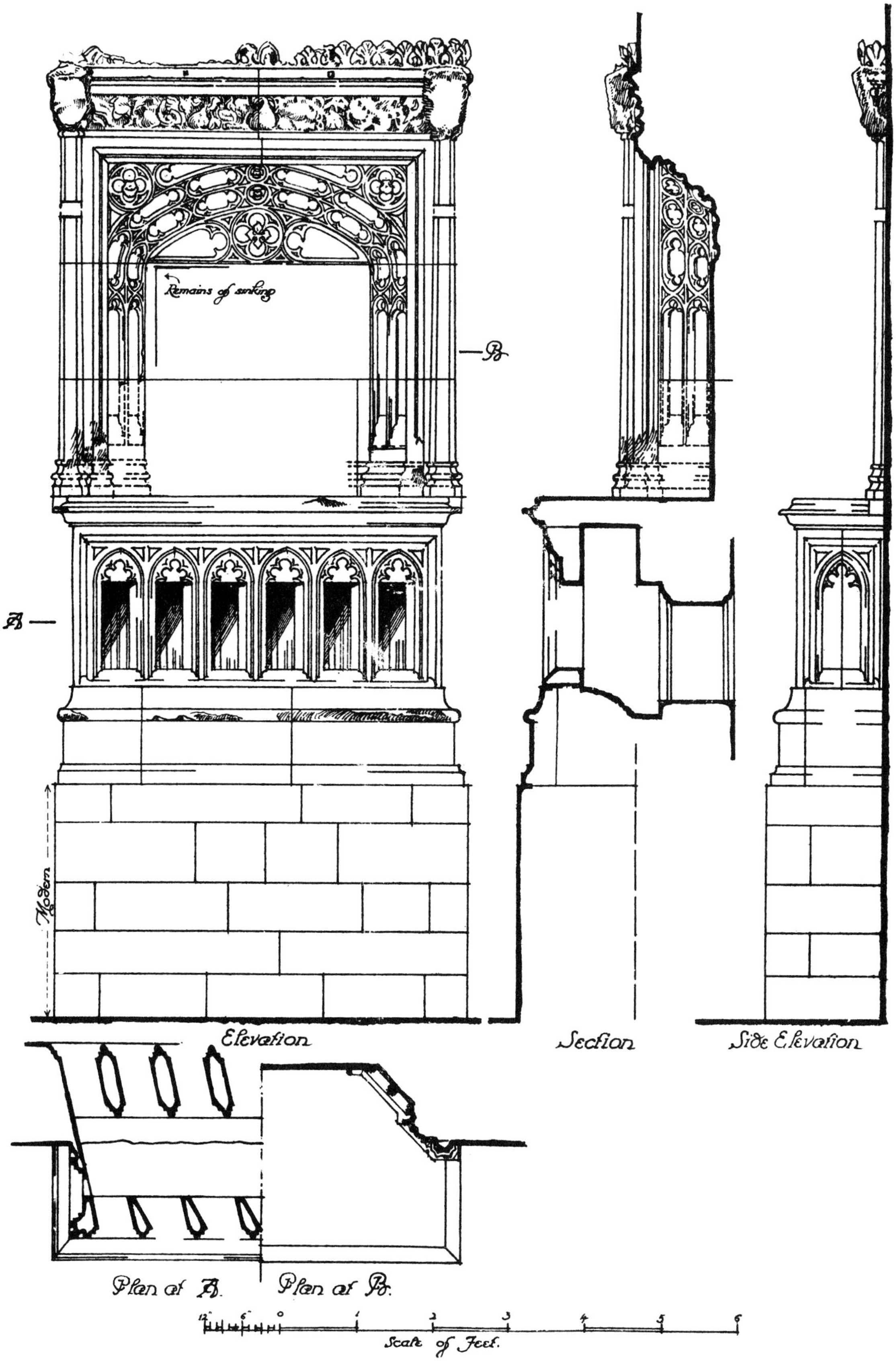
Remains of sinking
B
A
Modern
Elevation
Section
Side Elevation
Plan at A.
Plan at B.
12 6 0 1 2 3 4 5 6
Scale of Feet.

JOHANE ALFREY, 1525.

WILLIAM BOND, 1576

THE WILLIAM BOND MONUMENT
ST. HELEN'S CHURCH BISHOPSGATE

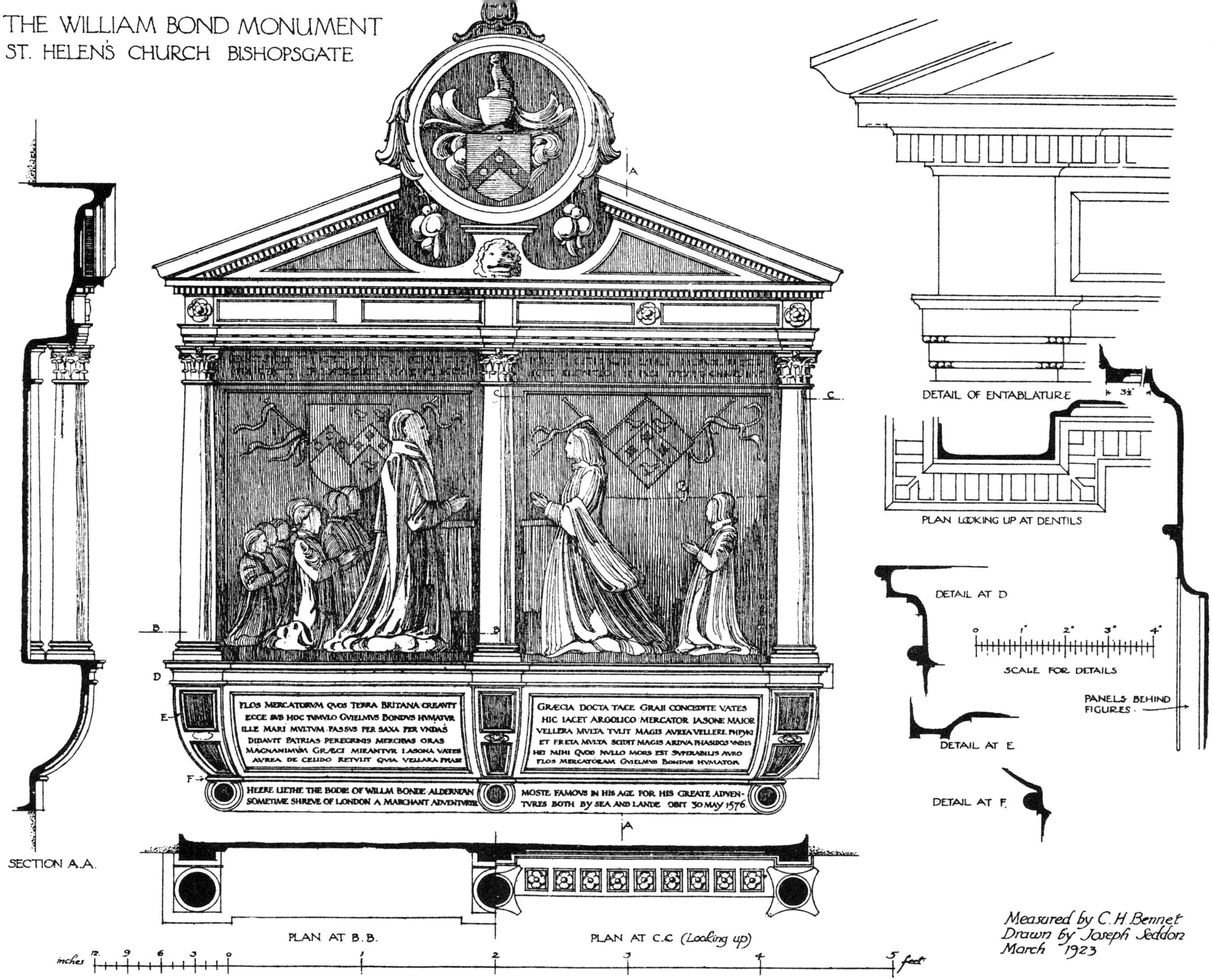
SECTION A.A.
DETAIL OF ENTABLATURE
PLAN LOOKING UP AT DENTILS
DETAIL AT D
SCALE FOR DETAILS
PANELS BEHIND FIGURES
DETAIL AT E
DETAIL AT F
FLOS MERCATORVM QVOS TERRA BRITANA CREAVIT
ECCE SVB HOC TVMVLO GVIELMVS BONDVS HVMATVR
ILLE MARI MVLTVM PASSVS PER SAXA PER VNDAS
DIDAVIT PATRIAS PEREGRINIS MERCIBAS ORAS
MAGNANIMVM GRÆCI MIRANTVR IASONA VATES
AVREA DE CELIDO RETVLIT QVIA VELLARA PHASI
GRÆCIA DOCTA TACE GRAII CONCEDITE VATES
HIC IACET ARGOLICO MERCATOR IASONE MAIOR
VELLERA MVLTA TVLIT MAGIS AVREA VELLERE PHRYXI
ET FRETA MVLTA SCIDIT MAGIS ARDVA PHASIDOS VNDIS
HEI MIHI QVOD NVLLO MORS EST SVPERABILIS AVRO
FLOS MERCATORAM GVIELMVS BONDVS HVMATOR
HEERE LIETHE THE BODIE OF WILLM BONDE ALDERMAN SOMETIME SHREVE OF LONDON A MARCHANT ADVENTVRER
MOSTE FAMOVS IN HIS AGE FOR HIS GREATE ADVENTVRES BOTH BY SEA AND LANDE OBIT 30 MAY 1576
PLAN AT B.B.
PLAN AT C.C (Looking up)
inches
feet

Measured by C. H. Bennet
Drawn by Joseph Seddon
March 1923

PETER GAUSSEN ESQ.
HE CLOSED A LIFE OF BENEVOLENCE
BY A DEATH OF PATIENCE AND RESIGNATION

PETER GAUSSEN, 1788

MEMORIÆ SACRVM

MARTIN BOND, 1643

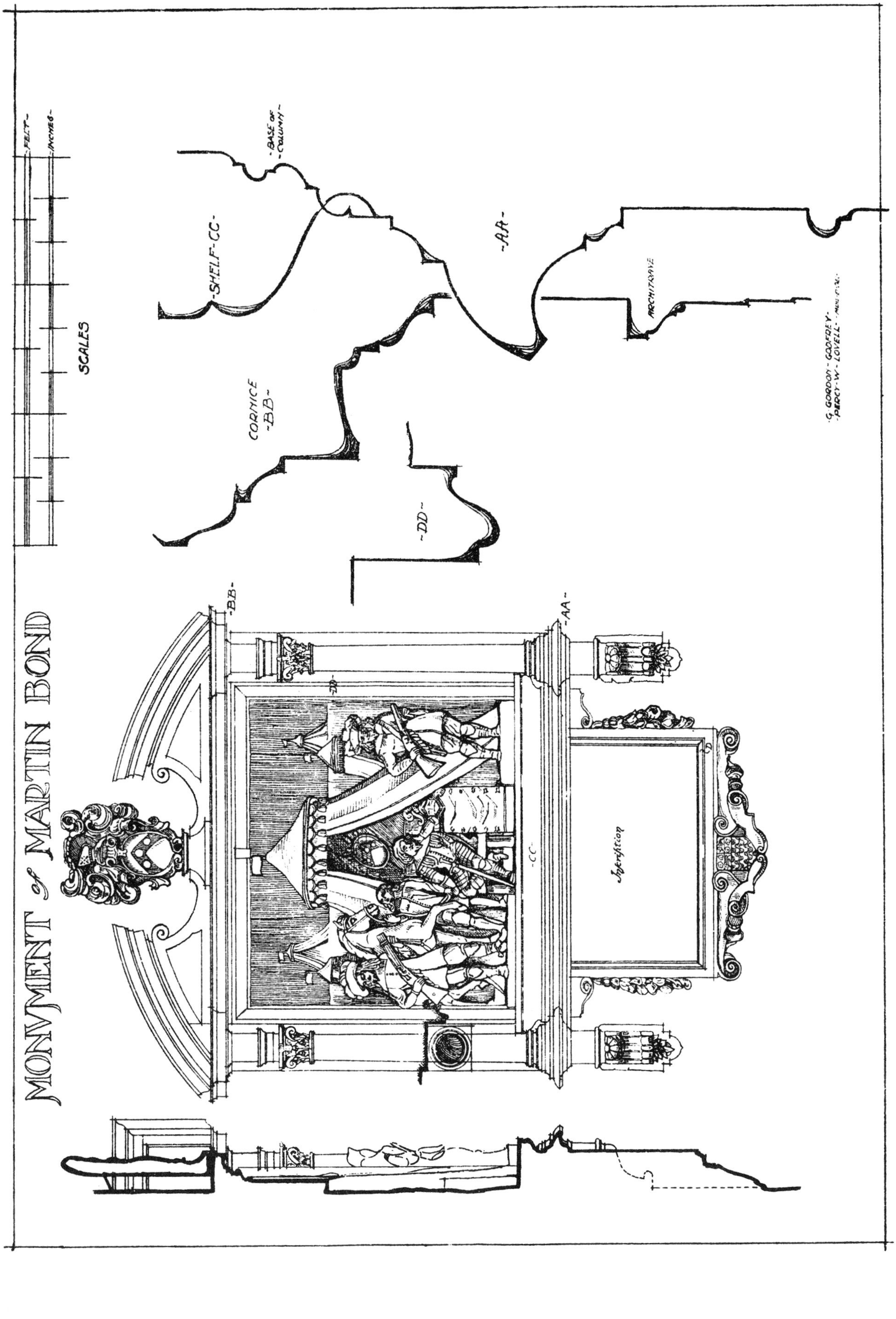
MONVMENT of MARTIN BOND
SCALES
FEET
INCHES
SHELF-CC
BASE OF COLUMN
AA
ARCHITRAVE
CORNICE BB
DD
BB
AA
CC
Inscription
G. GORDON GODFREY
PERCY W. LOVELL

I shall see God in my flesh.
Neere vnto this place lyeth buryed
the body of Valentine Mortoft Esq
haveing lived comfortably wth two
wives; the first Ellen Glover, by
whome hee had William, who was a
liveing at his death. His second wife
Margaret Eldest daughter of Sir
Hugh Hamersly Kt & Alderman of
London, by her hee had issue four
Sons, and three daughters of wch
hee left living one Son &
one Daughter.
Hee finished the course of 68 yeares
and yeilded vp his spirit to God Sept
16. 1641. Bequeathing his body to ye

VALENTINE MORTOFT, 1641

- INSCRIPTION -
- INSCRIPTION -
- ELEVATION -
SECTION -
2
1
0
3
6
9
1
FEET

VALENTINE MORTOFT, 1641.

ARMS FROM THE BANCROFT MONUMENT, 1727

HUGH PEMBERTON, 1500

PLATE 78

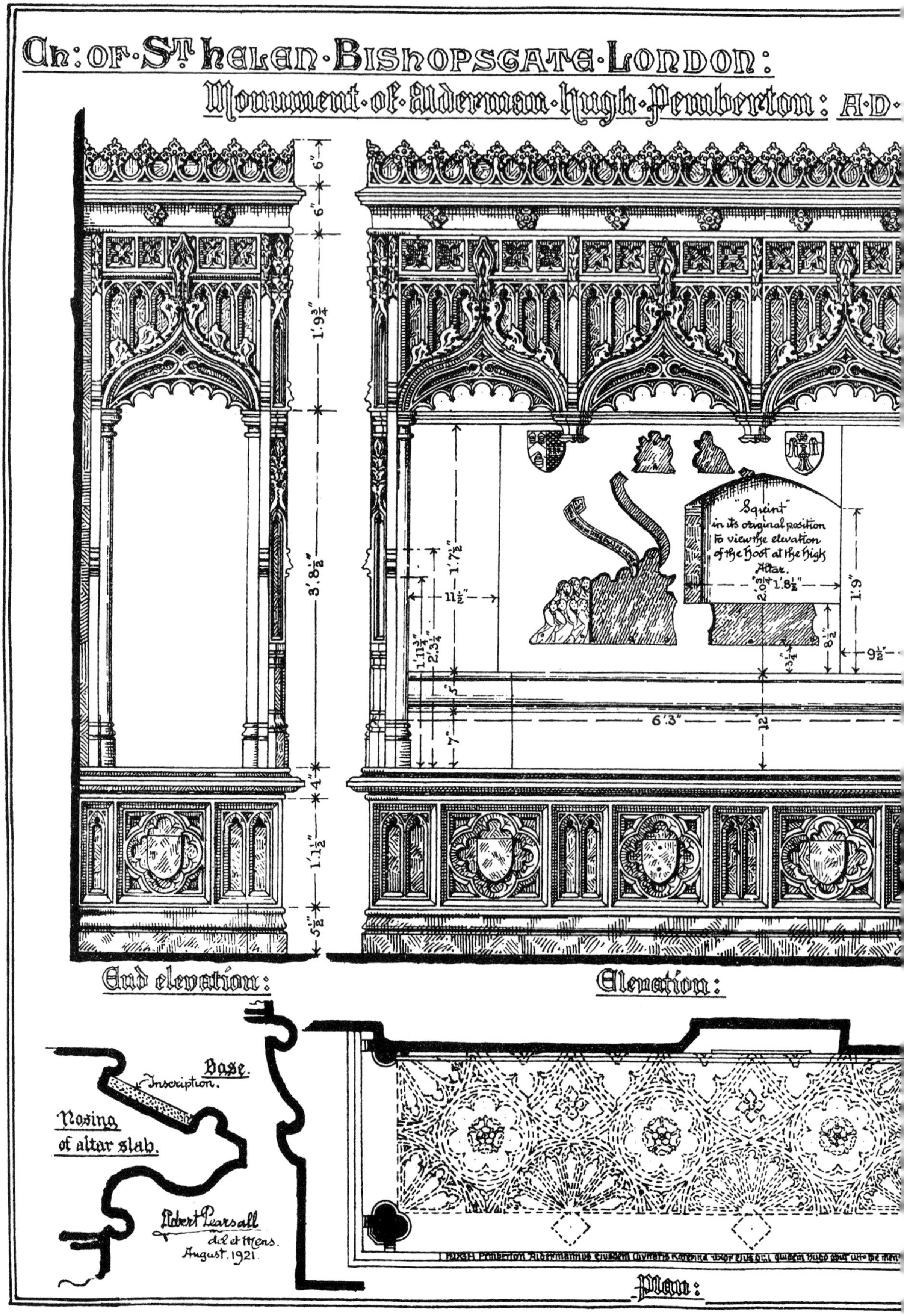
Ch: of St Helen·Bishopsgate·London:
Monument·of·Alderman·Hugh·Pemberton: A·D·
6"
6"
1'9¾"
3'8½"
4"
1'1½"
5½"
1'7½"
11½"
1'11¾"
2'3¾"
5"
7"
6'3"
12"
"Squint" in its original position to view the elevation of the Host at the High Altar.
1'8½"
1'9"
8½"
9½"
End elevation:
Elevation:
Base.
Inscription.
Nosing of altar slab.
Robert Pearsall del et mens. August. 1921.
Plan:

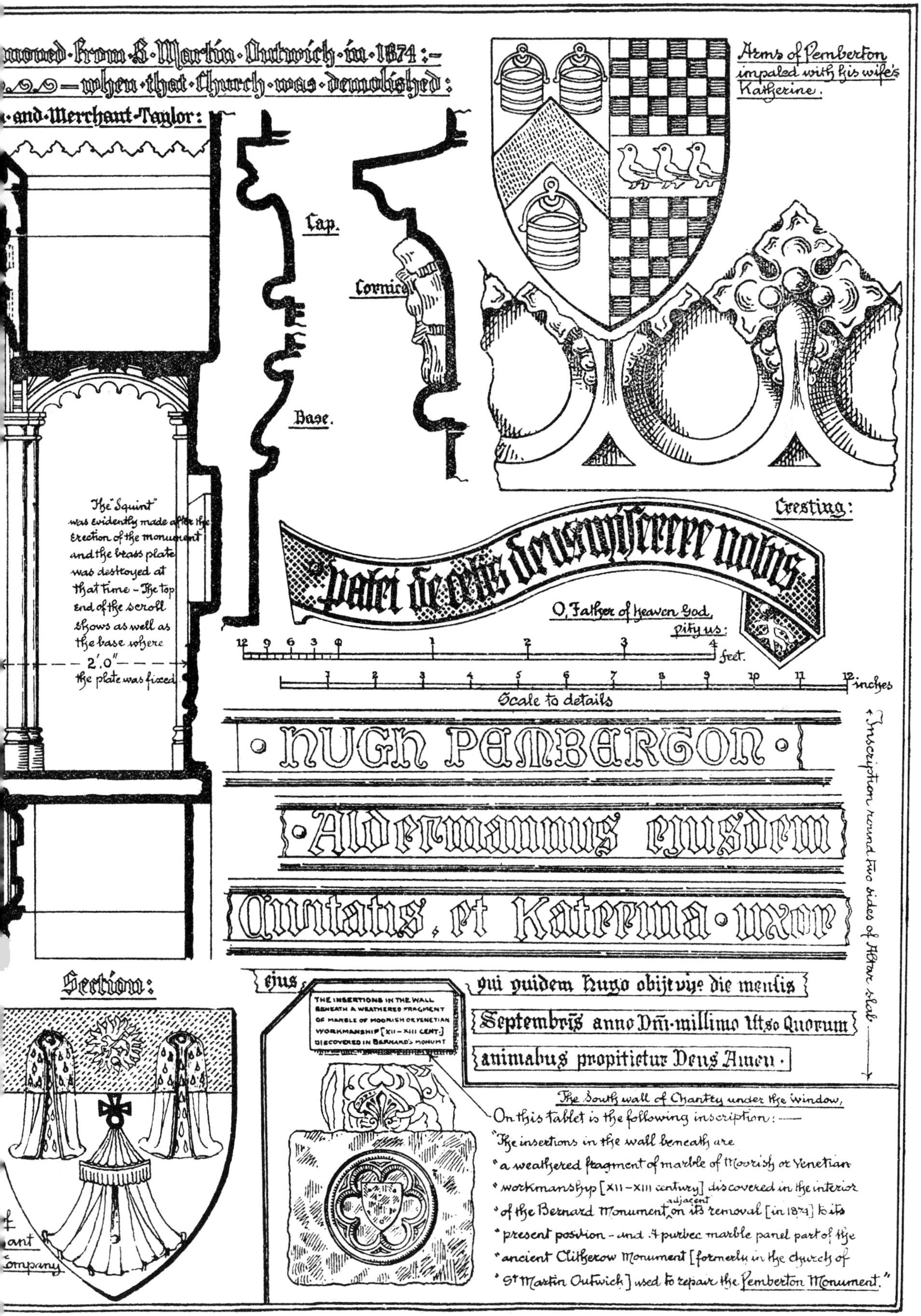

...moved · from · S · Martin · Outwich · in · 1874 :–
— when · that · Church · was · demolished :
... and · Merchant · Taylor :
Arms of Pemberton impaled with his wife's Katherine.
Cap.
Cornice
Base.
The "Squint" was evidently made after the erection of the monument and the brass plate was destroyed at that time – The top end of the scroll shows as well as the base where the plate was fixed.
2'.0"
Cresting:
pater de celis deus miserere nobis
O, Father of heaven God, pity us:
12 9 6 3 0 1 2 3 4 feet.
1 2 3 4 5 6 7 8 9 10 11 12 inches
Scale to details
· HUGH PEMBERTON ·
· Aldermannus ejusdem
Civitatis, et Katerina · uxor
ejus
qui quidem Hugo obijt viij° die mensis
Septembris anno Dñi millimo ...
animabus propitietur Deus Amen ·
Inscription round two sides of Altar slab
Section:
THE INSERTIONS IN THE WALL BENEATH A WEATHERED FRAGMENT OF MARBLE OF MOORISH OR VENETIAN WORKMANSHIP [XII – XIII CENT.] DISCOVERED IN BERNARD'S MONUMT
The South wall of Chantry under the window.
On this tablet is the following inscription:—
"The insertions in the wall beneath are
" a weathered fragment of marble of Moorish or Venetian
" workmanship [XII – XIII century] discovered in the interior
" of the Bernard Monument, on its adjacent removal [in 1874] to its
" present position – and A purbec marble panel part of the
" ancient Clitherow Monument [formerly in the church of
" St Martin Outwich] used to repair the Pemberton Monument."
...ant
Company

JOHN ROBINSON, 1599

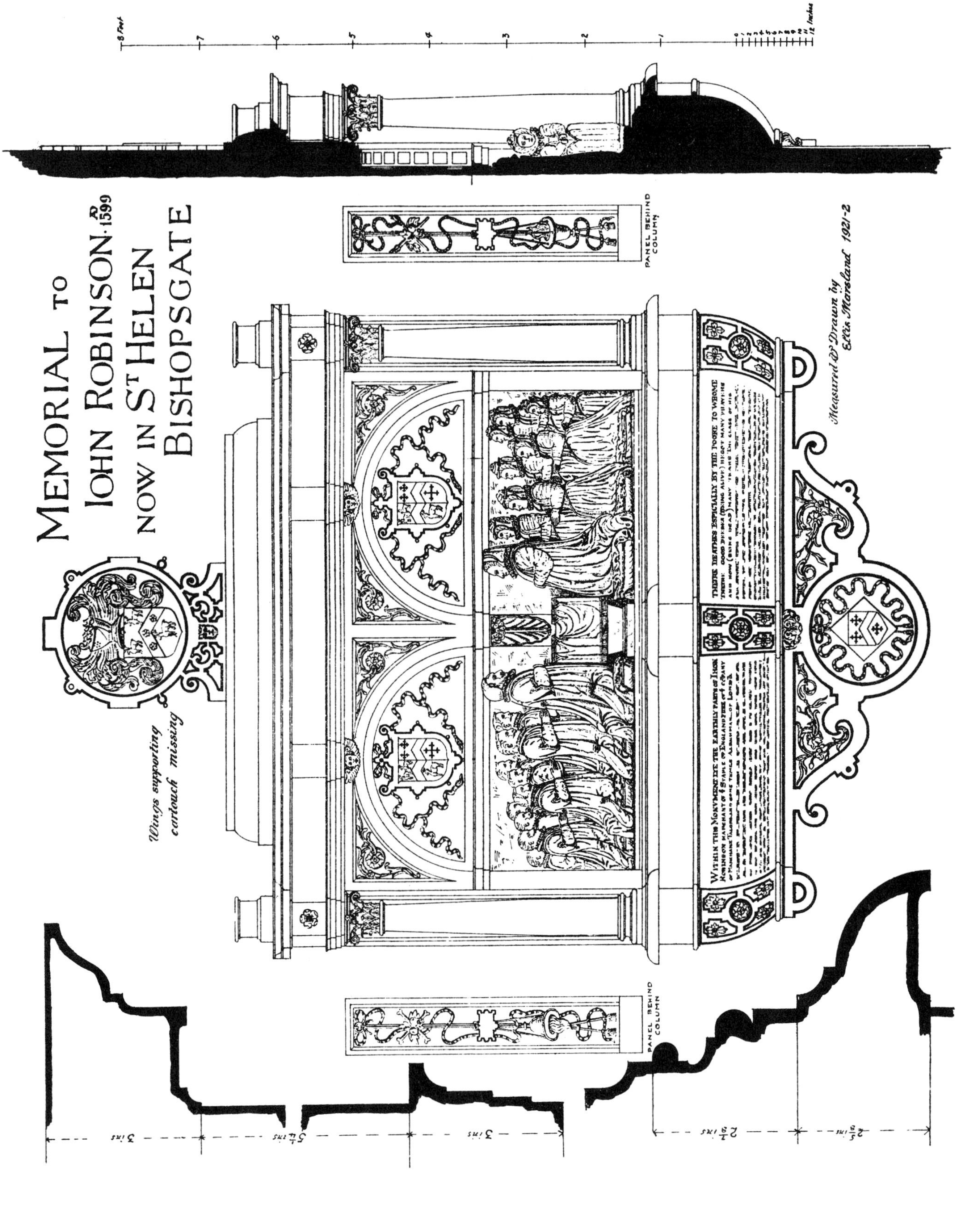
MEMORIAL TO
IOHN ROBINSON · Ob 1599
NOW IN St HELEN
BISHOPSGATE
Wings supporting cartouch missing
PANEL BEHIND COLUMN
PANEL BEHIND COLUMN
Measured & Drawn by Ellis Moreland 1921-2
8 Feet
7
6
5
4
3
2
1
12 Inches
3 ins
3 ins

SIR ANDREW JUDD, 1558

MONVMENT of SIR ANDREW JVDD
Ins 6 0 1 2 3 4 Feet.
Scale
TO RVSSIA AND MVSCOVIA
TO SPAYNE GINNY WITHOVTE FABLE
TRAVELD HE BY LAND AND SEA
BOTHE MAYRE OF LONDON AND STAPLE
THE COMMONWELTHE HE NORISHTE
SO WORTHILIE IN ALL HIS DAIES
THAT THE STATE FVLLWELL HIM LOVED
TO HIS PERPETVALL PRAYSE
THREE WYVES HE HAD ONE WAS MARY
FOWER SVNES ONE MAYDE HAD HE BY HER
ANNYS HAD NONE BY HIM TRVLY
BY DAME MARY HAD ONE DOWGHTIER
THVS IN THE MONTH OF SEPTEMBER
A THOWSAND FYVE HVNDERD FYFTEY
AND EYGHT DIED THIS WORTHIE STAPLAR
WORSHIPYNGE HIS POSTERYTYE
SR ANDREW JUDD KNT
Figures Omitted
Elevation
Section
Figures Omitted
Panel below
Bracket
Plan
T. Frank Green
mens et delt.

PLATE 83

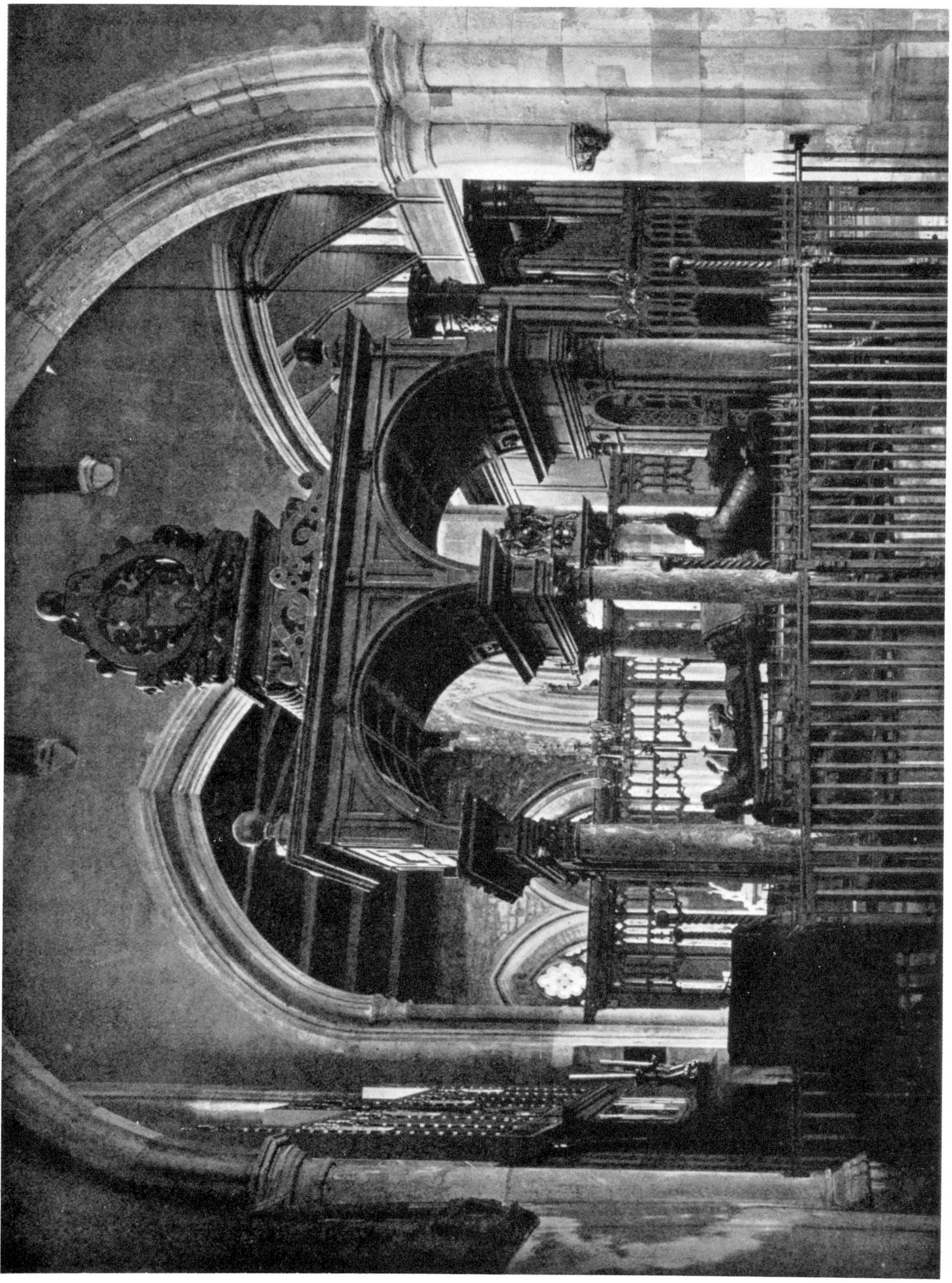

THE PICKERING MONUMENT

PLATE 84

THE PICKERING MONUMENT

FEET
INCHES
MOLDINGS
SCALES
CORNICE AT "A"
CORNICE AT "B"
EGG AND TONGUE
DENTILS
"C" BASE OF COLUMNS
"E"
"A"
"B"
"C"
"D"
"F"
PEDESTAL "D"
14½"
BASE OF CARTOUCHE "E"
BASE OF SARCOPHAGUS - "F"
FIGURE OMITTED
END ELEVATION
- SIDE ELEVATION -
- SECTION -
PWL. 1923

THE PICKERING MONUMENT.

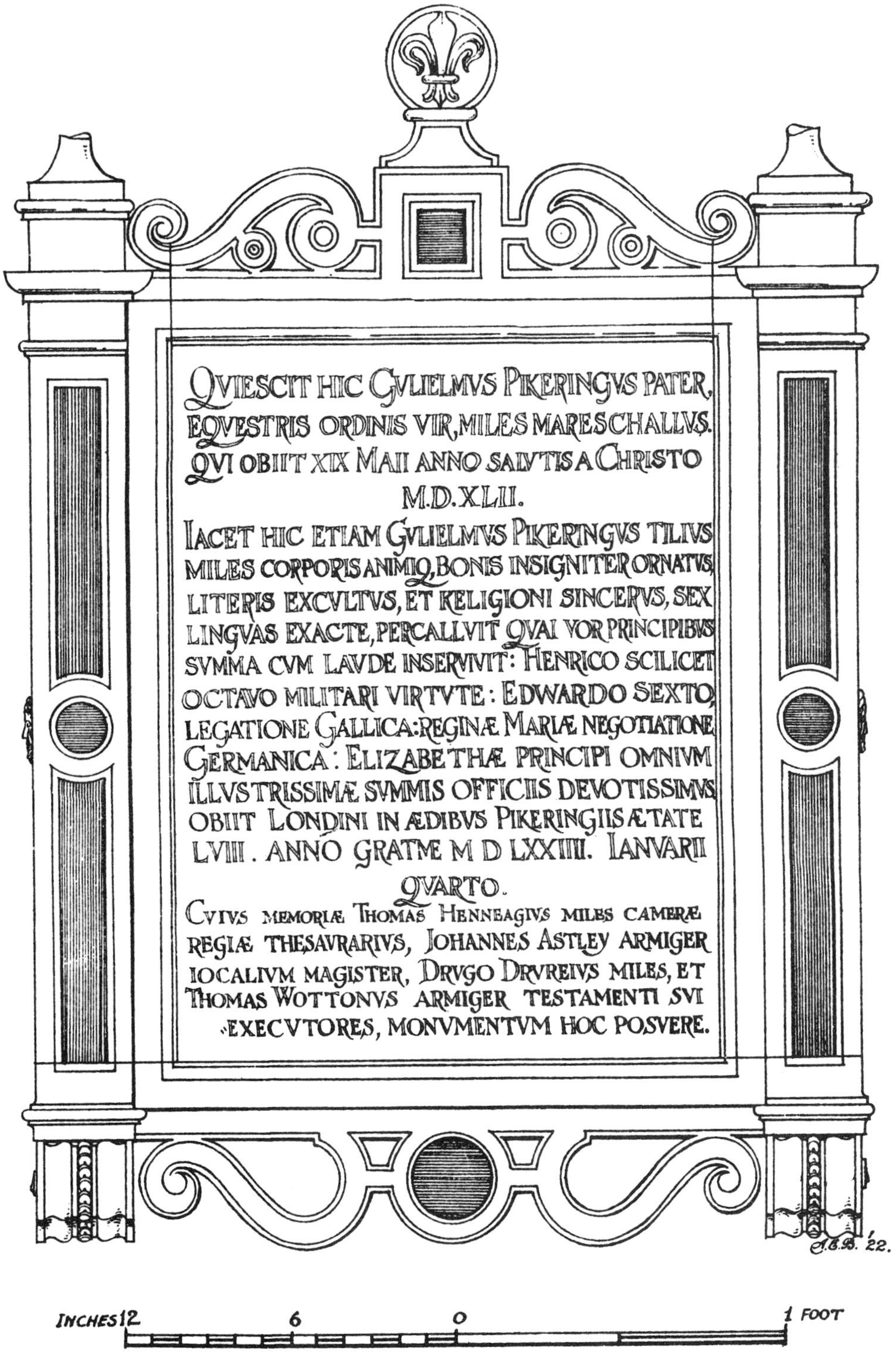
QVIESCIT HIC GVLIELMVS PIKERINGVS PATER,
EQVESTRIS ORDINIS VIR, MILES MARESCHALLVS.
QVI OBIIT XIX MAII ANNO SALVTIS A CHRISTO
M.D.XLII.
IACET HIC ETIAM GVLIELMVS PIKERINGVS TILIVS
MILES CORPORIS ANIMIQ, BONIS INSIGNITER ORNATVS,
LITERIS EXCVLTVS, ET KELIGIONI SINCERVS, SEX
LINGVAS EXACTE, PERCALLVIT QVAI VOR PRINCIPIBVS
SVMMA CVM LAVDE INSERVIVIT: HENRICO SCILICET
OCTAVO MILITARI VIRTVTE: EDWARDO SEXTO,
LEGATIONE GALLICA: REGINÆ MARIÆ NEGOTIATIONE
GERMANICA: ELIZABETHÆ PRINCIPI OMNIVM
ILLVSTRISSIMÆ SVMMIS OFFICIIS DEVOTISSIMVS
OBIIT LONDINI IN ÆDIBVS PIKERINGIIS ÆTATE
LVIII. ANNO GRATIÆ M D LXXIIII. IANVARII
QVARTO.
CVIVS MEMORIÆ THOMAS HENNEAGIVS MILES CAMERÆ
REGIÆ THESAVRARIVS, JOHANNES ASTLEY ARMIGER
IOCALIVM MAGISTER, DRVGO DRVREIVS MILES, ET
THOMAS WOTTONVS ARMIGER TESTAMENTI SVI
EXECVTORES, MONVMENTVM HOC POSVERE.
A.E.B. '22.
INCHES 12
6
0
1 FOOT

WILLIAM PICKERING, 1542, AND SIR WILLIAM PICKERING, 1574.

IOHANNES STANDISH
Rector de Therfeild in agro

JOHN STANDISH, 1686

PLATE 88

WILLIAM KIRWIN, 1594

PLATE 89

WILLIAM KIRWIN, 1594

SIR JOHN AND LADY CROSBY, 1476

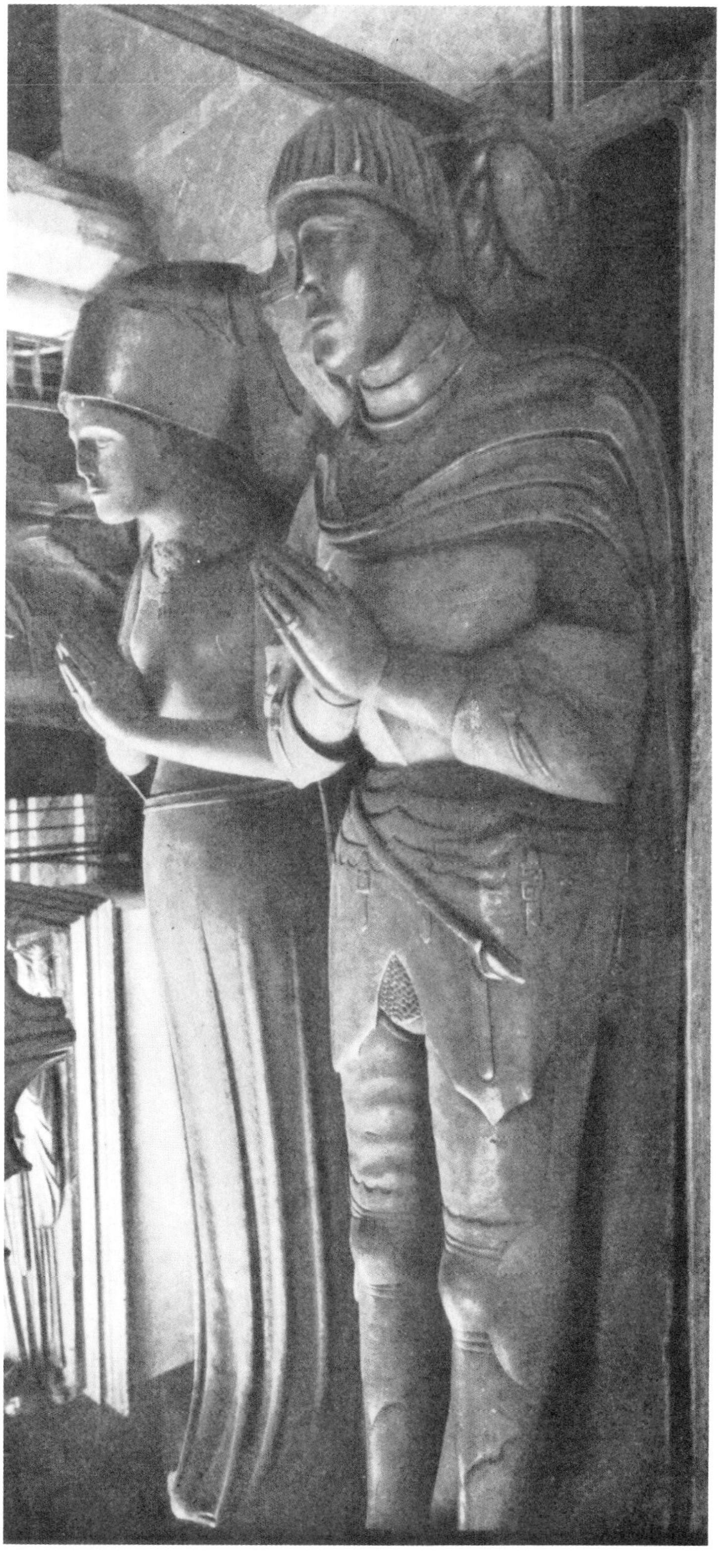

THE EFFIGIES OF
SIR JOHN AND LADY CROSBY, 1476

PLATE 92

TOMB OF SIR JOHN & LADY CROSBY

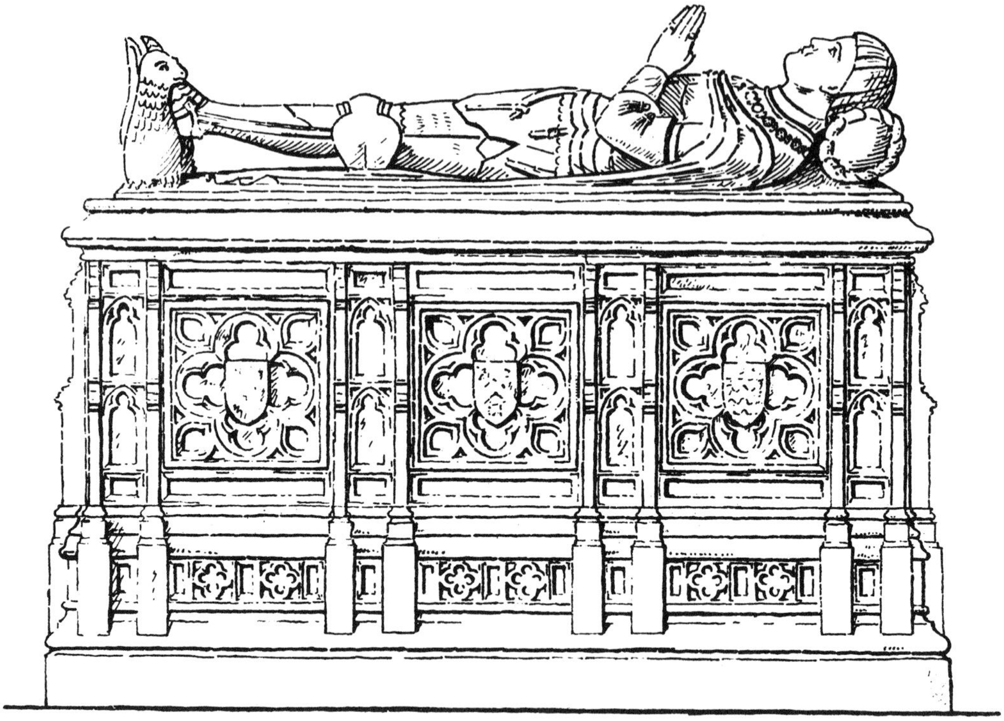

NORTH ELEVATION

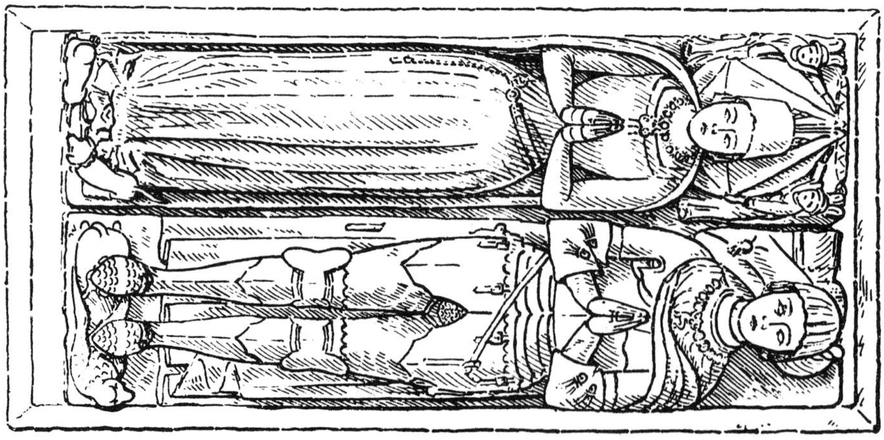

J.W. Bloe
1922

SCALE OF FEET

1
0
1
2
3
4
5
6

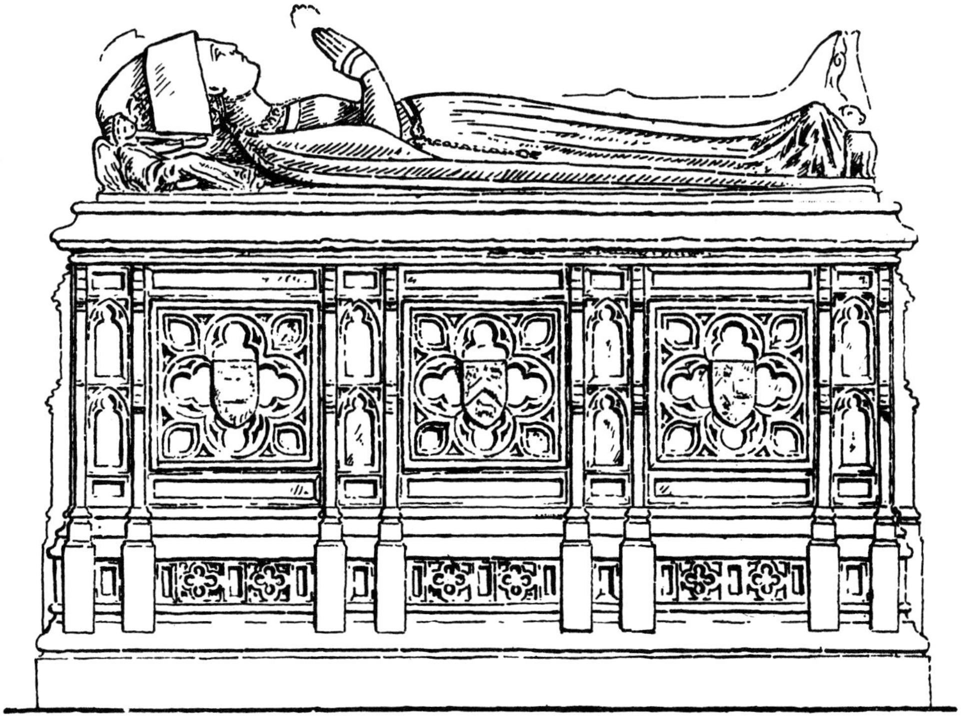

SOUTH ELEVATION

WEST ELEVATION

EAST ELEVATION

THE CROSBY MONUMENT, 1476

RICHARD STAPER, 1608

STAPER MONUMENT

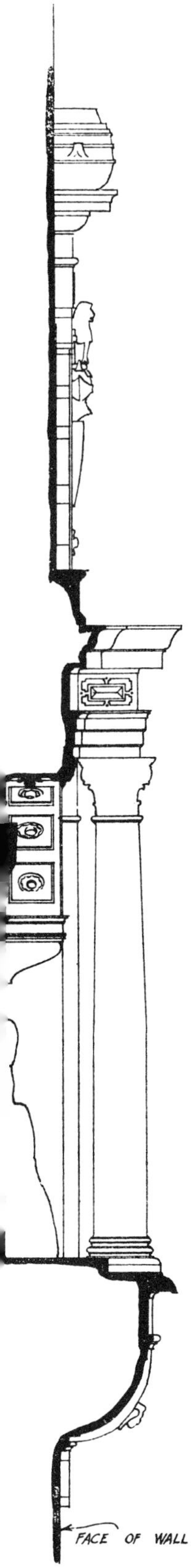
FACE OF WALL

SECTION

WOOD
WOOD
MISSING
MISSING
INSCRIPTION.
INSCRIPTION.

HERE RESTETH THE BODIE OF THE WORSHIPFVL RICHARD STAPER ELECTED ALDERMAN OF THIS CITTYE ANNO 1594. HEE WAS THE GREATEST MERCHANT IN HIS TYME, THE CHIEFEST ACTOR IN DISCOVERI OF THE TRADES OF TVRKEY AND EAST INDIA. A MAN HVMBLE IN PROSPERITY PAYNEFVL AND EVER READY IN THE AFFAYRES PVBLICQVE AND DISCREETELY CAREFVL OF HIS PRIVATE A LIBERAL HOWSEKEEPER, BOWNTIFVL TO THE POORE AN VPRIGHT DEALER IN WORLD AND A DIVOVT ASPIRER AFTER THE WORLD TO COME, MVCH BLEST IN HIS POSTERITY AND HAPPY IN HIS AND THEIR ALLYAVNCES. HE DYED THE LAST .IVNE ANNO DOMINE 1608

INTRAVIT VT EXIRIT.

PHILIP S HUDSON. 1923.
MENS ET DELT.

12 9 6 3 0 1 2 3 4 5 FEET

SCALE OF FEET

SIR JOHN SPENCER, 1609

PLATE 97

EFFIGIES ON THE SPENCER MONUMENT, 1609

HIC SITVS EST IOANNES SPENCER
EQVES, AVRATVS, CIVIS & SENATOR
LONDINENSIS, EIVSDEMQ CIVITATIS
PRÆTOR ANNO DÑI MDXCIIII
EX ALICIA BROMFELDIA
VNICAM RELIQVIT FILIAM
ETH GVILIELMO BARONI
ENVITAM OBIIT 3^c
SALVTIS MDCIX
SOCERO BENE MERITO
GVILIELMVS BARO COMPTON
GENER POSVIT
Measured by P. S. Hudson
Drawn by P. K. Kipps
SCALE OF FEET
12 ins 6 0 1 2 3 4 5 6 7 8 9 10

SIR JOHN SPENCER, 1609.

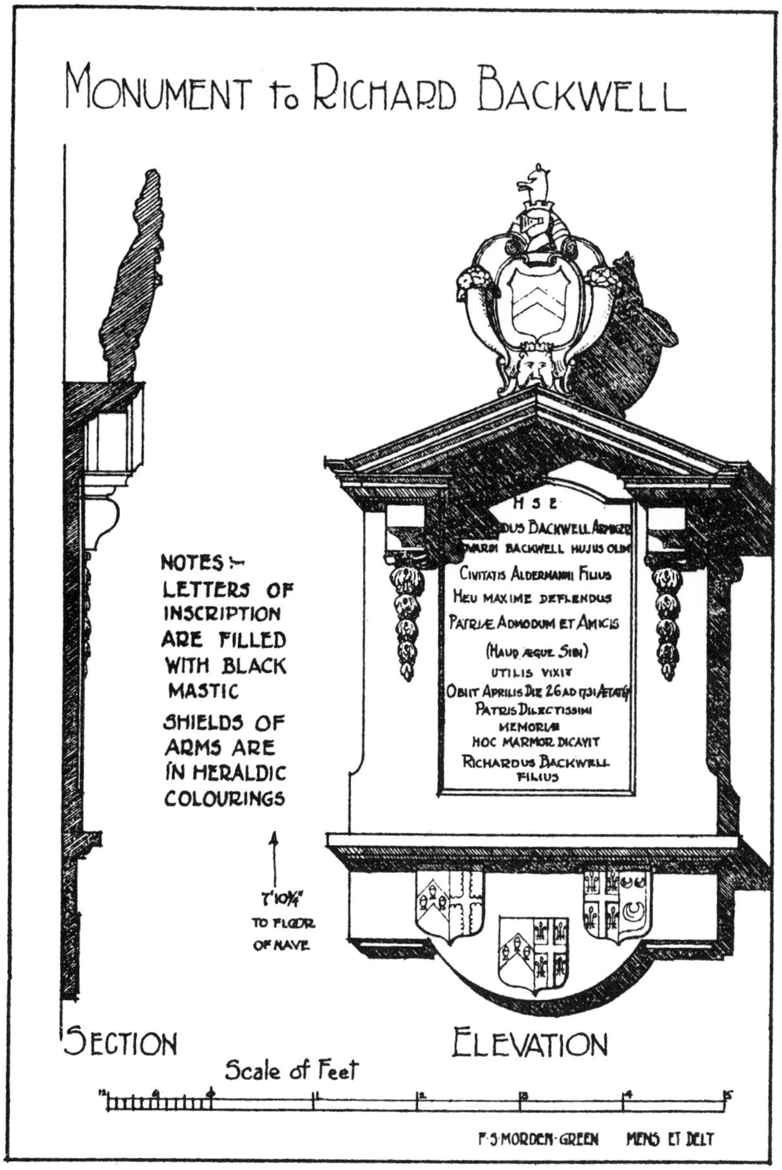
MONUMENT to RICHARD BACKWELL
NOTES:-
LETTERS OF INSCRIPTION ARE FILLED WITH BLACK MASTIC
SHIELDS OF ARMS ARE IN HERALDIC COLOURINGS
7'10¾" TO FLOOR OF NAVE
H S E
...DUS BACKWELL ARMIGER
...WARDI BACKWELL HUJUS OLIM
CIVITATIS ALDERMANNI FILIUS
HEU MAXIME DEFLENDUS
PATRIÆ ADMODUM ET AMICIS
(HAUD ÆQUE SIBI)
UTILIS VIXIT
OBIIT APRILIS DIE 26 AD 1731 ÆTATIS
PATRIS DILECTISSIMI
MEMORIÆ
HOC MARMOR DICAVIT
RICHARDUS BACKWELL
FILIUS
SECTION
ELEVATION
Scale of Feet
F·S·MORDEN·GREEN MENS ET DELT

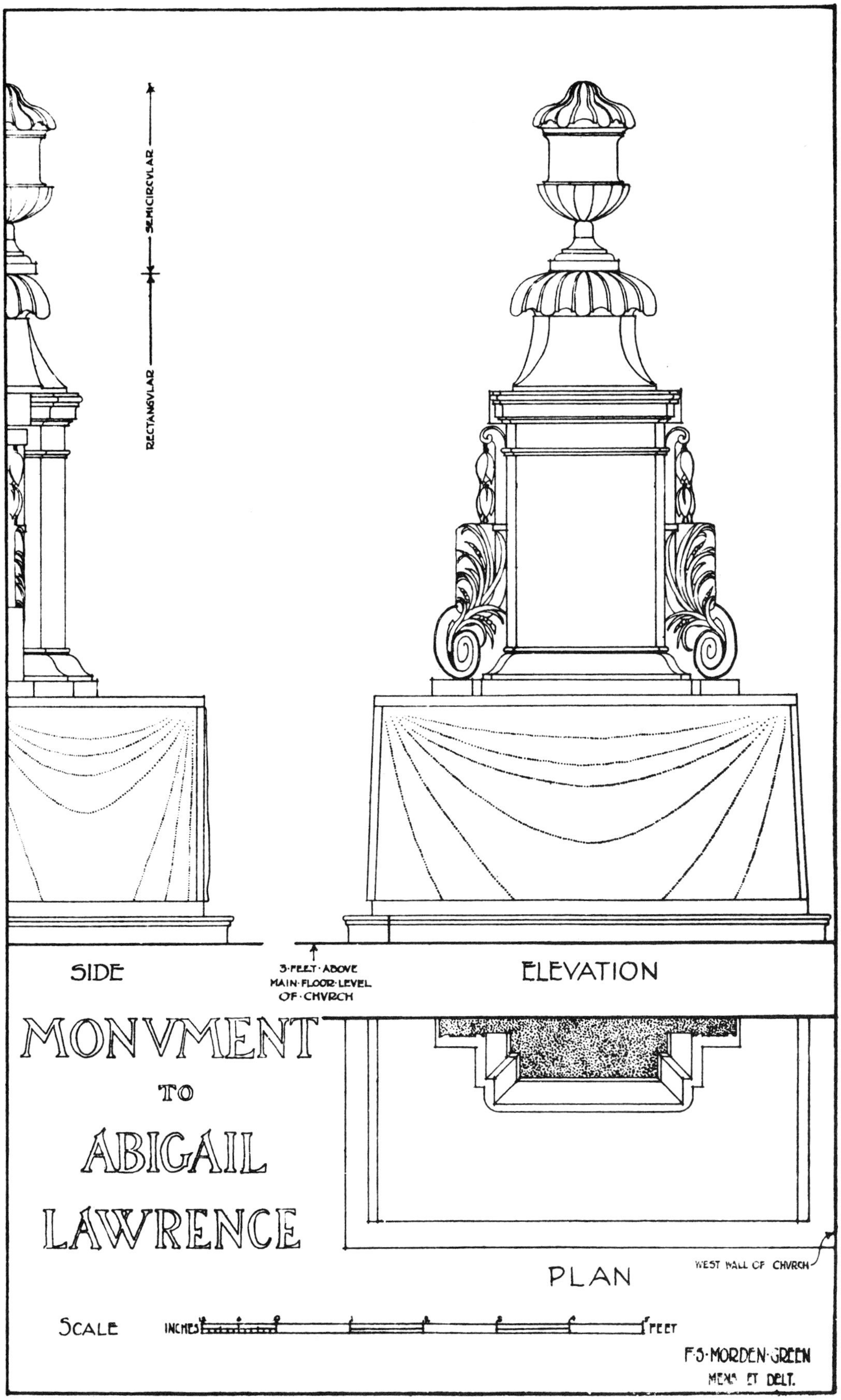
SEMICIRCVLAR
RECTANGVLAR
SIDE
3·FEET·ABOVE
MAIN·FLOOR·LEVEL
OF·CHVRCH
ELEVATION
MONVMENT
TO
ABIGAIL
LAWRENCE
PLAN
WEST WALL OF CHVRCH
SCALE
INCHES
FEET
F·S·MORDEN·GREEN
MENS ET DELT.

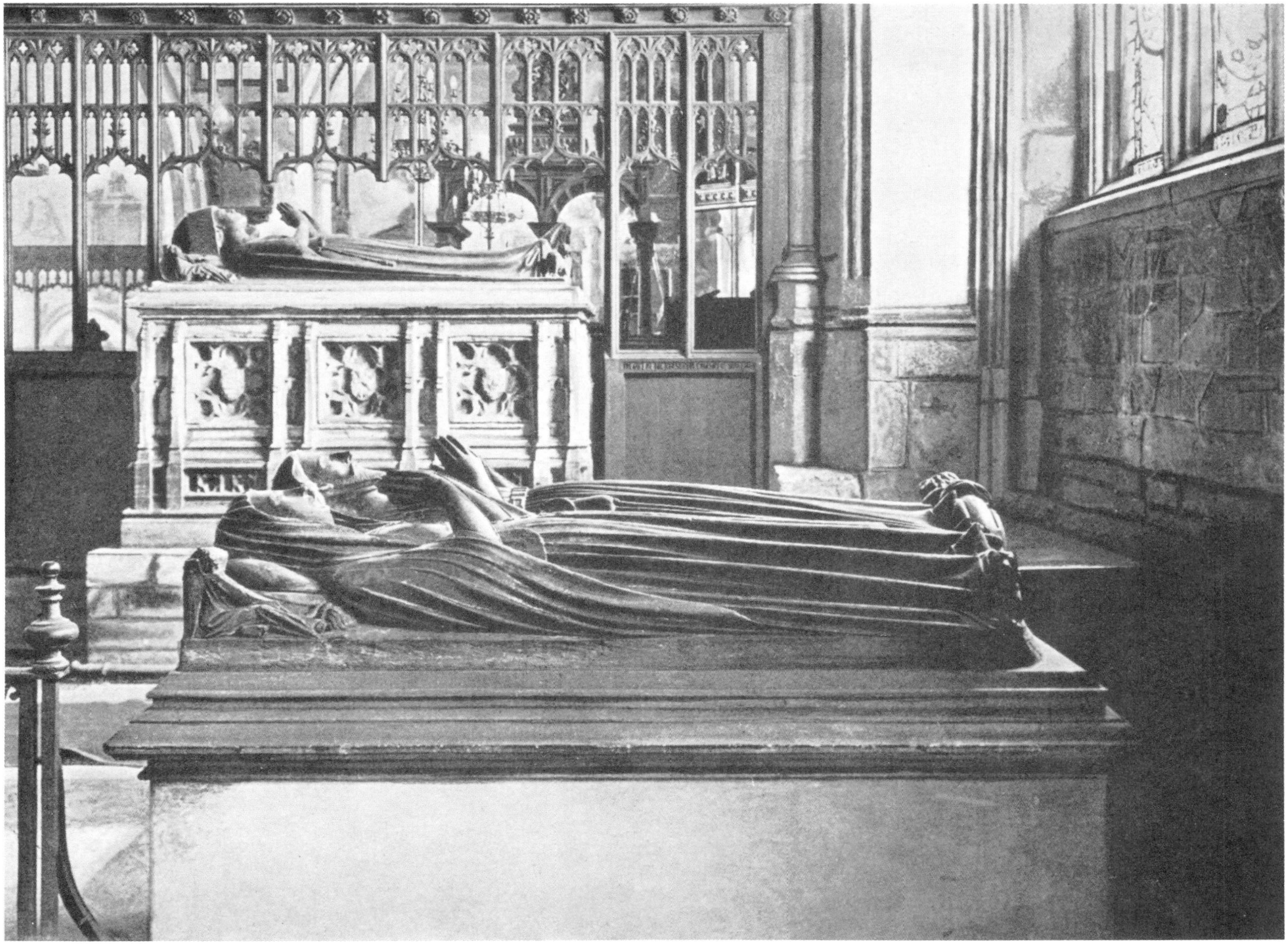

JOHN OTESWICH AND HIS WIFE, LATE 14TH CENTURY

PLATE 102

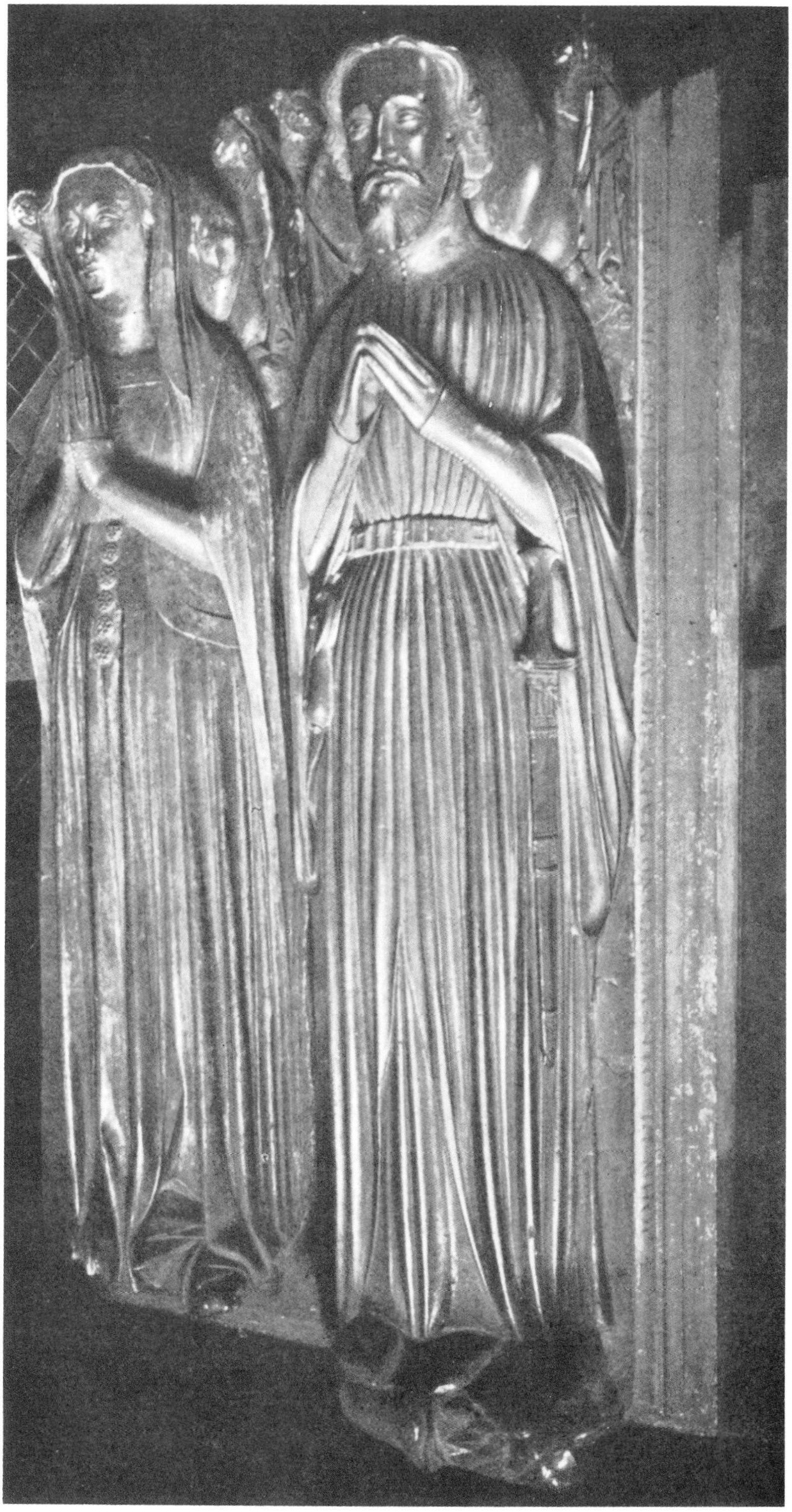

EFFIGIES OF JOHN OTESWICH AND HIS WIFE

PLATE 103

EFFIGIES OF JOHN DE OTESWYCH & MA

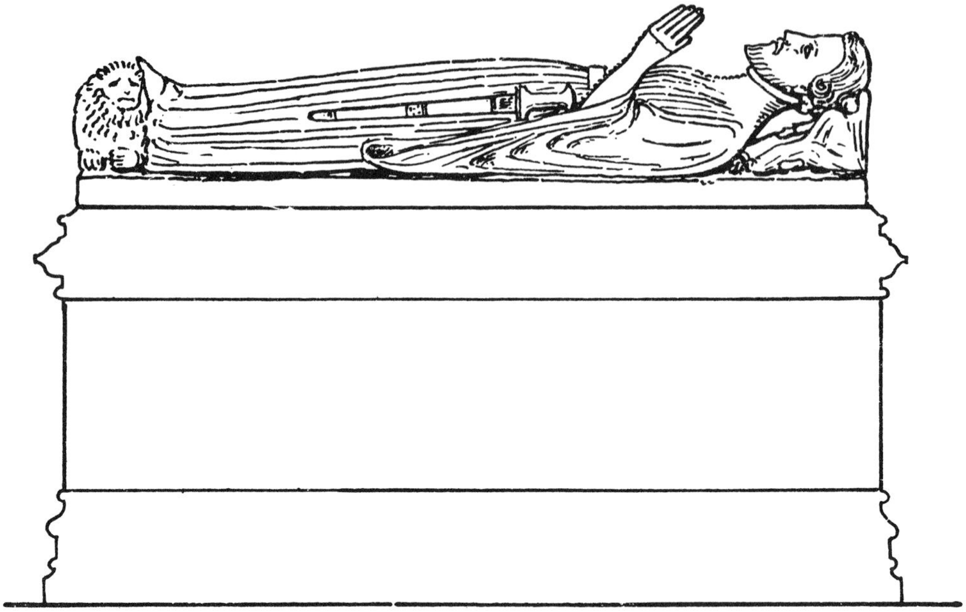

NORTH ELEVATION

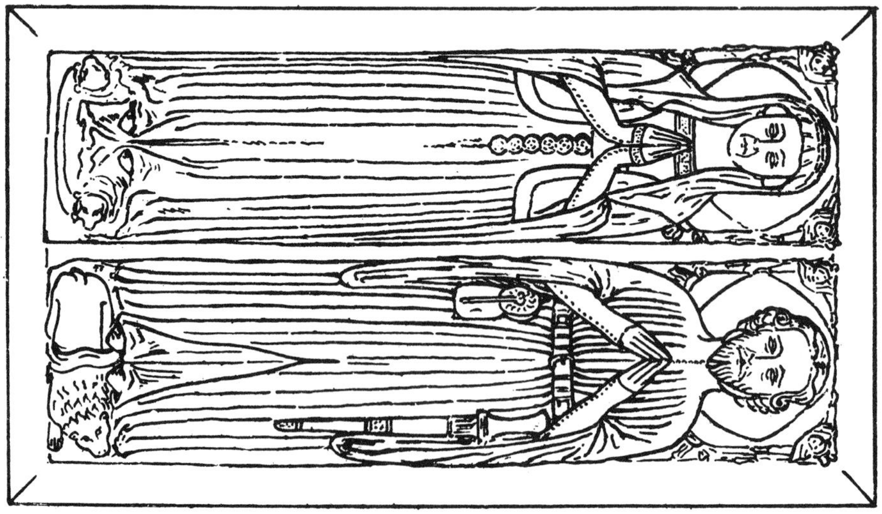

J.W. Bloe 1922

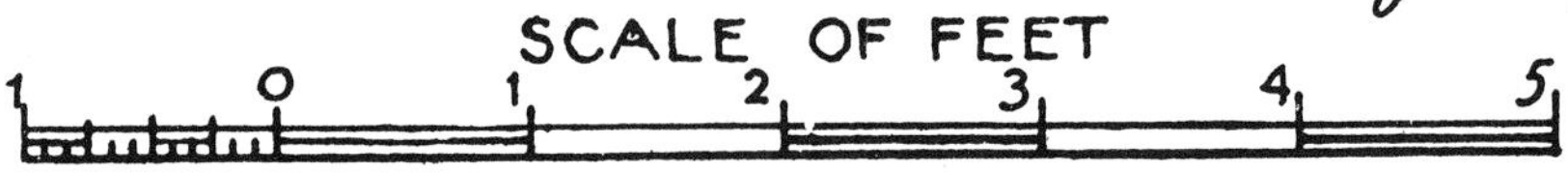
SCALE OF FEET
1
0
1
2
3
4
5

S WIFE.

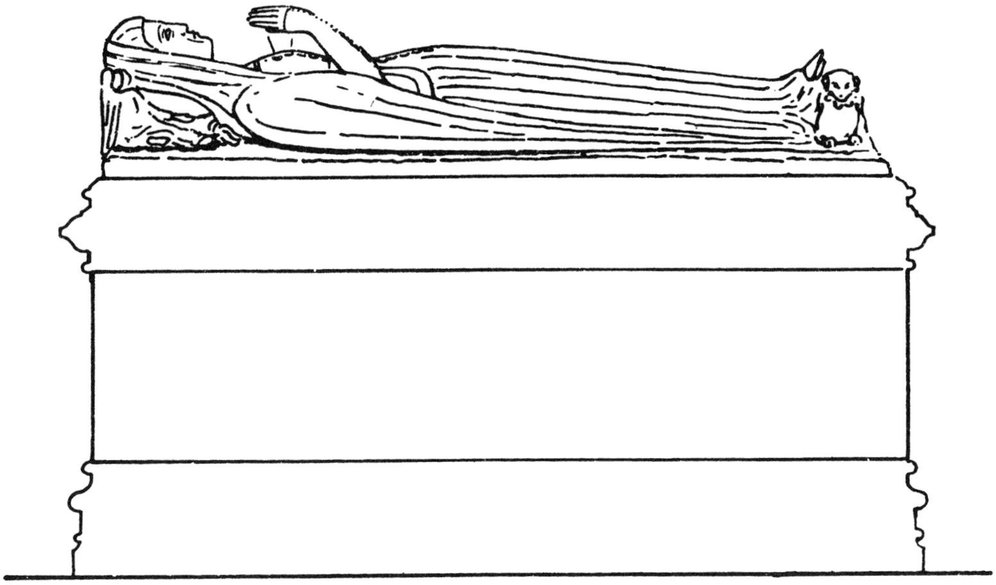

SOUTH ELEVATION

END ELEVATIONS

MONUMENTS IN THE SOUTH TRANSEPT

WALTER BERNARD, 1746

The Monument of Walter Bernard
Black
Black
Siena
Siena
Black Marble
Siena.
White
A.
B.
WALTER BERNARD Esq
Alderman & late Sheriff of this City
He dyed May the 4: 1706 aged 51.
White Marble
Stone
Side
Elevation
Section
at A
Plan
at B
J. Frank Gibbs
delt.

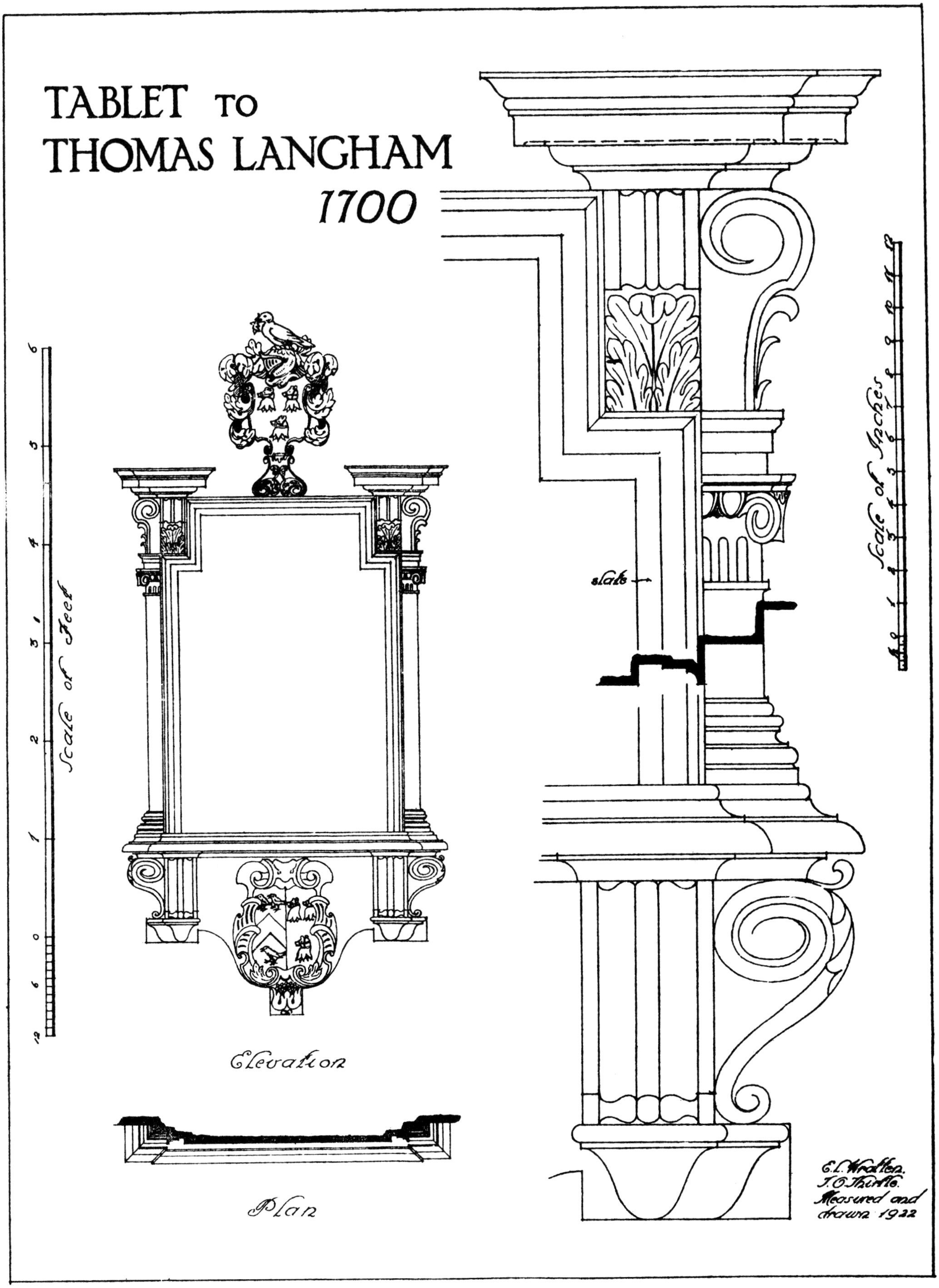
TABLET TO
THOMAS LANGHAM
1700
Scale of Feet
Scale of Inches
slate
Elevation
Plan
E.L. Wratten.
J.O. Thirtle.
Measured and
drawn 1922

Near this place are interr'd
the Bodies of
THOMAS LANGHAM
Citizen of LONDON
who died Decemb^{r}. 3^{d}. 1700;
And of ELEANOR his wife
who died Decemb^{r}. 2^{d}. 1694
And of REBEKAH their only Child
who was married to
BENIAMIN ROKEBY of LONDON Merch^{t}
& had Iſsue by him one ſon
LANGHAM ROKEBY & two daughters
REBEKAH & ELIZABETH:
ſhe died December 21st. 1692.

Non, nyſi per mortem patet iter ad Aſtra.
BENJAMIN ROKEBY Eſq,
dyed the 3^{d}. of February 173$\frac{2}{3}$ Aged 89.

MERCY
JESU

GERVASE RERESBY, 1704

M·S·
RACHEL
near this place
at the last day
ERNEST A MANN 1922

RACHEL CHAMBRELAN, 1687.

Epitaph
mented death of his honored friend

FLOOR SLAB
WILLIAM DRAX, 1669

FLOOR SLAB
WILLIAM FINCH, 1672

yeth Interrd the

FLOOR SLAB
GEORGE FINCH, 1710

FLOOR SLAB
JANE GAUSSEN, 1747

FLOOR SLAB
MAGDALENE BERCHERE, 1750

Here lyeth Interr'd
the body of Mrs
SARAH TRYON
one of ye Daughters of

FLOOR SLAB
SARAH TRYON, 1686

FLOOR SLAB
MARY BACKWELL, 1670

Honble Major Gen
GEORGE KELLUM

FLOOR SLAB
GEORGE KELLUM, 1732

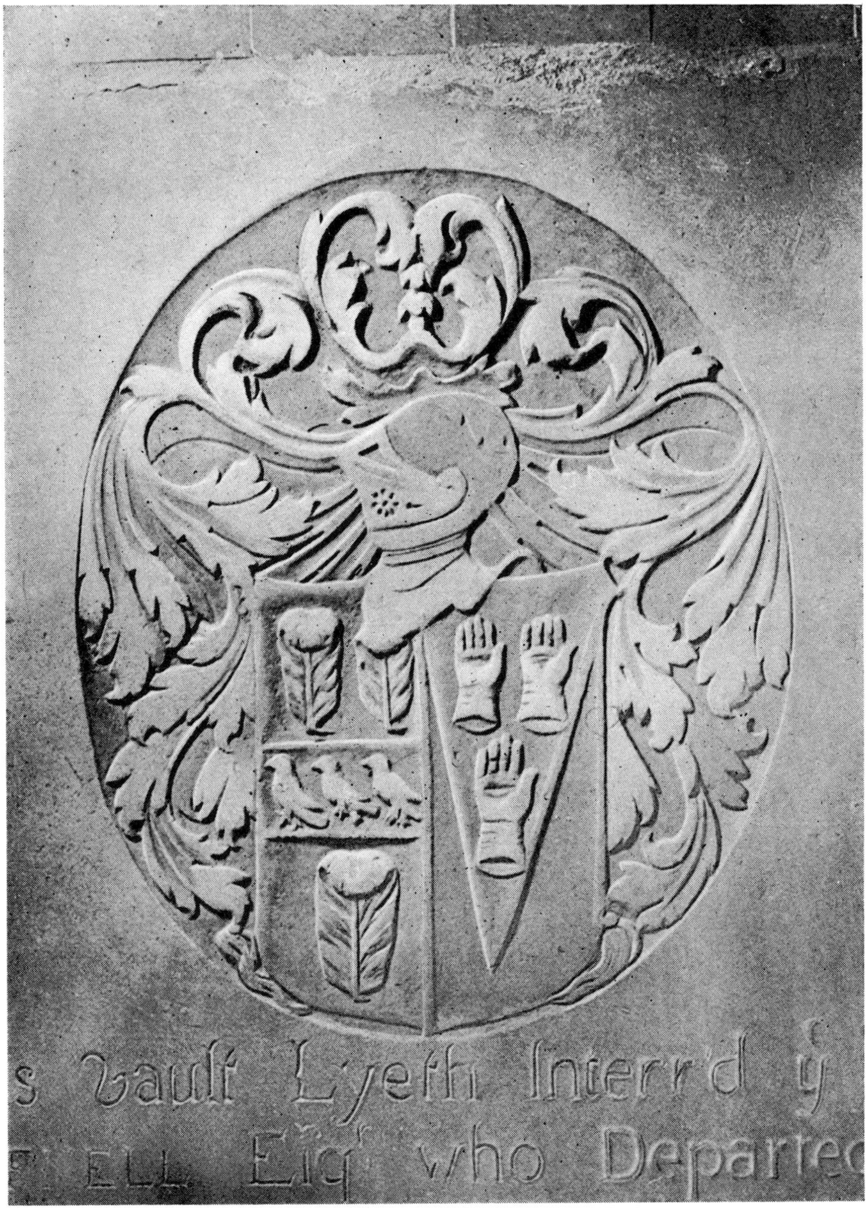
s Vault Lyeth Interr'd
who

FLOOR SLAB
JOHN TUFNELL, 1686

Scale, one and a half Inches to a Foot.

EDWARD SKEGGS, 1592

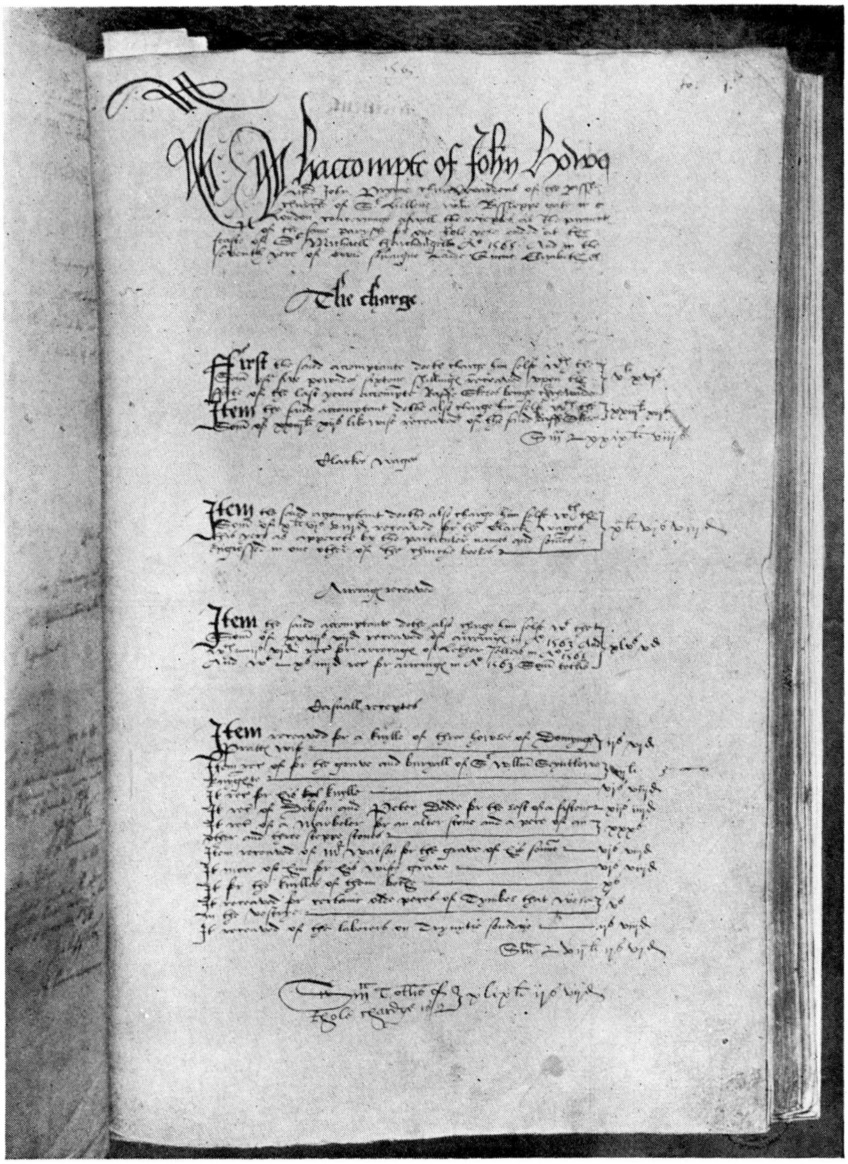
The charge

FIRST PAGE OF CHURCHWARDENS' ACCOUNTS, 1565

PLATE 122

SEAL OF ST. HELEN'S PRIORY

The PRIORY & CHURCH of St HELEN, BISHOPSGATE.

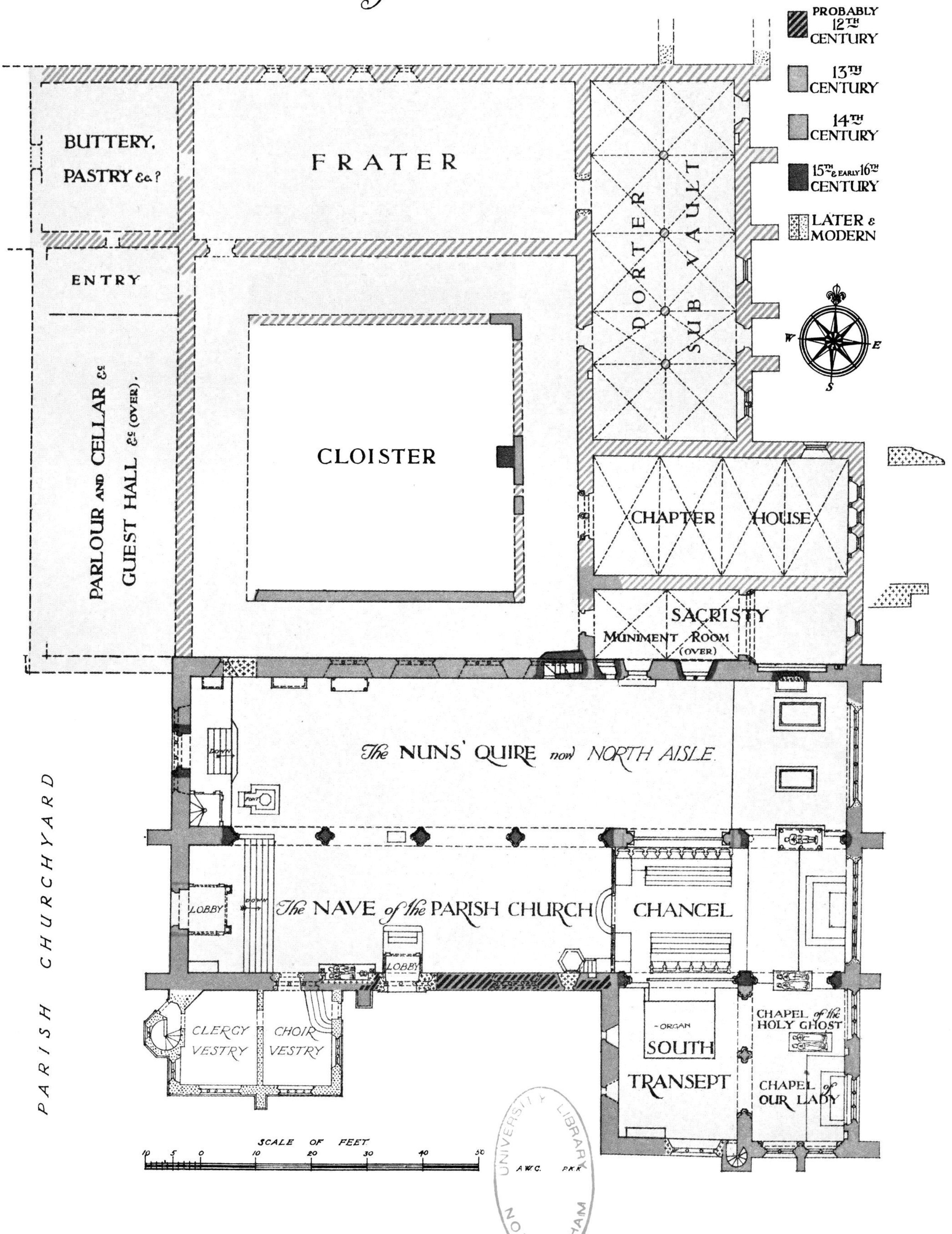
PROBABLY 12TH CENTURY
13TH CENTURY
14TH CENTURY
15TH & EARLY 16TH CENTURY
LATER & MODERN
W
E
S
BUTTERY, PASTRY &c.?
FRATER
DORTER SUB VAULT
ENTRY
PARLOUR AND CELLAR &c
GUEST HALL &c (OVER).
CLOISTER
CHAPTER HOUSE
SACRISTY
MUNIMENT ROOM (OVER)
The NUNS' QUIRE now NORTH AISLE.
DOWN
FONT
LOBBY
DOWN
The NAVE of the PARISH CHURCH
CHANCEL
LOBBY
ORGAN
SOUTH TRANSEPT
CHAPEL of the HOLY GHOST
CHAPEL of OUR LADY
CLERGY VESTRY
CHOIR VESTRY
PARISH CHURCHYARD
SCALE OF FEET
10 5 0 10 20 30 40 50
A.W.C. P.K.K.

[redacted]